AFRICAN LITERATURE IN THE DIGITAL AGE

Class and Sexual Politics in New Writing from Nigeria and Kenya

Shola Adenekan

James Currey
is an imprint of
Boydell & Brewer Ltd
PO Box 9, Woodbridge
Suffolk IP12 3DF (GB)
www.jamescurrey.com
and of
Boydell & Brewer Inc.
668 Mt Hope Avenue
Rochester, NY 14620–2731 (US)
www.boydellandbrewer.com

© Shola Adenekan 2021
First published in hardback 2021
Paperback edition 2023

All Rights Reserved. Except as permitted under current legislation no part of this work may be photocopied, stored in a retrieval system, published, performed in public, adapted, broadcast, transmitted, recorded or reproduced in any form or by any means, without the prior permission of the copyright owner

The right of Shola Adenekan to be identified as
the author of this work has been asserted in accordance with
sections 77 and 78 of the Copyright, Designs and Patents Act 1988

ISBN 978-1-84701-238-8 hardback
ISBN 978-1-84701-363-7 paperback

A catalogue record for this book is available from the British Library

The publisher has no responsibility for the continued existence or accuracy of URLs for external or third-party internet websites referred to in this book, and does not guarantee that any content on such websites is, or will remain, accurate or appropriate

This publication is printed on acid-free paper

Praise for *African Literature in the Digital Age: Class and Sexual Politics in New Writing from Nigeria and Kenya*

'Shola Adenekan breaks new ground with the first book-length study of African digital literature, as he examines how class and sexuality affect – and are affected by – the internet. Using Nigerian and Kenyan case studies, Adenekan makes far-reaching arguments about the ways in which the internet is revolutionizing African creative expression.'
Kwabena Opoku-Agyemang, University of Ghana, *Journal of the African Literature Association*

'the first substantial work on the contemporary African cyber literary experience. ... gives shape and substance to African digital literature while deepening understandings of class and sexuality in Kenya and Nigeria. Moreover, Adenekan's deployment of the network as an interpretative framework will prove applicable to other contexts, allowing us to read other regions of African digital production through the affordances of his study.'
Olajide Salawu, University of Alberta, *Journal of Postcolonial Writing*

'Shola Adenekan brings his considerable critical and forensic skills to bear in analyzing how online spaces have exploded the boundaries of what we think of as African literature in Kenya and Nigeria – from the erotic to the quotidian. Beyond celebrating the new work's formal innovation and its burgeoning audiences, Adenekan raises crucial questions about its class dimensions: Who has access to the internet? What market forces inspire and disseminate the new online literary bounty? Provocative, counterintuitive, but ultimately generous in its assessments, this ambitious study raises as many questions as it answers.'
Rhonda Cobham-Sander, Amherst College

'There are several reasons why *African Literature in the Digital Age* is a welcome addition to African literary scholarship. As the publisher of an online magazine, Adenekan is uniquely positioned to chronicle and theorise these developments he writes about, both as an insider and as an academic. His knowledge comes through in the range of materials he engages with. His analytic lens subverts the tyranny of the novelistic form in African literary studies, embracing texts ranging from poetry to short fiction, visual arts, and audiovisual forms. ... It is often the purpose of pioneer texts to lay the foundation upon which others can build, and *African Literature in the Digital Age* achieves much in this regard.'
Femi Eromosele, *English Academy Review*

'an important intervention ... interesting not only to scholars of African literature but also to those thinking more broadly about global writing throughout cyberspace.'
Lindsey Green-Simms, American University, Washington DC

'a refreshing analysis of the interface of digital circulation of African writing and emergent social identities, including urban middle-class sensibilities and non-heteronormative sexual desires. ... an indispensable book in contemporary Africanist cultural studies.'
Evan M. Mwangi, Northwestern University

AFRICAN ARTICULATIONS

ISSN 2054–5673

SERIES EDITORS
Stephanie Newell & Ranka Primorac

EDITORIAL ADVISORY BOARD
Akin Adesokan (Indiana University)
Jane Bryce (University of the West Indies)
James Ferguson (Stanford University)
Simon Gikandi (Princeton University)
Stefan Helgesson (Stockholm University)
Isabel Hofmeyr (University of the Witwatersrand)
Madhu Krishnan (University of Bristol)
Lydie Moudileno (University of Southern California)
Grace A. Musila (University of the Witwatersrand)
Caroline Rooney (University of Kent)
Meg Samuelson (University of Adelaide)
Jennifer Wenzel (Columbia University)

The series is open to submissions from the disciplines related to literature, cultural history, cultural studies, music and the arts.

African Articulations showcases cutting-edge research into Africa's cultural texts and practices, broadly understood to include written and oral literatures, visual arts, music, and public discourse and media of all kinds. Building on the idea of 'articulation' as a series of cultural connections, as a clearly voiced argument and as a dynamic social encounter, the series features monographs that open up innovative perspectives on the richness of African locations and networks. Refusing to concentrate solely on the internationally visible above the supposedly ephemeral local cultural spaces and networks, African Articulations provides indispensable resources for students and teachers of contemporary culture.

Please contact the series editors with an outline, or download the proposal form www.jamescurrey.com. Only send a full manuscript if requested to do so.

Stephanie Newell, Professor of English, Yale University   stephanie.newell@yale.edu
Ranka Primorac, Lecturer in English, University of Southampton   r.primorac@soton.ac.uk

Previously published volumes are listed at the back of this book

Dedicated to the memory of my father, Oladipupo Thomas Akanni Adenekan

Sun re o, Akanni, ara Ake

Contents

List of Illustrations	viii
Acknowledgements	ix
List of Abbreviations	x
Introduction: Kenyan and Nigerian Writers in the Digital Age	1
1 Network Thinking: Literary Networks in the Digital Age	21
2 Class and Poetry in the Digital Age	47
3 Class Consciousness in Online Fictions	63
4 Digital Queer: The Queering of African Literature	75
5 Middle-Class, Transnational, Queer, and African	97
6 'Ashewo no be job': The Figure of the Modern Girl in the Digital Age	113
7 The Erotic in New Writing from Nigeria	129
8 Social Media and the Aesthetics of the Quotidian	143
Conclusion: Connecting the Dots	165
Bibliography	173
Index	189

Illustrations

Figure 1   Literary Networks as represented in *Jumping Monkey Hill*. Image by Babatunde Idowu-Taylor, as commissioned by the author — 27

Figure 2   *Our love isn't fairytale* by Ella Chikezie. An image-poem posted on Instagram by the poet — 151

Figure 3   Bride wearing Aso-Oke Gele for her wedding. An image-poem by Dami Àjàyí aka #Jollypaps, posted on Instagram — 158

The author and publisher are grateful to all the institutions and individuals listed for permission to reproduce the materials in which they hold copyright. Every effort has been made to trace the copyright holders; apologies are offered for any omission, and the publisher will be pleased to add any necessary acknowledgement in subsequent editions.

Acknowledgements

They say it takes a village to raise a child, the publication of a book takes more than the author. *African Literature in the Digital Age* began as an idea, which came about after a discussion with Dr Wambui Mwangi, who was in 2007, a scholar of political economics at the University of Toronto. Wambui pointed out to me why the age we live in is different from the previous decades, because of the power of the internet. Wambui asked me to use everything I have to talk about what this moment in time means for African voices. Wambui, in her infinite generosity, introduced me via email to 'new' African voices such as Keguro Macharia and the late Binyavanga Wainaina. So thank you, Wambui.

Special thanks to the series' co-editor Prof Stephanie Newell, who has continuously been a source of inspiration. Thanks to Prof Newell's colleagues on the series Dr Ranka Primorac and Lynn Taylor. Many thanks to Renate Smith, my mother-in-law, who is my go-to editor. Thanks as well to Dr Ute Kuhlmann, who did a brilliant job with the final proofreading. My immense gratitude to the following people who, over the years, read the manuscript and made useful suggestions: Prof Rhonda Cobham Sander, Dr James Yeku, Dr Rebecca Jones, Dr Amatoritsero Ede, Prof Helen Cousins, Prof Conrad James, Dr Kwabena Opoku-Agyemang, Dr Stephanie Bosch Santana, Dr Charlotte Baker and Dr Stewart Brown.

I must also thank the many writers, thinkers and scholars in various digital communities, who allowed me to invade their space: Saraba magazine, USA-Africa Dialogue, Concerned Kenyan Writers group, Ederi, Krazitivity, the late Binyavanga Wainaina, Prof Unoma Azuah, Dr Dami Ajayi, Uche Peter Umez, Rasaq Malik Gbolahan, Ella Chikezie, Sitawa Nawalie, Sokari Ekine, Shailja Patel, Prof Oyeronke Oyewumi, Ikhide R. Ikheloa, Muthoni Garland, Prof Olu Oguibe, Prof Kole Ade Odutola, Dr Keguro Macharia, Romeo Oriogun, Prof Oyeniyi Okunoye, Salawu Olajide and many others, who are equally important.

My gratitude to the University of Bremen, Germany, for providing me the space to write and think through ideas and to Dr Helen Cousins, my first collaborator on online African literature, who has helped me think through some of my earliest ideas about this book.

My deepest thanks to my beautiful family for their love, support and steadfastness: Laura Smith, Ian and Renate Smith, Adefela Adenekan, Ifelola Adenekan, Adebayo Adenekan and Olayinka Adenekan.

Abbreviations

AA	Ashewos Anonymous
AfDB	The African Development Bank
BBC	The British Broadcasting Corporation
Brb	Be right back
CKW	Concerned Kenyan Writers
CNN	Cable News Network
ICC	International Criminal Court
IM	Instant messaging
IRN-Africa	The International Resource Network in Africa
KTN	Kenya Television Network
MMS	Multimedia messaging service
MS	Manuscript
NCC	Nigerian Communications Commission
OMG	Oh My God
SMS	Short message service
TED	Technology, Entertainment, Design
UK	United Kingdom
USA	United States of America

Introduction: Kenyan and Nigerian Writers in the Digital Age

On her Instagram page, on 28 March 2019, the Nigerian writer Chimamanda Ngozi Adichie is filmed dancing in front of a portrait of Andy Warhol. Adichie remarks on the video: 'And just because one was not blessed with the gift of rhythm does not mean that one should not, from time to time, make futile but enthusiastic attempts …'

While Adichie's dance steps may not constitute a literary work – just as Warhol's many self-photographs are not pure art, traditionally understood – the video becomes a prop that fashions the writer as both a literary icon and an icon of popular culture. It opens up the writer's personal space to the readers of her creative writings as well as to her social media followers, many of whom look up to her as an inspirational figure. At the time of writing this book, this short clip had garnered over one hundred thousand views and almost a thousand comments from Adichie's nearly four hundred thousand followers on Instagram. A week later, Adichie was involved in yet another poignant moment as a pop icon, when she graced the front cover of *Vogue* Brazil, becoming one of the few women of African descent to have ever been selected to feature there. As the Coronavirus pandemic sent much of the world into quarantine in April 2020, Adichie (5 April 2020) gave her readers and followers a view of how this torturous period in human history personally affected her:

> Last week, my family suffered a devastating tragedy, the very sudden death of my closest aunt, from a brain aneurysm. One day she was well and happy and the next day she was gone. Our time is filled with pain whose cause still does not feel fully true. We cry and yet we feel as though she is not really gone.
>
> And it is more surreal to grieve a sudden death in these strange times when the world has shut down, places once full are empty, heavy with the ghosts of silent gatherings, and across the world people are dying alone. Coronavirus is a menace in the air, a menace inside our heads. Every day I am reminded of how fragile, how breakable we are.
>
> My husband is a doctor and each morning when he leaves for work, I worry. My daughter coughs and I worry. My throat itches and I worry. On Facetime I watch my elderly parents. I admonish them gently: Don't let people come to the house. Don't read the rubbish news on whatsapp. This is a time to cope in the best way

we can. There are moments when our spirits will sag. Moments when we will feel tired after doing absolutely nothing. But how can we not? The world as it is today is foreign to us. It would be strange not to be shaken to our core.

Adichie uses the power of literature and that of her popularity to personalise the precarity of human life in the first half of 2020. Her statement underlines much about the way in which the personal and the literary collide in the digital age. We live in a world in which the African writer is not just our intellectual, but she is also our Agony Aunt. Her creative work and her personal life are used to reflect our lived experience.

From being referenced by celebrities such as Beyoncé, to interviewing Michelle Obama, and to her YouTube videos that have garnered millions of views, Adichie epitomises the visibility of African literature in a digital age. The Instagram moments are important to our comprehension of the way in which creative artists in the digital age have refashioned the concept of artistic self-presentation and self-fashioning that Warhol made popular through his now iconic self-portraits. Adichie's Instagram pages, like much of her digital presence, regularly showcase the writer as a cultural icon. On YouTube, she is the feminist and literary icon of our age, who gives a voice to women of African descent.

Anyone who has studied Adichie before she became a literary celebrity will know that her first preoccupation is telling the story of powerful Nigerian women, especially Igbo women, and the way in which these women have historically subverted patriarchy. Of course, fashion can also be a tool of subversion and of asserting one's identity, but it is only part of Adichie's sum total. The making of Adichie as an icon can be linked to the digital medium, one in which a story can be told in many different formats, to different audiences, in different settings. Some of her YouTube talks have become e-books, and these in turn have been converted to print books. But she also does a lot of live talks which are recorded and then uploaded online. Nonetheless, her major works of prose are first published in print.

While Adichie is arguably the most sought-after African writer, she is not the only African female writer leaving her marks on the digital landscape. The Kenyan-Somali British writer Warsan Shire is another important voice. Her YouTube videos are not only popular on social media, her poems are also used as status updates by many people on Twitter, Facebook, and Instagram. Another important female figure is the queer activist Sokari Ekine. In blogosphere and in book publishing, Ekine has brought visibility to, and critical engagements with, queer African writing and intellectualism with the help of her blog *Blacklooks.org*. The book she co-edited with Hakima Abbas, *Queer African Reader*, is one of the most important books on queer Africa.

In 2014, in a television studio in South London, United Kingdom, the Kenyan writer Binyavanga Wainaina is in a conversation with the Kenyan-Somali-British writer Diriye Osman about literature and life. In the video conversation, which was filmed for YouTube by the Iranian filmmaker and photographer Bahareh Hosseini, we see the two men read excerpts from their works; they talk about being middle-class Nairobians; they chat about multiple identities in a digital age; they discuss their lives as gay icons to many gay Africans; and the place of African literature in the age of popular culture.

Adichie, Osman, and Wainaina, who are writers with a middle-class background, signify the way in which middle-class consciousness permeates digital culture, including that of literature. This includes the everyday quotidian experience as well as monumental developments. We live in the age of digital celebrity, where one's cultural currency depends on Instagram followership and Facebook likes. On the one end of this spectrum are celebrities like Kim Kardashian who are notoriously famous not for their artistic talent but for the way they market themselves. On the other end are cultural icons like Adichie, Teju Cole, and Wainaina, whose digital currency relies on their brain power and how they use this to enlighten, challenge, and entertain us. Irina Dumitrescu surmises that: 'Celebrities feed the eternal hunger for newness without ever being truly new' (4). That sentiment is equally true in contemporary Africa, where the internet has become the main catalyst for a growing desire for new ideas, be it in politics, popular music, film or literature. In the field of African literature, the precursors to the age of Adichie and Wainaina can be found in a wide range of artistic endeavours by literary figures such as Wole Soyinka, Ngũgĩ wa Thiong'o and Chinua Achebe, who featured regularly in the media and at literary events. The difference, in terms of popularity, between the previous generation and the new generation is that in the age of the internet, popular culture and literature are not seen by many Africans as opposites. This is because the internet has amplified the image of the literary author beyond the confines of literary circles into the digital public domain. The authorial image is a marketable product that is very much in demand by the digital public. The author and the text are marketable products, which combined increase the marketability of the product. Taking advantage of this marketability, the literary market now uses the art of digital marketing to sell literature to a global audience. Literary events are promoted online, and publishing houses sometimes manage blogs and social media pages for their writers. You can read Adichie's creative writing on the same platform on which a pop-up YouTube video of the Nigerian pop star Burna Boy is playing, and the Adichie that is referenced by Beyoncé as a feminist icon is the same Adichie that school pupils want to study in the classroom.

The unexpected death of Wainaina from a stroke, in a Nairobi hospital in May 2019, has cemented his status as a literary icon and as an inspiration to many Africans, most notably among the youth on social media platforms. Cyberspace allowed Wainaina's followers and his literary friends to grieve him through his writing and through his queer activism. Others hosted events to celebrate his life on social media pages and in offline spaces across the continent. Today's literary celebrities are symbols of contemporary culture due to their offline and online lives. The physical demise of the author does not mean the end of his digital life and his relevance. Wainaina as a literary celebrity lives on in his works and the tributes that continue to appear on the internet. By using figures such Wainaina and Adichie as a point of departure, this introductory chapter lays the ground for the remaining chapters of the book, showing the way in which the elites of the digital age dominate issues such as sexuality and the experience of class in the twenty-first century.

Let there be no conflation between the everydayness and the 'spectacular' that *African Literature in the Digital Age* discusses, because the digital writings that speak to the big issues of our times also reflect everyday social-political engagements. One cannot talk about topical issues literature engages with without discussing the ordinary and the unspectacular it also portrays. The two themes can be examined side by side, or simultaneously, without creating confusion in the mind of the reader. This is not merely a juxtaposition; the literature that captures everyday ordinary existence is simultaneously addressing important social-political developments while also disabusing the outside world of an outdated anthropological perspective of the continent and its people. This is exemplified by Wainaina's well-received essay 'How to Write About Africa' (2005), in which he ridicules the trope of 'tribal' people who dance, sing and live in abject poverty, that has permeated mass media and academic projects on Africa for more than two centuries. The works of Wainaina and Adichie highlight how the immediacy of the internet, and its capability to integrate video, audio and images together, allows Africans, especially those who are educated and middle class, to depict their own Africa and their lived experience. While Wainaina's essay may be read as continuing a tradition of African writers writing back to the West, it is important to stress that for many writers from Kenya and Nigeria (Wainaina included) cyberspace is more of a site for African conversation and less of a preoccupation with responding to centuries-old stereotypes. The internet is seen as a tool that can bring about an era of progressive African ideas, especially in the context of sexuality. In her social media pages, for example, Adichie regularly asserts her African femininity as do Osman and Wainaina with their sexuality.

Every day in cyberspace, Nigerian and Kenyan writers use literature to respond to and influence events. When there was political upheaval in Kenya after the 2007 general elections, Kenyan writers came together to use literature to capture the experience of the victims, resulting in the 2016 social media literary project on Tumblr, the ICC Witness Project, that 'aims to give voice to some of the missing witnesses for the ICC trial'. Nigerian writers regularly use literature to respond to political events such as the activities of religious fundamentalists, for example attacks by Boko Haram.

Such interventions have become common in recent years with regard to Kenyan and Nigerian writers. It underlines the way in which the figure of the African writer has transformed from one that people only encounter through their creative writings to that of global intellectuals with a crossover appeal to the world of fashion and show business. *African Literature in the Digital Age* recognises this turn as a monumental paradigm shift because it signposts to us the possibility of the writer as a voice for a new era of openness; because it acts as a lens through which we can reflect on our understanding of African history, and articulate large as well as small-scale everyday political and cultural engagements. I ascribe this new visibility and transformation to one thing only – the digital age.

In the digital age, much of the creative writing being produced has a purpose, and I want to borrow Koleade Odutola's (16) terminology of 'cyber-framing' in discussing the way in which cyberspace offers digitally-wired Africans the chance to shape and reframe the way they and their societies are seen and perceived. Further, a concept of the potential to impact self-realisation in cyberspace can be parlayed to fictional narratives and poetry, especially in the implicit or stated position of fictional characters as embodiment of a social class and as belonging to a particular sexual orientation. Here, *African Literature in the Digital Age* sees African writers in cyberspace as agenda-setters within and outside of literature.

The ideas espoused in this book are foregrounded in the notion that for these writers and their contemporaries, and as well as their followers, the digital space intersects with the world of book publishing and with the lived experience outside the world of literature. Raine Koskimaa argues that the nature of literature in the digital age may be different from the cultural context of the past, especially with regard to the way in which literature is produced and distributed. He argues that we need 'to see literature as a media operating amongst others' (2). Koskimaa's argument is pertinent; the African writer in the twenty-first century needs to be seen both as an artist (in the traditional sense) and as an ambassador for popular culture. Within the conventions surrounding the online writing space, a writer is more intimately connected not only with other writers, but with her readers who might be from other parts of Africa or from the Diaspora. As Wainaina excitedly commented: 'There are 19-year-olds who've read all your work and they're based in Zimbabwe' (Spillman par. 42). Many readers of African fiction online are 'friends' of the writers on Facebook and follow them on Instagram and Twitter, and the writers are also 'friends' of those African readers. Readers and writers are able to see each other's personal life in pictures and in video with some writers regularly sharing family photos, activities, political thoughts and fashion tips with their readers on social media sites, alongside short stories and poetry.

Equally important is the fact that readers can leave comments on many of these platforms relating to the author's writing and extra-literary activities. These interactions instigate a dialogue about the writer's various interests. They highlight how these various interests intersect. The extra-textual material and engagements also alter and shape our conception of literature. Therefore, the nature of texts within the new media landscape is altered by the close interaction between the writer and her readers. It removes the tenets by which distinctions and value judgements are traditionally made about what is 'good' versus that which is 'popular', generally based on the reputation of the publishing house and on individual authorship. In this process, both writers and readers are starting to embrace different values regarding literature, as cyberspace abruptly frees up notions of literature for experimentation, collaboration and disconnection from specifics of place, politics and culture. The premise of this book is that this crossover appeal enables writers to perform the role of agenda setters, with the power to frame and determine their society's cultural values.

While cyberspace is important for this transformation of the figure of the African writer, *African Literature in the Digital Age* also recognises the notion of digital space is embedded in capitalist commercial mechanisms. Facebook, Instagram and YouTube are money-making ventures. Across the world, billions of people use social media every day, and these platforms are where our interior lives – including those of writers and other creative artists – are on constant display, alongside paid advertisements. For some writers, digital capital equals political and financial capital. The digital space is thus a site in which art and commercialisation exist in a symbiotic relationship.

Class Consciousness in a Digital Age

Debates about the nature of the social classes in Africa often tend to be divided between the romantic and the pessimistic. The late Tanzanian President Julius Kambarage Nyerere, who was an intellectual and a leading Pan-Africanist, held a romantic view of a precolonial Africa where class did not exist, and the 'elders sit under the big tree and talk until they agree' (quoted in Mohiddin 133). For Afro-romantics like Nyerere, class consciousness is one of the negative consequences of capitalism and colonialism, while in the past wealth as well as the means of production were controlled by the community for the benefit of every member. For Afro-pessimists on the other hand, there is no such thing as a class system in Africa simply because the means of productions and the nature of wealth creation are not at the same level as those of Western Europe and North America. Such a Euro-centric view of history is expressed by Henning Melber in the introduction to a book on the African middle classes, which he edited in 2016. Melber dismisses the definition of an African middle class by the African Development Bank

(AfDB) as being 'a far cry from the petty bourgeoisie featuring prominently in a proper class analysis, and is devoid of any analytic substance' (2). Melber not only ignores the knowledge production of a team of well-trained African economists who work at the AfDB, he at the same time fails to recognise other historical and economic developments that do not resemble that of Europe. For the Afro-romantics, the notion of class is un-African because they assume that Africans practised a form of socialism in the precolonial era, while the Afro-pessimists see class as un-African because they deem much of the continent as not being economically sophisticated enough to be class conscious. Over-simplification of history has been the bane of such analyses of class history in Africa. Precolonial Hausa texts such as the Tarikh es-Sudan and Tarikh al-Fattash depict social stratification among the Hausa-Fulani people: the yan Sarki were (and still are) the ruling classes; the barori were the warrior class who served at the pleasure of the emirs and the sultan; and the Talakawa are the poor and ordinary people (see also Szymon Chodak). As I argue in Chapter One, an African class structure existed in many precolonial monarchical African societies. My argument is that the foundation of most monarchies across the continent – before the advent of colonial rule – is the social strata that supported them.

In the current millennium, the digital network offers a unique opportunity to theorise a history of privilege, visibility, omission and marginalisation. These four elements are important because the digital space, as far as Kenya and Nigeria are concerned, is also a space dominated by those who historically enjoy certain class privileges and who possess cultural capital. Class matters because offline or physical-space social structures are re-enacted in one form or another in the digital space and, therefore we have to theorise the way in which class is reified in terms of access to the digital network, as well as the ability to maintain constant presence and actively participate in this network. One's ability to exert some influence on digital platforms depends on the ability to be constantly visible and to be constantly vocal. But digital influence requires one to be able to purchase digital data, which is the currency that buys digital participation.

Despite there being more Africans who are digitally connected than the population of the United States and that of the entire population of Europe put together, the fact that the languages of the digital African network are still largely English, French and Portuguese speak to the affordability of – and access to – Western-style education. Although, there are works written in local Kenyan and Nigerian languages such as Yoruba, Swahili, Sheng and Hausa, the bulk of what is being published digitally is in English. What this means is that the people with the best education money can buy constitute the bulk of digital literary networks. Many writers come from families that can be described as professional middle class, and they themselves are members of this class. Readers of literature posted online and publishers of online literary publications are also most likely to be members of the educated middle class.

Why Nigeria and Kenya?

The main focus of this book is on the works of writers of Nigerian and Kenyan descent, but the book also includes a discussion of South Africa as the third hub of African literary production in English, but without focusing on that country's internal debates around whiteness. These three national environments will be contextualised via references to the larger African literary canon as and when needed. I settled mainly on Nigeria and Kenya as case studies because these two countries arguably produce the majority of most-talked-about writers in Anglophone African literature. The body of written works and intellectual productions coming from, and relating to, both countries is the most extensive in Anglophone African literature, outside of South Africa. For example, these two countries have together produced most of the winners of the Caine Prize for African Writing. These include works that were originally published online such as Binyavanga Wainaina's *Discovering Home* (2002), Okwiri Oduor's *My Father's Head* (2013) and E.C. Osondu's *Waiting* (2008). Nigeria serves as the publishing hub for West Africa, while Kenya serves the same purpose for East Africa. In terms of literary networks, both countries have a history of literary collaborations between writers and scholars, which is discussed in the next chapter.

Furthermore, along with South Africa, Kenya and Nigeria possess the most digital hubs on the continent, thus putting them at the forefront of digital innovations in Africa. Many of the pioneering African bloggers come from Nigeria and Kenya, and digital culture is highly vibrant in these two countries, which is why both have caught the attention of digital conglomerates such as Google, Facebook and Twitter, all of which have business interests in Kenya and Nigeria.

It is important to stress that in the context of Nigeria and Kenya, written literature, be it in local languages or in the English language, must be analysed from the change in social structure brought about by the project of colonial modernity and the written culture that is the cornerstone of this modernity. For example, at the centre of the new social structure that emerged from the experience of colonialism is the discourse of sexuality. Stephanie Newell's important study of newspaper networks in West Africa points us to the people who exerted influence one way or another through the print publications they controlled, and through their engagements with the world of publishing. African female intellectuals like Oyeronke Oyewumi and Naminata Diabate alert us to the way in which colonial modernity and its written culture transformed our understanding of social status, as well as sexual and gender roles, and how this transformation created new moral codes that are mainly rooted in Euro-modernity. *African Literature in the*

Digital Age builds on such scholarship as it undertakes multiple explorations of middle-class domination of contemporary culture and how this domination is reflected in the thinking about class, sexuality and the quotidian. If Martin Burke signposts us to the 'conundrum of class' in America, this book argues for the need to study representational problems that one can only see from a robust analysis of the intersection of class and sexuality in the African context. While the digital age has allowed a lot of freedom in terms of communication, it is also an era that continues to reflect much of the dynamics of the print age. The material may be different, but it also carries many of the drawbacks of the past. The literary networks that emerged in Lagos and Nairobi in the first half of the last century were dominated by the new African middle class, whose members were largely educated by Europeans, and so participation in literary culture became a means of asserting one's status as a modern person. The 'new' modernity of the twenty-first century is closely linked to one's participation in digital culture. While this book will analyse the freedom that the digital space provides to writers, it also recognises that this space is a product of global capitalism, in which the unconnected are in danger of being overlooked and misrepresented because much of what is portrayed in fictional narratives is based on the African middle classes.

In theorising the representation that is emerging from the digital network, theorists need to take note of literature's focus on telling the middle-class African story, and that some of these depictions can be read as pathologising people who are not educated and who in the process are not part of Africa's literary network. The exclusivity of the English language, as previously discussed, may mean that the world view of those who are not connected to the digital network is not presented or represented in what is being published online in English. In the process, the lifestyle of the rich and the middle classes is glorified while that of poor Africans is portrayed discursively as materially and ideologically abject. Western proponents of the end of class such as David Bell and Joanne Hollows may argue that life-styling as seen in their popular media is an indication of the end of social group and the rise in social mobility, however, such representations may not capture the whole truth of digital development, not in the case of Nigeria and Kenya anyway. Therefore, we need to think about whether the idea of the middle-class African writer as the African cultural ambassador might not be rather problematic. Middle-class African writers may only be able to fully represent members of their own class as they are possibly somewhat ignorant of the way in which people outside their own social settings live. There are also nuances in contemporary Nigeria and Kenya that cannot be fully captured in English. Revathi Krishnaswamy aptly asks us to investigate 'what exactly are the "missing bits"' to which these cosmopolitan writers must reconcile themselves (141). The metropolitan perception of the contemporary African text is problematised by the presentation of the cosmopolitan writer as the mouthpiece of African culture. These writers, in turn, often play the role of the ultimate insider–outsider to an outside world that is often only too willing to accept them in such a role. Since literature is often used as evidence of lived experience, however, it is important to accept that works published within the digital network may not represent the entire postcolonial experience. The reality within which new creative works are produced and consumed needs to be queried in order for us to not ascribe responsibilities to young African writers to which they may not be able to aspire. Thus, the public persona of the twenty-first century writer as an autonomous conveyor of African realities, and as the true teller of the African story, may be as wrong as it is problematic.

Publishing in the Digital Age

As previously argued, there is an African public in the digital space which African writers target with their online writings. And since texts tend to move to where the audience is, it is therefore no surprise that a greater amount of creative writing, mostly short stories, poetry, plays and essays, are finding a home in this new media space in order to satisfy and address the demand of these digital communities. To some extent the internet has levelled the cultural and institutional ground between the ultra-elite African literature of the likes of Teju Cole and Mũkoma wa Ngũgĩ and the self-published authors who use online platforms to gain access to national public spheres. The established new voices like Cole and Mũkoma are very active on social media and are well known across the print and online mediums, but for those who are self-published the internet is an essential tool of visibility, through which they can gain a foothold in the world of literature, and also reach audiences that may not be part of the established literary circle. As demonstrated in some of the chapters, some of the newly emerging voices like Nigeria's Romeo Oriogun first gained critical attention and popular following first on social media before catching the attention of book publishers. The poet Warsan Shire was equally well known on Twitter and Tumblr to her almost one hundred thousand followers before she was published in several literary journals and anthologies. However, *African Literature in the Digital Age* shows that for most writers – regardless of their status in the literary world – the digital space provides an alternative to mainstream ideologies, and an opportunity to create new forms of expression. What some writers publish online may be ideologically different from what is published in the mainstream of print publication. For the established voices and those not yet known, the internet is an ideal platform to present their versions of self and society.

The problem with literature in Africa has never been a lack of African readers, as Newell argues, because there are already millions of potential readers in countries like Kenya and Nigeria. In addition to the problematic nature of the politics of book publishing where the main publishers and editors are based in Europe and North America, the problem with the literary market in

Africa is the space in which printed works of literature circulate, which limits their reach to certain sections of the urban areas. The traditional means of publishing normally involves a writer sending off a completed manuscript to a literary agent or a publisher. The manuscript is then reviewed by an editor who decides on the suitability of the material for publication. If a manuscript is accepted for publishing, the publisher takes on the financial risk of production and marketing in exchange for the income from future book sales, paying the writer a royalty on sold copies of the book. The problem, however, is often with finding a publisher willing to take that risk. From email conversations with some young writers it becomes clear that one constant worry is publishing in Nigeria and Kenya. Some of the writers point to the fact that even established local publishing houses often ask writers to finance the publication of their own work, and will further ask writers to sign a contract that will give the publishing house a substantial percentage of book sales, in other words the writer takes on all the risk and pays a royalty to the publisher. They argue that rather than submitting to such exploitation they will publish their works online. Another example of writers being asked to contribute financially was an email on the Nigerian writer listserv *Ederi*, sent by a Nigerian publisher, requesting a fee the equivalent of £50 sterling from writers whose stories were to be included in an anthology of short stories by emerging Nigerian writers.

Because of the problem of finding publishers, some writers self-publish by taking their manuscripts to printing presses, and then selling the published books themselves or through booksellers. The Kenyan writer Rasna Warah, in an email discussion on 4 November 2009, explains the advantage of taking the self-publishing route: 'You retain control over the product, for one, and in my case, you have access to the global market, which local publishers do not provide … so I am not complaining' (n. pag).

The digital space has helped in bringing visibility to those who have self-published as stated by the Nigerian romance writer Nkem Akinsoto, who uses the nom de plume Myne Whitman. She insists that she owes her self-publishing success to the internet:

> I will always be grateful for the vehicle the internet provides to a writer and published author like me to get my book out there. Setting up an active blog and publishing my book has served a double purpose for me; finding out the target audience for my kind of writing and building a platform too. If not for the social networking channels, *A Heart to Mend* would never have gone viral the way it did … I put up chapter one of the book on a free reading website and it became a massive hit. (2010)

A Google search of Whitman's novel shows a network of material relating to her writing: copies of the novel are available in print; as a download from Amazon; as a pdf copy, hosted by *Free-online-novels.com*; and there is a related Facebook site; a website and the blog. *Free-online-novels.com*, in particular, bills itself as 'helping to meet the desires of writers and readers', and Whitman's comments highlight the synergy between readers and writers in the digital space.

While creative writing published online still follows similar patterns to print, because many of these texts still try to mimic the material qualities of the printed page, new media technology provides a new avenue for many writers to move literature beyond the world of book publishing, by actually publishing short stories and poems directly on blogs, online magazines, social media pages and listservs. In Kenyan literature, for example, Binyavanga Wainaina's rise to critical acclaim arguably started when his online autobiographical fiction *Discovering Home* on the literary blog *Generator 21* (2002), won the Caine Prize for African Writing. From this, he launched the online literary magazine *Kwani?* In an interview with Rob Spillman, Wainaina recounts the role that the digital space is playing in African literature:

> You have all these young writers in Nigeria who know writers in Kenya because they met on Facebook and so-and-so's workshop. You start to get the sense of this piling up of power and production, which is now larger than the sum of any parts you can see. That certainly has meant more to writing out of the continent than any other thing. (Spillman par. 42)

Wainaina concedes that while there is still a place for the print medium, in his view, ultimately, 'We've all got to go digital. There's no question about it anymore. Print has to die' (Spillman par. 44). In part, this is because of the difficulty of accessing print copies within and outside of their countries of production, but equally Wainaina appears to be suggesting that the freedom associated with writing online accrues power to the writers and not to the publishers as in print production. Additionally, it is cheaper and faster to publish creative writing on the internet, and this work will potentially reach a wider audience, fuelled by a rapid uptake of internet and mobile phone technology within Africa.

Literature in Cyberspace

The 'internetting' of Kenyan and Nigerian literature arguably started between the mid- to late 1990s, when writers seeking to draw attention to their printed work started posting poems and short stories on personal blogs and on listservs such as *Krazitivity* and *Ederi* hosted by the likes of Yahoo and the now defunct Geocities. Some of these works also appeared on African-owned websites such as *Mashada.com, Nigeria.com, Africanwriters.com, African-writing.com, Chimurenga.com, odili.net* and *Nigeriavillagesquare.com*. By the turn of this century, some of the established literary magazines based within and outside Africa, not wanting to be left out of the internet race, started asking for short stories, essays and poems for their websites that would appeal to a growing online reading public. At the same time, more and more writers, seeking to increase control of their work, started putting creative writing on their personal pages on Facebook, Instagram and Tumblr, in addition to joining online writer collectives. The advent of social media and the surge in the number of young Africans with access to mobile phones further reinforced the idea in the minds of several writers that the future of African literature lies online.

This assumption may not be far-fetched; a report by the African Development Bank says that internet usage is a signifier of a middle-class lifestyle in Africa and the study uses internet penetration as one of its main markers for analysing the social classes on the continent. Another survey by Internet World Stats suggests that, as of June 2017, there are over forty-three million Kenyans online out of a total population of almost fifty million people, and the Nigerian Communications Commission estimates that, as of August 2017, there are over a hundred million Nigerians who have internet-enabled devices. The majority of the people living in both countries, therefore, have access to cyberspace.

Given these figures, one can see that African writers are not putting their work in cyberspace just for the sake of it; it is because communities – both local and global – are being constituted in this space. There are now several listservs, blogging communities and social media communities started by Kenyans and Nigerians. These include forums that target queer Africans, women, writers and readers. In the context of Nigeria and Kenya, marginalised groups such as the queer communities have found digital space the ideal site for their voices to be heard. These sites include *Blacklooks.org*, *Queer Kenya* and *Kabaka* magazine. Moreover, over two billion people around the world are on social media and are digitally connected. This means that there are two billion potential readers of African literature. And since texts tend to move to where the audience is, it is no surprise that a greater amount of creative writing, mostly short stories, poetry, plays and essays, is finding a home in this new media space in order to satisfy and address the demands of the digital community.

The Concept of Space and the Internetting of Literature

In an analysis of South African digital writing, Stephanie Bosch Santana argues that literature in cyberspace does not exist in a vacuum, nor is it removed from the offline world. She argues that 'there is reason to think that digital space is not so neutral, empty, or detached' (187). Santana's argument is germane: in the context of African literature, digital writing is connected to lived experience because it asks questions as much of psychic landscapes as of the material world. Therefore, the concept of space as used in *African Literature in the Digital Age* focuses on the literal uses of spaces by emerging voices as well as on the metaphorical uses of the idea. Here, this book is referring to the specificity of space, in which writers are located in either the physical geographical space or in the virtual space of the internet. This concept of space can therefore be seen as linked to the idea of attachment, and the argument is that African literature clearly makes its claim on the African condition – in the real texture of its lived life and history. This notion queries what is Africa and how is it presented. What kind of language is spoken on the streets of, say, Lagos, Nairobi, Douala or Lilongwe? And what is the value of experience, even as it is transformed by contact with a wider world that constitutes the condition of contemporary Africa?

Jenny Kennedy uses the term 'networked spaces' to describe the intricate link between the online and offline world. She argues that in the digital age, we need to make clear the distinction between 'place' and 'space'. The latter is infinite and can be inhabited by many different elements, but the former is rigid and only able to accommodate one thing at a time. Space for Kennedy, therefore, is where online and offline narratives converge and it is 'important in addressing the distinctions between online and offline for the contextualisation of social interactions' (3). Going by Kennedy's argument, the digital space can be seen as a site of multiple narratives that also reflects offline realities, at least to an extent. This is because the concept of space as expressed in this book is linked to the notion of having something in common with a community, such as a shared sense of Kenyanness, or a sense of being members of the professional middle classes, or of being gay. At times, these identities are also connected to Pan-African ideals.

Whilst online writers and readers congregate in mainly African-run online communities, non-Africans are allowed to become members of these communities as fellow digital citizens. One common factor within these online communities is that members are mostly people with the means and the skills to fully understand and engage with African literature written in English. And since English seems to be the language that many members of the educated middle and upper classes use in online forums, we see class manifesting and vocalising itself in the online space more than in the physical space. This happens because the writer can maintain some distance from the expectation of the geographical society and instead expresses herself as a middle-class African writing within a mainly middle-class digital space, without having to explain herself or her fictional characters. The digital space also enables the writer to address themes such as homosexuality and prostitution in fiction and poetry, which may have been considered taboo subjects in the physical space, especially by book publishers as well as by political and religious authorities. The physical space is thus being visualised by some of the emerging voices as restrictive as well as patriarchal, which is symbolised by the book form, while cyberspace represents freedom and democracy. In turn, one can argue that fictional narratives reflect both the restrictions of the printed word and the freedom of online publishing.

Structure of the Book

Although creative works published online and in print are the main focus of this study, I also used conversations on listservs and social media as supporting evidence in my analysis. In the course of carrying out this study, I joined online groups including *Ederi, USA-Africa Dialogue, Krazitivity, Concerned Kenyan Writers*, as well as various social media pages and blogs on African literature in addition to writers' blogs and social media pages. Having access to these privileged conversations gave me an invaluable insight into the world view of these writers in a way that would have been impossible twenty years ago.

African Literature in the Digital Age can be categorised into two, albeit interrelated parts; the first three chapters focus mainly on class consciousness, especially middle-class identity and what literature tells us about the relationship between those who can be classified as members of the African middle classes and those on the lower rung of the economic ladder. In these chapters, what this book is trying to do with regard to class is to not base its analysis completely on the Marxian understanding of the word. I recognise and accept that Marxists have provided robust arguments on class identity and consciousness, but as I have argued in this Introduction, ideas about status awareness are not exclusively European nor are they exclusively Marxist. Olaudah Equiano's narrative points to class awareness in precolonial Nigeria, before the subjects were enslaved. The life of enslaved figures in the Americas, such as Abdulrahman Ibrahim Ibn Sori and Ayuba Suleiman Diallo, are stories of class consciousness, in which the subjects are fully conscious of their social status in their respective West African societies. Likewise, the poetry and songs of the Yoruba, the Swahili and the Hausa, are replete with ideas about one's position on the social ladder. Wole Soyinka's *Death and the King's Horseman* (1975) – which is loosely based on a true story – depicts sexual, economic, gender and political privileges enjoyed by the ruling classes over ordinary members of the society, as well as how these privileges were disrupted by colonial rule. In addition, the story of Obi Okonkwo in Chinua Achebe's *No Longer at Ease* (1960) represents the dynamic of class aspiration in a Euro-modernist era. The life and aspiration of Nigeria's lower middle classes and working classes in the 1960s were captured by the writers of Onitsha pamphlet literature (which I get to in Chapter One), many of whom were themselves members of these social classes. I will also argue that, like these fictional narratives by two members of the first generation of modern African writers, several novels published by some members of the second generation, especially books published in the popular Pacesetter series of the 1980s, reflect contemporary concerns in Kenya and Nigeria, such as sexuality and spirituality that are mediated through the lens of class.

Chapter One addresses an under-theorised aspect of African literature with its analysis of digital literary networks and their importance to our understanding of literary history in Nigeria and Kenya. I use Patrick Jagoda's idea of 'network ambivalence' to think through questions about what the digital network means for African literature, writers and the African digital public, as well as the millions who are not part of literary networks. I show why literary networks provide an important means to theorise the intersection of global politics, class and literature. In Chapters Two and Three, *African Literature in the Digital Age* builds on Adichie's interview with the UK *Guardian*'s journalist Stephen Moss, in 2007, in which she argues that, while the outside world may not realise it, class distinction exists in Africa. For some African writers, especially emerging voices, the digital space is the site where class consciousness can be articulated and projected. My position is that in the quest to show this side of Africa, there is a middle-class consciousness in the literature being published in the online space, which may be leading to the pathologising of the lower-class fictional characters. This point is further extended in Chapter Five, where I surmise that fictional representations of queer Africans largely revolve around middle-class gays and lesbians, and this means that poor people are missing from literary imagination. Perhaps this is because most of the writers and readers in the online space are middle-class Africans, with some of them identifying with the global middle class, rather than with those who exist in the periphery of the online space. Suffice to say that while online African literature may be imaginatively exploiting the freedom of cyberspace and the digital age, class and sexual identities depicted in some of the new writing show us that freedom from constraint can also mean imprisonment in alternate structures of economic power, denial and frustration.

In Chapter Two, we see writers reprising the oral tradition, the same way in which poets did some centuries ago. Here, I make the point that while publishers and editors are often the only authority in the way texts are constructed and consumed in the print space, some of the writers are embracing the freedom of the digital space by posting work straight online in their blogs, listservs and social networking spaces. In the process, they are bypassing the traditional gatekeeping roles synonymous with the world of print publishing. Like the ancient griot, the twenty-first century poet is allowing texts to be mediated upon by readers, and texts are in turn very flexible. This fits into the new ways of doing art that the Kenyan poet Shailja Patel alludes to in one of her poems (August 2010).

The next four chapters then build on the first three by examining the intersectional links between the discourse of class and the issues of sex, sexuality and body politics. I base my analysis on the impact of modernity on these discourses. I am interested in using contemporary history to show the way in which writers over the course of a century have used their role as cultural ambassadors to comment on African sexuality, while forcefully foregrounding their opinion on what constitutes African tradition and what is alien. At the centre of a new social structure that emerged in the late nineteenth and early twentieth centuries is the way in which attitudes to sex becomes a marker of progress versus barbarity, as well as what constitutes Africanness and Europeanness. This reflects a global trend at the turn of the last century, when certain attitudes towards sex and sexuality are ascribed to a particular social class. Michael Trask observes a similar trend in the context of American literary modernism, by surmising that: 'the elites of modern society chose to couch class difference in the language of sexual illicitness, viewing innovative and unsettling social arrangements as an extension of the irregular or perverse desires that sexology deliberated' (1). The social climate in America and Europe at the turn of the last century filtered through to the emerging middle classes in Kenya and Nigeria, if one examines magazines, newspapers and newsletters that were published during that time. African language publications in the 1920s, such as *Muigwithania* in Nairobi, founded and edited by Jomo Kenyatta, and *Eleti-Ofe*, in Lagos – which often featured poetry by the young Nnamdi Azikiwe – regularly argued that sexual enjoyment is frivolous and uncivilised. Many writers and journalists who came into their own in the early decades of the twentieth century, in publications such as *Akede Eko* (Nigeria) and *Muigwithania* (Kenya), used literature and journalism to argue for moral purity and a sense of purpose. As discussed in some of the chapters in this book, this preoccupation with sexual permissiveness mirrors what the middle classes of Europe saw in their own working classes. Local news publications in both Nairobi and Lagos often republish columns from Western magazines that warn against sexual frivolity. As a brand-new middle class emerged from the colonial project, the people who constituted this group sought to differentiate themselves from the European middle class that refused to see them as equals, and also from non-educated Africans, whom they considered as backward. Attitudes to sex – especially where women and homosexuality were concerned – became one of the ways in which class distinction was expressed. In the process, the educated middle class used the discourse of sexual desire as a means to straddle the divide between the tradition of the colonisers and that of the colonised. And as it tried to negotiate its place in the turbulent era of the early twentieth century, this new middle class borrows from European and African views of the world. However, the middle-class sensibility of the twenty-first century differs to a large extent from the orthodoxy of the past. Many of today's writers use their status as cultural ambassadors to argue for a more liberal attitude towards sexuality. In doing this, they foreground their message in aspects of African history they consider as sexually liberal, rather than borrow from the West's sexual revolution of the 1960s or the Stonewall campaign of the similar era. This reflects an aesthetic strategy on the part of a new generation of writers and thinkers.

In Chapters Four, Five and Six, I use the intersections of class and sexuality to unpack the queering of the online African space. In my study of digital queer Africa, I see this moment of queering of African literature starting to happen when emerging voices take a different approach from the older generation in their representation of homosexual characters. In these chapters, I show that the agenda of literature is not just concerned with exposing the endemic corruption of the postcolonial state but that it is now challenging the hypocrisy and lies surrounding African sexuality and history. We see the middle-class African writer in the online space using literature to attack homophobia; fictional narrators even show us that homophobia and capitalism are intractably linked. Thus, writers project themselves not as mimics or as agents of capitalist globalism, but as people who use literature and the internet to disrupt the agenda of global capitalism.

The chapters on female sexuality are foregrounded in the discourses of body politics, the history and the impact of the project of colonial modernity on contemporary ideas of what constitutes African sexuality. Roy Porter calls for a closer engagement with body politics. He points out that 'body history must be part of big history. It must display the body as the inexhaustible generator of representations for society at large, and as a crossroads of power, the new pineal gland mediating between personal and public, private and political' (11–13). More than two decades on, some of the young African writers and poets in the online space are using literature to depict the African body as a category of historical analysis. And as literary studies about African bodies have brought about continuous encounters, clashes and border-crossings between varieties of spaces, *African Literature in the Digital Age* looks at the African body as represented in online creative works and the sexual politics that have long surrounded this body. Some of these writers are using the freedom of the digital space to focus attention on marginalised bodies, especially the history of spectrality surrounding those Africans who do not conform to the prevailing sexual norm.

While literature in the print age helped articulate the idea of nationhood and Pan-Africanism, online literature along with the rise of the middle class is now arguably the catalyst for the 'coming out' of African marginalised identities. Similar tactics to those used in fictional representations of the figure of the African homosexual are employed by some writers who look at the figure of the sex worker and that of the modern girl. In discussing the figure of the modern girl, a term often interchanged with 'the Good Time Girl', this book reiterates one of its key arguments – that writings and ideas from the past have a great influence on current discussions on sexuality and class. According to Alys Eve Weinbaum et al., 'The Modern Girl appeared quite literarily around the world in the first half of the twentieth century' (1). Weinbaum and her fellow contributors demonstrate how this figure was also part of the discussions as far back as the 1920s in major Southern African cities (see also Jennifer Cole and Lynn M. Thomas).

African Literature in the Digital Age builds on such discussions in scholarship by showing that the trope of the modern girl still permeates literature published in the digital age. It shows that the modern girl was a fixation with writers and editors of small magazines in Nigeria, and that a new generation of writers from Kenya and Nigeria is now portraying their own rendition of the modern girl in the digital era. In this regard, we see the African writer returning to the role of the reporter of current events and the recorder of history. My usage of modern girl is the description of a woman, usually young, who does not conform to societal norms all of the time. These can be standards of dressing, speaking, posture and attitude to sex and gender roles. By discussing the trope of the modern girl in the digital age, I am trying to unpack the way in which Euro-American class anxiety over young women's behaviour, and the behaviour of the working classes of Europe and North America, became a colonial anxiety over the behaviour of the colonised from the early part of the last century, and how this anxiety was adopted by the new African middle classes during and after colonial rule. This book fills a critical gap by highlighting how some of the emerging works in the online writing space show that prostitution (or sex work) is a form of capitalist exploitation in the context of globalisation, and how it is also a form of female empowerment when we look at the way in which modernity's dictated gender performances are being disrupted by fictional female characters.

Chapter Six, takes a more cautionary approach by warning that not all emerging writers in the online space take similar liberal attitudes towards African sexuality. Tracing the impact of colonial modernity on African literature, this chapter shows that fictional works in the online space can also mimic some of the conservatism of the past. Chapter Seven addresses another under-theorised theme – the erotic in African literature. Foregrounding my arguments on the work of Audre Lorde, I place the erotic as an aesthetic strategy used by some emerging voices to challenge history, and as a means of empowering female readers. In Chapter Eight, *African Literature in the Digital Age* ends with an exploration of the importance of the quotidian, the commonplace and the ritual, to our understanding of African societies. It stresses that while literary scholars and journalists tend to mainly focus on the spectacular and the abnormal when it comes to African societies, African humanity can only be truly captured by an examination of the everyday. People love, take their children to school, laugh and cry, just like in other parts of the world.

Whether striking a liberal pose in their poetry and fictional representations or standing as vanguards of morality, the online writing space shows the new way in which African writers use literature to depict everyday political engagements. Kenyan and Nigerian creative works within cyberspace show the internet as a site of cultural performance and politics, and what is being published and consumed by readers in the digital space is relevant and important in this new media age.

Network Thinking: Literary Networks in the Digital Age

1

For many Nigerian and Kenyan writers in the new media space, cyberspace sometimes serves as a debut platform for what may later appear in print, but most of these works (sometimes fragmented and, at times, short, intricate pieces) remain within cyberspace. This chapter analyses online writings as reflecting the dynamics of interconnectedness, especially the way in which cultural practices are organised around not just the individual (the author) but also around the collective, in a global network that is the world wide web. This chapter uses the concept of 'network' in analysing the many layers of relationship between the analogue terrain of print publication and that of the digital. Having studied computing for my first degree, my understanding of the concept of 'network' and its application are both loosely based on networking morphology taught in information technology classes, which relates to the different structures and forms of networks. As a literary theorist, I apply the metaphor of network in unpacking the types of connections to be found within African literatures and within the community of global literatures.

Manuel Castells and Patrick Jagoda provide robust analyses on the concept of the network. Castells sees networks in terms of the global power structure. Networks, he argues, 'can expand indefinitely, incorporating any new node by simply reconfiguring themselves, on the condition that these new nodes do not represent an obstacle to fulfilling key instructions in their program' (1996, 695). In *The Rise of the Network Society* (1996), Castells sees digital networks as disrupting the global order because various digital entities are now able to bypass previously constituted authorities. Building on Castells's theory on the intersection of network and power, Jagoda argues that networks are both cultural and material structures (2016, 2–3). From these two arguments, one can surmise that a network is made up of interconnected entities with shared – and sometimes divergent – interests. In computing, these interests revolve around information and data, and this is the foundation of today's internet and the digital space. On a more rudimentary level, a spiderweb can be conceived as representing the structure of a hub-and-spoke network. The spiderweb as a network has spokes in many different directions that are connected to a central hub, which is the spider itself. The idea of the spider as a network has been part of African and African diasporic folklore. In West Africa, Anansi the trickster spider is a figure in oral tradition that can be read as a metaphor for the way in which oral networks operated long before the project of colonial modernity. During the four centuries of the transatlantic slave trade, the power of African narrative is embodied by the way in which its oral network – through enslaved Africans – carried the story of Anansi to the Americas. In the twenty-first century, the figure of Anansi is now part of the digital network with various re-tellings of this story in digital formats and with different renditions. In this regard, networks in the African context can be seen through information architecture as well as through the metaphors provided in oral productions and creative writings. Applying this terminology to literature, I see the network as a composition of interconnected groups of people or – to use information iechnology terminology – nodes that make up the world of literature. These literary entities do not have equal status, rather their power depends on the dynamic of location, race, gender and class. On the continent in general, networks can be said to encompass the psychic and the material world.

Network theory is gaining currency in literary studies, and examples include Gillian Russell and Clara Tuite's co-edited book, *Romantic Sociability: Social Networks and Literary Culture in Britain, 1770–1840* (2002), Dan Edelstein and Chloe Edmondson's *Networks of Enlightenment: Digital Approaches to the Republic of Letters* (2019) and Andrew O. Winckles and Angela Rehbein's *Women's Literary Networks and Romanticism: 'A Tribe of Authoresses'* (2017). These books speak to the quantitative turn in literary studies as they extract from literary texts the sociability that enabled small magazines and literary societies to make an impact on European literature from the Enlightenment period to the modernist era. With the rise of digital humanities, such use of data mining is gaining ground across literary studies. However, network concepts are only just beginning to be applied to the literary endeavours in the digital age.

Jagoda shows that in the context of the United States of America, the current understanding of the word 'network' has been largely influenced by the world of politics, news media and information technology. The same argument could be said to apply to both Nigeria and Kenya. For example, journalists and politicians in both countries use the term 'terrorist networks' in discussing the activities of radical Islamic groups – Boko Haram and Al Shabab – which operate in Nigeria and Kenya, respectively. This reference to radical organisations as networks or axes has become part of the political lexicon in several Western countries. Writers and publishers are also using the word 'network' to describe their literary circles as well as their relationships with other organisations. For example, in the 'About Us' section of its website, Kwani Trust says that it 'is a Kenyan based literary network dedicated to developing quality creative writing and committed to the growth of the creative industry through the publishing and distribution of contemporary African writing, offering training opportunities, producing literary events and establishing and maintaining global literary networks. Our vision is to create a society that uses its stories to see itself more coherently.'

Kwani's operation offers a good example of local, continental and global interconnectedness. In addition to the flow of information between the global South and North, and the various concepts of network that emerged from it, Kwani's many relationships speak to the dynamic of networks in a digital age, especially the multidirectional flow of information, relationships and data. The concept of networks that I borrowed from the world of computer science and information technology reflects what Jagoda refers to as inviting 'an understanding of the world that is open to random links, messy structures, and unforeseen complications' (2010, 209). Jagoda's argument is germane to the way digital networks operate; they are democratic tools that allow people from different parts of the globe to interact and communicate with one another in real time, but, simultaneously, they allow political and corporate entities to monitor people and enforce surveillance laws and in the process censor and stifle dissenting voices. Networks therefore also have their disadvantages and in that way are a reflection of our world and its complex interconnectedness.

In literary as in computer networks, the objective of any network is to meet the needs of its users, which in the case of a digital literary network are the members of that particular network. As discussed later in this chapter in the context of Nigeria and Kenya, the members of digital literary networks can be writers, readers, publishers, bloggers, editors and scholars. Writers also function as readers, and readers may function as publishers. There are also scholars who are creative writers, and who also function as publishers. So, as in computer science, the entities in a literary network and the processes that bring them together are multidirectional and interconnected. The concept of networks, therefore, speaks to the cross-connection between various entities, and these entities are not constrained by physical boundaries. For example, members of a literary network include people based in Kenya and Nigeria, across the African continent, and people based outside of Africa. The key things required to enable participation in these digital literary networks are membership and access to an internet-enabled device.

In this regard, literary circles such as listservs and online communities that require either membership and/or have gatekeepers will be regarded as 'closed networks', while those on open platforms such as social media sites will be deemed 'open networks'. In closed networks, the gatekeepers – moderators – grant memberships to those who want to join the community. In the examples that I will be using in this chapters, moderators on email lists and online magazines enforce house rules and have the power to remove or suspend a member's account, and there are by-laws that guide members of such literary communities. A moderated network is thus close-knit and is composed of members whose interests are far more aligned than an open network. Conversations in a closed network tend to be more tangible and with objectives in mind. For example, the ideas for the establishment of digital-print publishers such as Okada Books, Farafina and Cassava Republics (Nigeria), as well as *Storymoja* and *Kwani?* (Kenya) were initially discussed among members of literary networks that sprang up in the first decade of the new millennium. In an open network, membership is less monitored, as all that is required in the case of Twitter and Instagram, is that you have an account with these platforms.

Thinking with Network

Thinking 'with' the idea of networks has changed how literary theorists approach literature. John Edward Terrell, Termeh Shafie and Mark Golitko argue that: 'Network thinking lets us scientifically understand the world around us as one of connections that shape observed phenomena, rather than as one where the intrinsic properties of people, genes, or particles determine outcomes' (n.pag). In all fields of human endeavours, people are influenced by ideas within and outside of their field of specialisation. In the digital age, many people who are digitally wired have some connection to various digital entities, be it as members of WhatsApp groups or Facebook groups. These entities are in turn digitally connected to other groups due to the way in which the internet operates. On social media platforms, photography, video, art and literature often go together. And indeed, African writers have embraced a variety of media tools in their works. Emmanuel Iduma, Chuma Nwokolo, Teju Cole and Diriye Osman operate within a transmedia space by marrying prose texts with art, photography and animation across several social media sites, while others such as Biyi Bandele have tried their hands at film productions. Literary voices such as Warsan Shire and Chimamanda Adichie regularly collaborate with video producers and photographers on digital projects. These varying layers of interconnectedness inform my theorisation of network, as does the metaphorical representation in literary texts. In what follows, I use examples from creative writings, photography as well as digital films, to argue that the local is intricately linked to the global. Moreover, such connections focus not only on representing the present but also on interpreting the past. I also want to argue that network thinking can let us see the place of Nigerian and Kenyan literature in the world of letters.

With regard to digital networks, Diana Saco divides discussions on the benefits of the internet into two schools of thought: those who believe that the cyberspace is changing societies in a positive way because it allows for the free and democratic exchange of ideas across multiple interconnected platforms; and those who see the internet as numbing people's minds because of information overload and purveying inaccurate or incomplete information. Digital networks also carry much of the hangover of market economies, because networks privilege some groups while marginalising others. Given this complexity, I place my analysis of digital literary networks in the context of Nigeria and Kenya within these settings: as a starting point for studying the power dynamic within global literary networks; as providing a means to articulate literary history and development; as giving good insight into the way in which class operates within Kenyan and Nigerian literary circles; as recognition there is a digital network aesthetic that is being produced by Nigerian and Kenyan writers; and as insight that digital networks can be read as material metaphors.

Networks and the Literary Marketplace

Chimamanda Ngozi Adichie's short story *Jumping Monkey Hill* (2006) provides a useful starting point for analysing network structures in the context of literature and thinking about social organisation and the emergence of digital network aesthetics with regard to Nigerian and Kenyan literary histories. Originally published online by Granta, it foregrounds the way literary networks – embedded in transnational capitalism – link to power dynamics within and outside the world of literature. The story centres on the experience of Ujunwa, an aspiring Nigerian author, at a workshop in South Africa for emerging African literary voices who have been selected as cultural ambassadors for the continent. The workshop is the brainchild of Edward Campbell, an Oxford-educated Briton, who is an old Africa hand. Edward knows his Africa and the African stories he thinks are authentic, and he is quick to tell us that 'African literature had been his cause for forty years, a life-long passion that started at Oxford.' Edward derives his power from his many connections in the world of literature. One of the workshop's participants warns that Edward is 'connected and could find them a London agent; there was no need to antagonize the man, no need to close doors to opportunity.'

Jumping Monkey Hill reflects the power imbalances in the global literary networks to which African writers have access. Like minerals and raw materials, literary texts are part of the market economy. They also generate sociability since social connections are built around literature. Moreover, by using a workshop as a backdrop, Adichie alerts us to the politics of literary networks: attending a writing workshop, like doing a Master of Fine Arts (MFA) degree, is now the sine qua non – an essential route to getting your name known in the literary marketplace. The narrator underlines the intricacies of powerful literary networks and the importance of such writing workshops to their operations; *Jumping Monkey Hill* is supported by the British Council and funded by a fictitious Chamberlain Arts Foundation, and the latter is the patron of 'the Lipton African Writers' Prize', which is another idea developed by Edward. Adichie thus robustly uses the fictional character of Edward as a metaphor for the literary marketplace.

When Ujunwa presents her short story about a middle-class Lagos female banker who challenges patriarchy, her story is deemed by Edward as 'agenda writing'. When a female Senegalese tearfully asserts, 'I am Senegalese! I am Senegalese!', after he dismisses her short story about two African lesbians, Edward quips: 'I think she had too much of that excellent Bordeaux.'

Adichie uses this particular conversation to sensitise us to the way in which homophobia is embedded in the politics of postcolonial publishing. Edward's statement shows that not only is same-sex desire viewed as un-African, it is also deemed as the postcolonial Other. The fact that the Senegalese writer is a woman – as is the fictional gay character in the work she presents at the workshop – signifies the marginal place of female African writers in the literary marketplace. Queer female writers are even more marginalised. Edward epitomises the patriarchal nature of powerful literary networks. This male-centric nature of the world of literature is further accentuated when Ujunwa informs us that Edward favours a male writer from Uganda over the women. Although all the African participants are middle class, it is the fictional male Ugandan writer who is privileged, and therefore we are shown the way in which class, gender and race intersect. *Jumping Monkey Hill* shows the way in which African female narratives are sometimes straightjacketed and the voices of female writers stifled. Women's experience of literary networks may in fact differ negatively from that of men. One can, therefore, argue that Adichie uses this story to ask questions about who gets to be heard in the literary marketplace and who is seen as a bona fide ambassador for Africa. Being heard is as important as being seen. The female voices of *Jumping Monkey Hill* are seen by Edward, but he refuses to hear them.

The Ugandan writer occupies a position of privilege over his female African contemporaries, but he occupies a lesser position on the status ladder in comparison to Edward, who is a Caucasian from England. *Jumping Monkey Hill* can also be read as suggesting that some African men are complicit in the marginalisation of African women. For example, rather than standing up for the female participants, the Ugandan laughs at Edward's bad jokes, and it is no surprise that he is chosen as the group leader. The Ugandan here becomes Frantz Fanon's 'palatable negro' – a symbol of neocolonialism, who allows himself to be silenced, and who is reduced to mumbling; a man-child.

There is a saying in the world of electronic and computer networks, that not all networks are equal; some are more equal than others. The same maxim applies to literary networks. Edward in *Jumping Monkey Hill* can be read as embodying the powerful London literary network – a network of literary agents, editors, publishers, bookshops, art organisations, university academics, bodies awarding literary prizes, journalists and readers. The Euro-centric conception of the literary world forms the basis of Pascale Casanova's much quoted book, *The World Republic of Letters* (2007), in which she argues that the hubs of literature are located in the Western metropolises of London, New York and Paris. These hubs combined canonise literary texts and influence what constitutes literary aesthetics.

I use Figure 1 to imagine literary networks as represented in *Jumping Monkey Hill*:

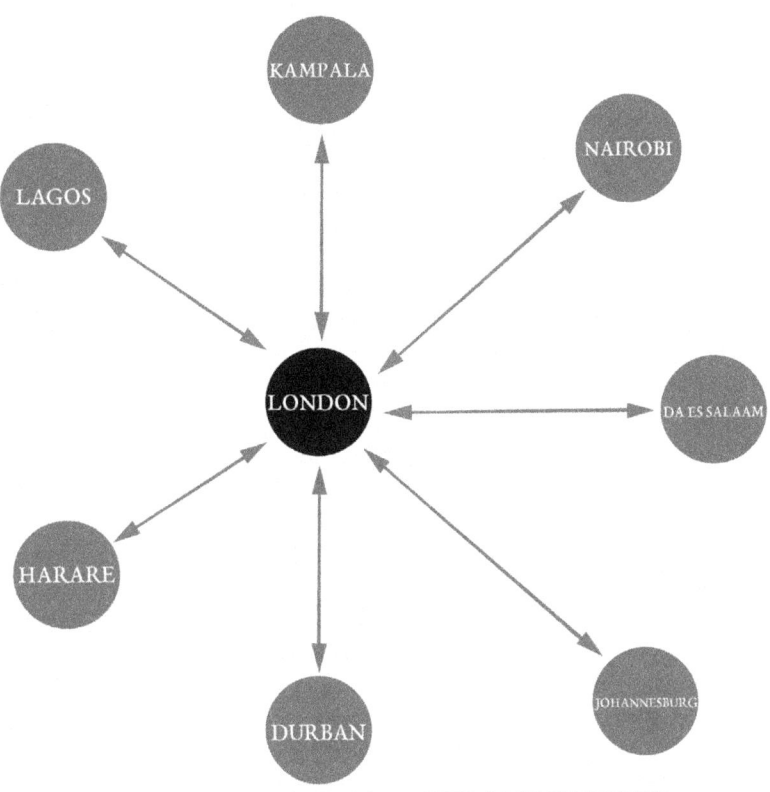

ANGLOPHONE AFRICAN LITERARY NETWORK

Figure 1   Network visualisation of Adichie's *Jumping Monkey Hill*. Image by Babatunde Idowu-Taylor, as commissioned by the author.

Through the metaphor of computer networks, Lagos, Nairobi, Kampala, Johannesburg and Harare, are sub-hubs, and are connected to London as the main hub. London functions strategically as the gatekeeper of Anglophone literature. Not only do the literary networks of London (and New York) influence the idea of aesthetics in the context of Anglophone writing, they are also the centres of canonisation because no literary figure has attained their eminence without the 'sanction' of the literary networks of the West. Africa's position in relation of Casanova's *Republic of Letters*, becomes explicit in *Jumping Monkey Hill*, as the protagonist informs us that:

> The white South African woman was from Durban, while the black man came from Johannesburg. The Tanzanian man came from Dar es Salaam, the Ugandan man from Kampala, the Zimbabwean woman from Harare, the Kenyan man from Nairobi, and the Senegalese woman, the youngest at twenty-three, had flown in from Paris, where she was at university. (n.pag)

The sub-hubs of Lagos and Nairobi are, in turn, connected to their own local sub-hubs. Furthermore, *Jumping Monkey Hill*, like the Figure 1 image, highlights the relationship between subgroups within the global middle class. Edward and his wife, who co-host the writing workshop, are middle class, and so are the emerging African voices they host. Indeed, all the African participants at the workshop in *Jumping Monkey Hill* are members of the professional middle class, who live in cosmopolitan cities. These cities represent the locale of literary power – local and global – as well as the cross-connections that one associates with networks. The relationship between these members of the global middle class, however, is not equal. In the world of book publishing, the London literary network that Edward represents, often provides mentorship and access to Africa-based literary networks, but that patronage comes at a price – adherence to certain expectations of what an African story should consider. Western patronage of African literature thus becomes one more strategy of political and cultural control. It privileges works that fulfil our fantasies about Africa while suppressing those that counter that narrative. Its financial power sets the aesthetic agenda, and thus determines who or what gets projected as authentic – the self. Literary networks in the world of book publishing thus re-enact the dynamic of global political and economic structure.

In *Jumping Monkey Hill*, Edward lusts after Ujunwa even as he typecasts her as the African with the chip on her shoulder. He considers her and the Senegalese writer as not African enough because their demeanour runs counter to the subservient African that powerful figures such as Edward Campbell expect. Edward's attempt at silencing Ujunwa in addition to ogling her – while praising the Ugandan writer – fits into a space that Olu Oguibe argues is 'the hierarchical location of the [European] *Self* over the [African] *Other*, of the white critical and artistic establishment over the African artist' (*Art, Identity, Boundaries* 349).

Networks in Nigeria

In both Nigeria and Kenya, the literary networks that came about through the print culture of the nineteenth and twentieth centuries provide a means to analyse the way in which a reading culture emerged to create a new public that was mainly composed of those who could read and write. It gives an opportunity to investigate the way in which print cultures not only produced new artistic genres, but also how they produced new and competing ideas about civilisation, progress and modernity. The literary histories of both countries can therefore be best understood if one studies the workings of the people who form the circle of writers, publishers, readers and politicians. This is because literature expresses not only the world view of those who constitute a literary circle, but also carries the exigency of the society from which they emanate from. In a way, literary networks are small worlds. The emergence of a network often occurs as a response to a 'crisis' (or crises) that impacts the world of literature. These may include a crisis of aesthetics; a crisis of politics; the exclusion, omission and marginalisation of some aspects of literary representations; and the dissatisfaction by a collection of people who inhabit the literary sphere.

For example, in 1920s' Nigeria, the project of colonial modernity, and the narratives that came with it – portraying Africans as savages – led to the emergence of a circle of writers, mostly Lagos-based, who used literature and journalism to counter Europeans' depictions of Africans. This new network built on the print culture and network that was started in the mid-nineteenth century by African and European missionaries that included public figures like Bishop Samuel Ajayi Crowther, who authored the first Yoruba dictionary in 1852. Like their precursors, some of the writers of the early twentieth century wrote in both Yoruba and English, so as to cater to a growing reading public all over Nigeria. They banded together to create publications such as *Eko Akete*, *Akede Eko* and *Eleti-Ofe*. While these three Lagos-based publications were newspapers, writers also published poems and short stories in them, and they often used literature to critique European modernity. At the same, writers also queried their own communities. They shared and critiqued works across multiple print platforms. This sociability enabled them to publish a range of publications that articulated the tragedy of colonialism not only in Nigeria, but also across the continent, and they articulated the experience of racism in the Diaspora, especially in Britain and the United States. These networks also organised book readings and educational programmes in Yoruba and English, in community halls across Nigeria, Cameroon and West Africa. They saw their task as preparing the younger generation for the oncoming postcolonial era. Among the notable personalities in these literary networks was Nnamdi Azikiwe, who became the first president of Nigeria in 1960, and who wrote a series of poems in the early 1920s that were published in *Eleti-Ofe*.

Working together across different print publications gave writers of this era good publicity for their works and in the process, they gained access to the literary marketplace of Lagos and beyond. Azikiwe, who was based in Calabar at the time, was able to sell his writings to Lagos publications, and this publicity enabled him to create a political profile for himself prior to moving to Lagos and becoming one of Lagos's political elites. The journalist and editor Isaac Bamidele Thomas, popularly known as I.B. Thomas, also became prominent and marketable by publishing his works in several prominent publications that existed in Lagos at the time. One issue of *Akede Eko* shows the writer-editor travelling to London, sporting a bag with the inscription 'Akede Eko'. On such visits, Thomas provided a link between the Diaspora literary circles in the UK, and the home-based networks in Nigeria. Such images enhanced his reputation as a political figure representing the nationalist movement that was gaining ground against British imperial rule. Literature combined with journalism enhanced Thomas's sociability, which, in turn, provided him with political and cultural capital, and that gave him the financial capital to turn *Akede Eko* into a powerful journalistic, political and literary tool.

Like today's literary networks, the networks of the previous decades did not just connect writers, readers and publishers in Nigeria, they communicated with networks outside of the country. For example, they created local forums for short stories and poems published overseas through republication. Literature also became a medium through which writers and readers expressed solidarity with the African Diaspora. An example of this is when the Ghanaian educator and intellectual Dr James Emman Kwegyir Aggrey died in Harlem, New York, in 1927, poems were written in his memory by writers in *Akede Eko* and *Eleti-Ofe*, and lectures were organised in Nigeria to celebrate his life and contribution to Pan-Africanism. In poems, short stories and essays, writers within these networks pontificated on the issues confronting their societies at the time, including the notion of modernity and the place of African cultures within modernity. They engaged fellow writers and readers in print publications and in debating societies in cities such as Lagos, Ibadan and Calabar. It was this atmosphere of interconnectedness that provided the context for the first Yoruba language novel, I.B. Thomas's *Itan Igbesi Aiye emi "Ṣẹgilọla" "Ẹlẹyinju-Ẹgẹ," "Ẹlẹgbẹrun ọkọ l'aiye*. The novel, which examines the modern girl's sexuality in a patriarchal time in history, is full of network metaphors, as the female protagonist builds a network along the West African coast through her sexual relationships with men of different races.

Across the Niger, in northern Nigeria, a small literary network was founded by a colonial official, Rupert East, who, in 1933, started a literary project at Katsina College. According to Graham Furniss, East's sole objective was to encourage the Nigerian students and staff of the college to 'write novels/novellas of around 20,000 words that he would then publish through the renamed Literature Bureau' (Furniss 11). East sees the project as being 'neither for the edification of the mind, nor the good of the soul' (12). East's sentiment and prejudice show that the network that he founded – unlike the Lagos networks that were started by Nigerians – was a project that was geared to be part of the colonial government's educational policy. Also worth noting is that the people he selected were mainly males from the ruling classes of northern Nigeria, among whom was a young Abubakar Tafawa Balewa, who later became the first and only Prime Minister of Nigeria after colonial rule.

Some four decades after the 1920s, a new network of artisans and lower middle-class people emerged in East Nigeria. Onitsha market literature, which emerged from the city of Onitsha, is a good example of a literary network that disrupts the idea that literary networks are mainly constituted of educated professional middle-class men and women. The writers, publishers, printers and booksellers who made the genre popular were not university-educated, and the literature that emerged from this circle continues to capture literary imagination in light of the amount of scholarly research on the genre. This research is epitomised by the scholarly works of Emmanuel N. Obiechina and Donatus I. Nwoga as well as the collection that has been digitised by the University of Kansas, USA.

Not only did literary networks inspire new genres of literature as discussed above, they also helped to cement the idea of national literature, by nurturing writers who changed the course of global literary history. For example, the establishment of the Mbari Club by Ulli Beier at the University of Ibadan brought attention to the emerging talents Wole Soyinka, John Pepper Clark, Chinua Achebe and Mabel Segun. In the years leading to independence in Kenya, new literary networks also emerged at the University of Nairobi, with the establishment of the Chemi Chemi literary club by the South African writer and scholar Es'kia Mphalele, who had previously been the managing editor of the Mbari Club. Mphalele was a good networker, who linked the literary networks in Ibadan and Nairobi together, which in turn encouraged the movement of creative figures between East and West Africa.

Networks in Kenya

A rich literary history existed in Kenya, long before Mphalele arrived in Nairobi. Much has been written on the Swahili literary traditions that began in the thirteenth century by several notable scholars including Alamin A. Mazrui, who came from a long line of Swahili intellectuals. In Kenya, as in Nigeria, European missionaries and colonialists introduced the printing press. According to Maurice N. Amutabi, the first printed press in Kenya, the *Taveta Chronicle*, was set up in 1895 to propagate European ideas as superior to the African ways of life. And as a response, a network of journalists, writers, editors, marketers and readers began to emerge in the early twentieth century. The *African Standard* (now *East African Standard*), which was owned by A.M. Jevanjee, was the leader of the pack of newspapers in the first decade of that century. It was later followed by the young Jomo Kenyatta's *Muigwithania*, which was arguably the first Kikuyu language newspaper of note. With regard to these print publication networks, Simon Gikandi uses his father's cousin – the renowned Kikuyu writer and journalist Gakaara wa Wanjaũ – as an example to provide an interesting account of how, in the first half of the last century, the printing press helped to bring about a new literary network in Kenya, made up of writers, journalists printers, editors and readers. Gikandi argues that: 'In the colonial world, it was assumed by colonizer and colonized alike that the very existence of the printed book produced new subjects and transformed customs and manners' (205). What Gikandi's argument demonstrates is that, as in Nigeria, printing presses in Kenya, as well as newspapers, small magazines and books of colonial and postcolonial era, including those written in Kenyan and Indian languages, produced new cultural forms such as written short stories, didactic Christian texts and journalism while cementing old oral traditions that made new publics possible. Race, class and gender also intersect with regard to these networks. For example, there were publications owned by Africans with an African readership that published mainly in Kenyan languages, while at the same time, there were publications in Indian languages like Gujarati, which targeted South Asians living in Kenya. There were also publications in the English language targeting European, African and Indian middle classes. The people who managed these networks were men, and analyses were written mainly from a man's perspective.

In both Kenya and Nigeria, early signs of anti-colonial struggles in colonial West and East Africa can be found in the various networks of print publications that existed during the colonial era. Gakaara for instance, in 1946, established a published network by the name African Book Writers Limited, which according to Cristiana Pugliese, was 'the first company of writers in Kenya and, possibly, one of the first in the whole of Sub-Saharan Africa' (178). It seems as if one of Gakaara's main objectives for starting a literary network, was to challenge the colonial view of Kikuyuness and Kenyanness, as he and his contemporaries place the Kikuyu language at the centre of the production, and address their readers from this viewpoint. Gakaara especially produced literature that incurred the wrath of colonial officials who proceeded to jailed him for eight years. Such subversive assertions and literary activism make print culture in Kenya and Nigeria significant, particularly through the literary networks' foregrounding of the epistemic violence of colonialism and an emergent activist response to this. The works of writers writing in both English and the Kenyan languages, from the first decade of the twentieth century, provided Kenyans with an avenue to tell their own stories from an African perspective.

Post-independence Literary Circles

In the 1970s and 1980s, new literary circles of serious and middlebrow literature emerged that catered to the expanding middle classes in Kenya as well as Nigeria. Heinemann's African Writers Series edited by Chinua Achebe, for example, provided a platform on which serious writers from across the continent were published, while Macmillan's Pacesetter Series can be seen as having catered for those less interested in the serious tone set by Heinemann. These publishing platforms respond to the demand of the African literature market, as readers are looking for stories that address concerns about politics, love, romance, growing urbanisation and the disillusionment with the postcolonial state. The writers in this period not only address themes within their countries of origin, but they also introduce African readers to everyday life in other African countries, and in that respect, they are also Pan-Africanist writers. The popularity of both serious and middlebrow titles among Africans also show that there was a lucrative market for African literature that attracted foreign publishers such as Macmillan and Heinemann.

Although there are female writers like Charity Waciuma and Grace Ogot from Kenya and Flora Nwapa and Mabel Segun from Nigeria, most of the literary figures I have mentioned in previous paragraphs are male, because literary circles in the last century were male-centric. This is an issue that was raised by the Ghanaian writer Ama Ata Aidoo in the documentary *The Art of Ama Ata Aidoo* (2014). The list of writers and publishers of Onitsha Market Literature features only a few women. Although there were African women writers, editors and readers, men largely dominated much of the critical engagement with African literature and were often (albeit erroneously) seen as the leaders – the 'authentic' voice of African writing.

The Literary Networks of the Twenty-first Century

The digital networks I am going to be discussing in this section can be read as the twenty-first century's version of the small magazines and clubs that I have discussed above. Since they are constituted as cyber-communities, they can also be seen as the digital version of the village square where artists gather to perform for the discerning public. Like the literary networks of the print era, digital networks emerge as a response to the challenges of the twenty-first century. Just as the print culture helped to create the literary networks of the last century, the rise of the digital culture in the twenty-first century led to the birth of new literary networks in Nigeria and Kenya. The increase in internet uptake generates a new kind of sociability, one in which lovers of African literature can come together to write and discuss literature in addition to other issues such as politics, cultural practices and news stories.

Not only does the internet age allow for this new kind of sociability which does not require physical presence, it also brings new and cheaper means of publishing creative writings. The disillusionment expressed by the fictional character of Ujunwa in *Jumping Monkey Hill*, reflects the disenchantment with the world of book publishing by many within the literary circles of Nigeria and Kenya, with many writers and would-be publishers looking for means to publish African literature on their own terms. New literary networks emerged from the digital space out of a growing disquiet about the nature of patronage of African literature by Western institutions, and about what constitutes African writing. Should writers still stick to the format created by the likes of Ngũgĩ and Achebe, or should they experiment and tell their own story?

Jumping Monkey Hill not only questions the power dynamic in the global literary network, it reflects the conversations taking place across many literary listservs about the place of African literature in the global space. In a cross-posted post on *Krazitivity*, Tunde Leye articulates this disquiet as part of his choice for self-publishing and for publishing on digital platforms:

> So it was that when the great Chinua Achebe died, there were all sorts of cries from all sorts of corners for us to revive the good old days of Nigerian publishing, to bring the publishing industry back to its old glory ... Virtually all of their books, even Fagunwa's book written in Yoruba and Tutuola's in Pidgin-English were published by foreign publishing houses. Fast forward to the next generation after these men, the Okey Ndibes and Pius Adesanmis generation, and the same thing applies. In the generation that is emerging after Mr. Ndibe's, Chimamanda Adichie, Teju Cole and Nnedi Okorafor's generation, it is the same ... The confinement of Nigerian writing to a certain straitjacket is a direct result of this – the foreign publisher is in business after all and will publish only the Nigerian stories that conform to the expectations of their readers, and which they can sell. The single story which we often scream hoarse about has its roots here. We simply have not given our authors the opportunity to tell our own stories, from the multiplicity of angles and spanning the old and emerging Africa without going through the prism of foreign Western publishing. (n.pag)

Similar sentiments are expressed by Keguro Macharia and Wambui Mwangi in their explanation on the formation of the Koroga network:

> [W]e as Koroga artists are constantly bombarded with images of 'Africa' that do not resemble either our memories or our imaginaries. As Africans, our subjective and concrete experiences of 'home' are constantly over-written, always framed by other voices and imaginaries about Africa. Western imaginaries frame Africa with such authority that the visual symbols used by the Kenyan government in its official images are indistinguishable from those deployed by a colonial government

insistent on spectacularly empty vistas, 'exotic' wildlife and the picaresque 'authentic' pastoralist peoples. (2)

The two statements suggest that people within the literary networks of Nigeria and Kenya are aware of the politics of book publishing and want to subvert it by forming their own networks with the aim of publishing on their own terms. This attempt is not borne out of the need to respond directly to the West, as Ngũgĩ and Achebe did, but several writers are more interested in re-orientating fellow Africans towards African aesthetics that speak to the complexity of their societies, to a complex history and to cultures that continue to evolve in an ever-changing world. Additionally, some of the writers and fellow artists operating within these literary circles are alluding to the idea that much of the most authentic writing that reflects the 'real' Africa can be found in small online magazines run by Africans and on listservs, in addition to those self-published on blogs and on social media platforms. These works have the African digital communities as their targeted audience, and they often take on subjects such as sex work and same-sex desire that may not be well represented in the traditional publishing industry.

Another factor for the creation of digital networks was a hostile political atmosphere in both Nigeria and Kenya during the mid- to late 1990s, which led to many writers leaving for exile in Europe and North America. As internet technology took off in the mid-1990s, groups of writers began to congregate on websites such as the now defunct *Nigeria.com*, and literary networks began to emerge as listservs on digital services provided by companies like Yahoo, Microsoft and Google. This development arose from the perceived freedom of the internet, which offers people a safe space to combine politics and literature, without being monitored or attacked by the authorities.

Krazitivity is one of Nigeria's most important literary networks to have emerged from the digital space, because of the impetus it gave to, and continues to give, to Nigerian literature. *Krazitivity* came into being because of the determination of a group of mostly creative writers, but also journalists, artists, scholars, publishers and avid readers, who wanted to extend the parameters of Nigerian literature by focusing on producing literary texts that address the Nigerian condition, that of Africa and its Diaspora. *Krazitivity* is a treasure trove for researchers interested in digital literary networks, but unfortunately the conversations as well as much of the literature posted on its forum cannot be used in this book due to the bye-laws guiding members, of which this author is one.

Krazitivity, interestingly, started as a network of online-savvy Nigerians in Nigeria and its Diaspora on 10 September 2001 – one day before the infamous attacks in New York and Washington, DC. The list of its founding members read like a list of Who-Is-Who of Nigerian literature, with figures like Olu Oguibe, Sola Osofisan, Akin Adesokan, Ogaga Ifowodo, Remi Raji, Koleade Odutola, Amatoritsere Ede, Ikhide Ikheloa, Okey Ndibe, Folasayo Dele-Ogunrinde, Toyin Akinosho, Chika Unigwe and Esiaba Irobi. Not long after it took off, *Krazitivity* members included notable figures such as Bibi Bakare-Yusuf, Lola Shoneyin, Chuma Nwokolo, Sefi Atta, Jeremy Weate, Chris Abani, Ike Anya, Chimamanda Adichie, Molara Wood, Helon Habila and Sarah Ladipo Mayinka, among others.

Among the objectives set by the original members of the listserv is: '[t]he VISION to provide a cerebral space for writers, artists, and thinkers of Nigerian affiliation to construct synergies, debate and review issues, critique and appraise themselves, exchange information, propound ideas, assess them, and troubleshoot the myriad ramifications of Africa's interface with the world' (n.pag).

This mission statement highlights the importance of literary networks for the survival and the development of literature. Every day, and at times several times daily, writers, scholars, journalists, artists, publishers and readers indulge in some or all of the elements stated above in *Krazitivity*'s objectives. For example, discussions around alternative means of disseminating African literature led to the establishments of creative writing websites such as *Africanwriters.com* and *African-writing.com*. Members of this network were also part of initiatives such as the Abuja Writers Forum and Ebedi Residency. Ebedi is an international residency project for African writers that is financed by the writer-cum-politician Wale Okediran. Ebedi started in 2010 and was opened by the eminent playwright Femi Osofisan. Abuja Writers Forum offers a monthly creative writing workshop, as well as training in creative writing for up-and-coming writers writing in English and in Nigerian languages.

The emergence of similar literary circles in Kenya in the first decade of the twenty-first century underlines the notions of literature for experimentation, collaboration and disconnection from specifics of place, politics and culture. Kwani Trust is arguably Kenya's most influential literary network due to the way it has helped shape literary outputs from the country. *Kwani?* network was founded in 2003, as a digital publication launched by Binyavanga Wainaina, after he won the Caine Prize for African Writing. The publication soon grew into Kenya's most formidable literary network with members that include literary editors, writers, journalists and public relations professionals. Kwani Trust not only publishes creative writings in print and digital forms, it also organises workshops for up-and-coming writers to help them hone their creative writing skills. Kwani published Yvonne Adhiambo Owuor's short story, *Weight of Whispers*, which won the 2003 Caine Prize. Additionally, Kwani runs literary festivals in the Kenyan cities of Lamu and Nairobi, and also maintains alliances with other literary networks on the continent and worldwide. Many of its members, for example, were instrumental in forming the Concerned Kenyan Writers group (CKW), a closed literary network that is also a listserv.

The sociability and alliances that one sees in Kwani in particular, and in Kenyan digital networks in general, provide robust insight into network production. For example, Tony Mochama's short story, *The Road to Eldoret*, was written as part of a group of writers' collective response to Kenya's post-election violence of 2007. It was first published as a short story in a collaborative project by the CKW literary network, before it was published on the *Kwani?* website, and it later became part of a short story collection *The Road to Eldoret and Other Stories* (2009), issued by Nairobi's Brown Bear Insignia publishers. There is also Billy Kahora's *The True Story of David Munyakei: Goldenberg Whistleblower*, which was first published three years earlier in 2005, as a short story *Munyakei on the Coast*, on Wambui Mwangi's blog Diary of a Mad Kenyan Woman. The story was also serialised in 2006, in an online magazine, *The New Black Magazine*. The story then developed into book length in 2008, when it was published by *Kwani?* Kahora, Mwangi, the publishers of *Kwani? Magazine*, and the publisher of *The New Black Magazine* (the author of this book), all belong to the CKW group. What becomes obvious is, that in addition to creative writers, there is a set of facilitators involved in the production of texts in a digital age, and these facilitators often belong to the same network. Given the energy many network members have brought to African literature, it is no gainsaying that digital literary networks are incubators of new literary innovations and they can be seen as the platforms that breathe new life into Africa's literary culture.

Network Aesthetics

While much of this chapter is about alliances and shared values that networks foster, it is also worth pointing out that alliances do not always work out. Members often disagree on issues such as aesthetics and politics. For example, *Ederi* network came into being due to disagreements within the *Krazitivity* group. And when in February 2018, Chimamanda Adichie questioned the very essence of postcolonial studies, she was derided by writers within her literary circles, including the Kenyan writer Shailja Patel, who posted a rejoinder on Twitter. However, this section is not about network dissents, but focuses on the importance of alliances, interconnectedness and cross-connections to what constitutes the arts in the digital age.

In his seminal work, 'African Aesthetics' (2001), Rowland Abiodun predicts a disavowal of the usual Euro-centric anthropological approach to African aesthetics. He sees a return to an African aesthetic tradition that makes use of sound, sight and soul. Abiodun talks about how the philosophy of African aesthetics is as grounded in the individual as it is in the community. While he does not directly use the word 'network' in his essay, Abiodun uses the example of the Yoruba art world in signposting to us how a network of people works together to determine aesthetics. Abiodun starts with the word Aṣa, which, depending on the context, can be used to describe 'new style' or 'tradition'. In the Yoruba world, according to Abiodun, experts on beauty are art critics, who are known as 'Amẹwa'. He surmises: 'When used in the context of Yoruba artistic discourse, "aṣa" refers to a style or the result of a creative and intelligent combination of styles from a wide range of available options within the culture' (17). If one applies Abiodun's theory, in the Yoruba world as in many Nigerian and Kenyan societies, artists including writers draw their inspirations from a wide range of traditions and media. In the twenty-first century, this tradition of Yoruba people's 'aṣa' is giving birth to a new style-'aṣa', one in which artists are collaborating within a network. A literary network is an extension of the experience of the collective; the sum total of how a group sees the world, although each member may not agree on any issues most of the time. Networks are about alliances and social groupings as much as they are about shared aesthetics. Our conception of aesthetics within the digital platform is incomplete if we omit the various elements on which it is based. The written is interlinked with the visual and the auditory. They all come together to provide aesthetically pleasing arts. This development reprises Abiodun's notion of African aesthetics.

In building on Abiodun's thesis, I am drawn to the *Koroga* project initially started on Tumblr, in which the individual artist and the community have come together to define African aesthetics in the digital space. In Kenya, between 2010 and 2013, several new voices – poets, intellectuals and photographers – came together to start *Koroga*, a digital project that marries poetry with photography. *Koroga* is conceived as a series of collaborative projects between a network of photographers and poets, who are based in Kenya, Africa and its Diaspora. In this regard, it provides an innovative way of reimagining the potentials of African poetics through its connection with another art form – photography. And since networks in their mode of operation are often about collaborative endeavours rather than individual efforts, *Koroga* allows us to see, and even imagine, what happens when artists across different genres come together. For the artists, the purpose is not only to challenge each other to provide a more robust African story, but also to nurture members.

There are fifty-five projects in total. Each project is framed as a postcard – a symbol of network communication that has been around for over a century. Each postcard is a proof of the *Koroga* collective's commitment to the ethics of creating not just aesthetically pleasing work, but one that is rooted in lived experience. *Koroga* is also not focused mainly on Kenyan politics, but the poets and photographers provide a wider lens to chronicle the quotidian of twenty-first-century life. Each *Koroga* as a postcard can be read as a specially conceived message to the digital public that occupies the network known as the world wide web. In a statement on *Koroga*'s page on the social media site Tumblr Keguro Macharia, one of the project founders, points out that *Koroga*:

'is another African story, a story of what we see and how we see, of meetings and transformations, of looking and seeing, of seeing and writing, of speaking into being the worlds we know, and those we are always imagining'. Macharia deploys network metaphors in asserting that *Koroga* is about the complexity of Africa; that there is not one Africa but many Africas, just as network thinking is not a straight line but several lines connected to hubs. The power of poetry lies in the fact that it often holds a mirror to the individual soul as well as to the soul of a society: prodding conscience; asking questions about and elucidating the human experience. In the *Koroga* project, photography provides a visual depiction of what poetry does. As Macharia has argued, photography in modern Africa provides Africans with the chance to wrestle the narrative of seeing away from a Western aesthetic that often uses photography to portray the continent as the embodiment of abnormality and the antithesis of the West. In addition, the poets and photographers provide a wider lens to chronicle the quotidian of twenty-first century life. The latter will be discussed further in the next chapter.

Koroga feels and reads like a digital exhibition, with its 'curators' explicitly stating their intention to challenge the enduring presentation of Africa to the outside world by book publishers and journalists from the metropolitan centres of the West. But *Koroga* should also be read as a rejection of the current state of Africa's indigenous book publishing. There are of course, local publishing houses in Nairobi, Lagos and Johannesburg, but the subject matters covered by *Koroga* may be deemed unsuitable by publishers who want their books to be adopted in school curricula. An example of this could be found in Wambui Wamae Kamiru Collymore's poem *Nightdresses*, with a photograph by Wambui Mwangi.

In the image-poetry posted on *Koroga*'s Tumblr page, the speaker is a sex worker, who is unashamedly puncturing the fake morality of a female onlooker and her society when it comes to the way the community views women who refuse to conform to accepted sexual norms. The vivid image portrayed in the poetry may be deemed unsuitable for a poetry book that will be marketed for the school curriculum, but the power of the literary network enables the poet and the photographer to give voice to the figure of the prostitute. Postcards by their nature are not concealed and the message in a postcard is open to anyone who may encounter it. 'The postcard,' argues Alon Confino, 'also eliminated the veil of secrecy, privacy, and personal property associated with letters' (179). *Nightdresses* as a postcard reveals the inner workings of Nairobi's libidinal economy, in which the sex worker is the principal actor. The sexual market is one in which female sex workers walk the streets of Nairobi in revealing dresses that they hope will attract clients. *Nightdresses* challenges a postcolonial history of secrecy around sex works, which in turn marginalises and punishes female sex workers, while leaving the male patrons of sex work untouched. The literary network in the digital age (in the context of *Koroga*) then becomes a community that uses literature to bring the private into the open. The figure of the prostitute also becomes a symbol that challenges the hypocrisy of the society on moral issues.

Koroga is a digital project that robustly narrates the complexity of Africa. Macharia and his co-curator Wambui Mwangi realise that reframing Africa's image is a daunting task that can only be accomplished by a group of creative artists, and that these artists should share similar world views, especially in terms of the place of African arts in the world. Perhaps the curators also realised that the digital space provides a cheaper and more viable means of doing this. Being students of history, Macharia and Mwangi know that across many African societies the poetic and the visual often intersect, and *Koroga* can be read as reprise of the history of symbiotic relationships between different art forms. *Koroga* is grounded in aesthetically pleasing formats, in which well-thought-out poems are woven into beautiful photographs.

This book will keep returning to *Koroga* because it is a project that exemplifies network capability. Although primarily hosted on Tumblr, *Koroga* projects are cross-hosted on a network of digital platforms. For example, in 2010, I was asked by its curators Wambui Mwangi and Keguro Macharia to run parts of the project on *newblackmagazine.com* – an online magazine that I publish. The projects can also be found on Facebook, Twitter and a few other blogs. In the process, *Koroga* creates new publics and new articulation of Kenyanness and Africanness. It shows digital African networks as sites of not just raw data, but, as Macharia reminds us, as sites that generate their own theory. For example, if we are asking questions such as: is there an African digital aesthetic? Should works of arts communicate direct social and political messages? Who should be their public and how should these works be shown? *Koroga* offers a space to theorise on these questions.

Koroga as Material Metaphor

Koroga can be seen as an embodiment of the strength of the network that is based on the collective. Each postcard reflects the argument that network aesthetics in the digital age can best be appreciated through a transmedia format – that is a combination of many different media forms across multiple platforms. Not that the novel or the printed book no longer matter, but there is a different aesthetic standard for what is published in the digital space because of the nature of the media from which it emerges. *Koroga* provides the space to look at the way in which digital networks and different technological entities connect to one another.

A good example of this aesthetic is the *Koroga* project entitled, *The Writing on the Screen*. In this collaboration between Ngwatillo Mawiyoo and Andrew Njoroge, *Koroga* sees poetography as an aesthetic strategy that places Africa at the heart of digital visibility. The image in this postcard is centred around a female broadcaster for KTN (Kenya Television Network) – a news network that is the first privately owned television station in Anglophone Africa. Networks provide a useful means to imagine and build new networks, and in this network context, KTN is a model for many non-governmental digital media broadcasters across the continent, because at its inception it was known for its fiercely independent journalism that places Kenya and Africa at the core of its news network operations. One can therefore read this postcard as signalling the intention of *Koroga* to follow in the step of KTN, as a powerful network that speaks truth to power. The possibility alluded to by the speaker in the accompanying poem may be read as *Koroga*'s intention to be a network that can serve as an inspiration for the birth of new networks. The network speaks to a renewal and an imaging of a Kenya which is different from much of the portrayals in Western media. It imagines a self-confident nation and continent.

Social Media Platforms as Literary Networks

In an email conversation on *Ederi* listserv, the Nigerian writer and publisher Richard Ali points to the sociability and multiple negotiations between the world of book publishing and that of digital publishing:

> The writers in my generation do a lot of talking amongst themselves. For example, I met a girl on Facebook, I liked her short stories and we got talking, she had an MS, I read the first chapters and was bowled over, so I edited for her, tried to bring out something a bit better from the first half of her MS, she sent first chapters to a small press in America and they accepted and, while they didn't pay her an advance, they gave her a contract, published her and made her books available in print and via Amazon [she's working on making it available in Nigeria now]. I've never met the girl, still haven't. Yet, we are Facebook buddies and belong to a small Nerdz Lounge on Blackberry Messenger. A lot of the conversation the internet has fostered in this my dubbed Unapologetic Generation is within ourselves.

What this statement by Ali (who is also a co-owner of Paressia Book Publishers) illustrates is the place of digital media for understanding literary networks of African writers in the second decade of the twenty-first century. We cannot robustly theorise African literature without analysing its digital network. The printed book and the digital network have a symbiotic relationship and they breathe life into each other. This relationship shows the way in which technology continuously intervenes in African arts and in African subjectivity. Technology regularly encourages the birth of new textual genres in Africa. For example, the literature that came out of the last century mediated between African and European traditions, spawning new models of fiction, poetry and theatre. A good example is the contemporary Yoruba Ewi poetry. The work of its leading exponent, Lanrewaju Adepoju, combines the Yoruba oral tradition with audio-visual technology as well as the computer. The digital age continues this tradition of generating and sharing African stories through technology. And in the process, technology is allowing writers to respond in real time to a changing society and to a changing world.

New networks are built on social media between different writers, who may not have met in real-life. They tag each other's work on Twitter and Facebook, in an attempt to create awareness for themselves and their works. Tagging, as a means of building networks, also allows writers to comment on each other's work – the aesthetic merit and timeliness. Additionally, writers and readers are now more closely connected than in the past. Offline public engagements are announced online, and writers regularly use digital platforms to announce book publication dates and to point readers to where they can purchase their work. Writers create content on Facebook and may develop these materials for a book project or for YouTube. These writers may be active across several digital networks, while also actively engaging with several offline associations. This multidirectional relationship speaks to the multilayeredness of the relationships between social networks and other digital platforms, as well as between offline platforms. These fluid and multiple negotiations between print and online mediums represent the way in which online and offline social interactions are not set in stone, and like their texts, many of these writers move seamlessly between these platforms. One can also argue that the online and the offline worlds of African literature are interrelated and are becoming increasingly blended. One major difference, however, lies in the fact that writers think the online space offers them greater freedom for self-expression and that it brings them closer to readers and fellow writers alike, in a way that may have been impossible in the book age.

While on 1 June 1962, several African writers had to travel to Makarere University in Kampala, Uganda, to meet other writers at the first conference on African literature, today, many young writers meet instead on social media (Instagram, Facebook and Twitter), listservs and on blogs. They communicate with each other daily from the comfort of their homes, internet cafés, offices or even on public transport. While writers are still attending conferences and retreats, much of the organisation is now done online. In the 'golden' age of the printed book, most literary events took place in capital cities, but nowadays, because even few and geographically scattered people can find one another easily online and then organising a get-together, offline meetings are no longer concentrated in major national literary network hubs like Lagos, Abuja or Nairobi. For example, there are regular and impromptu literary gatherings in sub-hubs like Kisumu, Ilesha, Port-Harcourt, Ibadan, Minna and Kano. And these events attract members of the public as well as budding and established writers.

In the digital space, many writers, young and old, regularly publish work in cyberspace with the expectation that readers will comment on this work. When the eminent poet Niyi Osundare sought to respond to the election of Busola Saraki as the new leader of the Nigerian Senate House, he posted his poem on the Facebook page of a popular Nigerian digital news media organisation, *Saharareporters.com*. Osundare's *Blues for the New Senate King*, has drawn commendations and condemnations from readers and the poem has been shared across different social media platforms. Some writers, meanwhile, invite readers into their personal space, as they are 'friends' of their readers on Facebook and on Twitter. In social networking, the word 'friend' is simultaneously a noun and a verb for the writer and her readers. A reader can add a writer to her (the reader's) friend-list, which is to 'friend' the writer, or vice-versa. If the 'friend' request is accepted, both the writer and the reader become virtual friends, able to see each other's personal life in pictures and in videos. On Twitter, several African writers ask their readers to 'follow' them through tweets. Some of these writers regularly share family photos, reports on daily activities, political thoughts and fashion tips with their readers on social media, alongside short stories and poetry.

Networks in Digital Films

Elzbieta Winiecka enjoins literary theorists to see beyond the literariness of creative writings, because 'when we observe new writing practices taking shape online, in an ethereal, virtual and interactive digital environment, we need to rethink the ontological, aesthetic, political, and social properties of what we have been accustomed to give the enigmatic and circumspect appellations of literature and literariness' (34). This is an argument that echoes the one I make consistently in this book; *African Literature in the Digital Age* invites us to rethink our approach to the traditional means of textual analysis, in which the focus is mainly on the text. In the age of the internet, literary aesthetics should also include the multimedia formats that co-exist with the written text on our screen. The value judgement that we made on what constituted literature in the past no longer holds water in the twenty-first century.

Therefore, if, as highlighted in the previous section of this chapter, the poetography of *Koroga* signposts us to the aesthetics of print and news media networks and the possibilities such network productions offer the African imagination, I want to explore the way in which emerging multimedia creative endeavours are using fictional characters to create material and metaphoric network symbols. Patrick Jagoda (2016) makes a convincing case for using films to unpack network aesthetics. Jagoda's argument is foregrounded on cinematic experimentations that speak to an interconnectedness, which can be robustly articulated through the application of network analogies. Film productions on the African continent provide the ideal site for the application of network thinking. After all, in countries like Nigeria, scriptwriters and filmmakers have been able to circumvent the lack of financial support from the national government and corporate bodies, to successfully challenge the domination of Hollywood and Bollywood, by producing films that have made the local film industry, Nollywood, a global phenomenon. And since the digital space offers African writers and multimedia artists, as well as film producers a vibrant and less costly platform to experiment, it is no surprise that scriptwriters are producing works that incorporate local and foreign concepts into films that can be found on platforms such as YouTube.

A good example of such projects is the diversity of Makmende films, which are available on YouTube. These short films are made by different groups but are connected through the original Makmende character. For example, Makmende 2, produced on 24 July 2013, is an adaptation that is loosely based on the original Makmende 1 film. The original is a 5.25-minute music video entitled *Forever People (Do It So Delicious)* that was first posted on YouTube on 14 March 2010, by the popular Kenyan musical group Just A Band. It is Kenya's first viral video and by the start of 2019, it had garnered over 800,000 views. In the song, Makmende is the crime-fighting hero with the ability to make the impossible possible. Dina Ligaga points out that the word 'Makmende' is a Sheng word that came out the phrase 'Go ahead, make my day,' uttered by Clint Eastwood's Dirty Harry character in the Hollywood film *Sudden Impact* (6). While, according to Patrick Jagoda (2016), network films in the American context are sites of chaos and happenstances, both Makmende 1 and Makmende 2 emanate from the aesthetics of refashioning: the original comes out of a music video by a popular band, in which a professional actor is hired to act the part of the fictional hero Makmende. The adaptation (Makmende 2) reimagines the original Makmende as having a son who possesses superhero powers, who, at the end of the twenty-one-minute film, is compared to the American superhero Superman.

James Yeku uses the term 'online fan fiction writing' to describe the genres of African remediation that show 'that digital media platforms of literary and cultural representations function as creative spaces for mini-narratives, which can force scholars to think of African literature in an age of digital reproduction differently' (262). Yeku argues that in the age of Web 2.0, the notion of authorship is disrupted by fans who use new media technologies to rewrite original pieces of works, and in the process new subjectivities are created, and the new works take on a life of their own. In light of Yeku's theory, one can argue that the different versions of Makmende can be analysed as showing us the way in which digital African stories within digital networks are being retold by fans of the original stories through intertextual and intervisual mediation. This argument is predicated on the fact that YouTube is a social media network of artists and publics, whose mode of operation is based on participatory and multidirectional practices. The implications for creative works on this platform is that they can be rearranged and modified in many new ways by the digital public as a response to their aesthetic values. A musical genre gives birth to a cinematic genre, which then gives birth to a new postcolonial vocabulary. This digital enablement also gives birth to a new discourse among the audience on YouTube, some of whom suggest that Kenya needs a Makmende to clean up corruption in politics and crime in the society. The new versions in the process not only pay homage to the original, but they also add value to it, as exemplified by the fact that the original Makmende is an internet sensation with far more 'likes' from users than any of the remixes.

YouTube as a social media network enables the multiplicity of different subjects and subjectivities from one or several sources. These different variants can be thought of as coming out of a network, with the potential to form their own networks, which are also linked to other networks, especially in the digital space. As mentioned, Makmende 1 derives its name from Sheng, a postcolonial urban language that came out of Swahili and English languages, in addition to a sprinkle of other indigenous Kenyan languages such as Kikuyu and Luo. The Sheng version of the word is in itself based on an archetypal Hollywood movie, with a lead character that Ligaga surmises is modelled as a Blaxploitation figure with Afro hairstyle and flare trousers. Here, we can see the original version as reflecting global interconnectedness. Makmende 1 – through the fans of the fictional character and the music group Just A Band – then takes on different life forms by the many renditions available on YouTube and online forums, of which Makmende 2 is only one. Other versions of Makmende include Ben Karanja's *Makmende Goes After Hitler*, in which short clips from several Hollywood movies are mashed together with a short clip from the original Makmende film. There is Mugambi Nthiga's *Makmende Rescues Eve and Gaetano from Taste of Daynjah*, in which the superhero rescues two kidnapped journalists from the hands of their abductors. Another version is a martial-arts animation entitled *Makmende (aka Bushido Brown) dies fighting Stinkmeaners Hateocracy*. The longest of the versions is Makmende 2, a futuristic science fiction, in which the son of Makmende comes from outer space to continue his father's legacy. With this inheritance, he gets to fight earthlings and aliens on earth and in outer space.

The remediation that one sees in Makmende 2 can be read as digital network aesthetic being a continuation of previous aesthetic traditions, but in the process new subjectivities are produced, and a new future is envisioned. While Makmende 1 is an ordinary man who fights corruption and criminals with his martial arts skills, the son exists in a futuristic virtual world and is confronted with different realities, in which he uses machines that fly between the earth and space, in addition to his martial-arts skills. Digital aesthetics as argued previously is rooted in experimentation, and also in playfulness. The role of the fan and the author is not delineated as the fan can become the author through the refashioning of a creative work, and that remediated work can also be refashioned by new fans. Before the digital age, a particular piece of art was normally associated with a single creator, but the way in which creators and fans interact on platforms such as YouTube, and the affordability of writing and producing in digital space means that the way we judge aesthetics and the value we place on such judgement has changed. The author or the artist interacts in real-time every day with her fans, something that did not exist in the past. As digital networks link different cultural spaces together they are thus embedded in a state of flux where there is not just one reality but many realities.

If the concept of network as discussed in this chapter seems applicable to a vast array of artistic endeavours, it is because the very idea of network speaks to limitless possibilities. Human beings are network beings, and if no man is an island it is because we are always seeking to build a connection with others, from the family level to the societal and national levels. We produce tools and ideas that make connections possible. Networks are not solely ideas that came out of modern technologies, they are notions that societies have been using for many centuries. The Swahili coastal civilisation came about through a network that connects Africa with Asia, the old Oyo Kingdom of Yoruba people operated as a network run by powerful kings, chiefs and their underlings. The Underground Railroad was a network of people that brought freedom to many enslaved Africans in the United States and Canada. These monumental eras in African and African diasporic history signpost us to the power and the robustness of network. Network controls and subjugates, it also frees people and builds new cultural forms. These elements, in my view, should be borne in mind as we think about network and its many varieties.

Class and Poetry in the Digital Age 2

Back in 1999, Terry Harpold predicted that Africa would epitomise the heart of digital darkness. Harpold uses Joseph Conrad's *Heart of Darkness* in pointing out the futility of imagining an African digital age. He surmises that no studies or data available at the time can 'account for the extreme local obstacles which must be overcome before anything like a viable African internet is possible' (par. 22). Two decades or so later, not only does Africa have more mobile phone users than Europe but internet usage on the continent is also growing rapidly. As discussed in this book, the past decade has also seen a boom in online-based communities, websites and social media pages that target Africans at home and overseas. As in most African countries, leading politicians in both Kenya and Nigeria target online readers as potential voters on platforms such as Facebook and Twitter. The Nigerian and Kenyan presidents, for example, maintain an active social media presence, with millions of followers. Governors and legislators in these two countries are also active on social media. Poets often try to speak truth to power, while politicians use this space daily to communicate with the same audience that poetry is targeting. Readers are equally likely to be educated and they often use social media to partake in political discussions and to follow popular culture, in addition to using these mediums for historical and cultural events. Such poets and their readers can therefore be regarded as people who possess cultural and digital capital. They are members of Africa's digerati. Elżbieta Winiecka describes digerati as 'people who actively participate in creating a new type of culture, based on the generation, transmission, and management of [digital] information' (34). And giving the power that these writers and readers have, one can argue that class intersects with the poetic and the political in the digital age.

As demonstrated throughout this book, for many poets from Kenya and Nigeria, literature in cyberspace is not entirely separate from book publishing nor from an oral performance in a physical space, as they use online mediums in a way that suggests orature, that the print platform and cyberspace complement one another, and that they are both germane to African literature in a new age. For example, poetry posted on Facebook may be performed for members of the public in the real space of Lagos and Nairobi, and the recording of those performances may be posted on YouTube and Facebook for consumption by the online public. Young poets such as David Ishaya Osu (Nigeria), Dami Ajayi (Nigeria), Jumoke Verissimo (Nigeria), Saddiq M. Dzukogi (Nigeria) and Redscar McOdindo K'Oyuga (Kenya) publish poems almost every week on Facebook, many of which later form part of print collections. The poetry of established voices such as Shailja Patel (Kenya), Sitawa Namwalie (Kenya), Amatoritsero Ede (Nigeria) and Niyi Osundare (Nigeria) are also part of social media poetry culture and their works may appear as part of a collection of creative book projects. These processes arguably involve reshaping the text for different formats, and through this process the creative piece is unfixed and susceptible to changes. These textual movements across spoken words, the print medium and cyberspace speak to the malleability of texts, and also to the transnational middle-class lifestyle – and upbringing – of several members of a new generation of African voices.

Historicising Class

African literature in English has always been a product of middle-class authors because when the European missionaries introduced the printing press to Nigeria and Kenya, one of their main goals was to create a new African middle class that would be able to read and write in English, as J.F.A Ajayi surmises: 'the emergence of such a class was perhaps the most concrete feature of the social revolution that the missionaries envisaged.' (18). Although there were several publications in African languages, English was the institutional language of the print culture, even as it was used to subvert colonial rule. It was, and still is, the language with which many middle-class Africans communicate amongst themselves and their tool of communication with the outside world. It is also an aspirational tool that those who are below the middle class see as a means of social climbing. So there is an intersection between class and literature. For example, the life and aspirations of Nigeria's and Kenya's lower middle classes and working classes in the 1960s were captured by the writers of pamphlet literature, many of whom were themselves members of these social classes. Fictional narratives by members of the first generation of modern African writers, and as well as several novels published by some members of the second generation, especially books published in the popular Pacesetter series of the 1980s, reflect contemporary concerns such as sexuality and spirituality mediated through the lens of class. We also see class concerns in the writing of many members of the third generation of writers who are publishing their works online and in print. Examples include Teju Cole's *Every Day is for the Thief* (2007), Chika Unigwe's *On Black Sisters Street* (2009) and Chimamanda Ngozi Adichie's *Americanah* (2013). These works may utilise European aesthetic

The Old and the New

While Karin Barber in *The Anthropology of Texts, Persons, and Publics* (2007) enjoins us to rethink our obsession with traditional ways of thinking of texts and asserts that all texts deserve our attention. Susan Arndt likewise argues that new texts such as cybertexts 'are informed by previous texts just as much as they happen to inform future ones … Discourses meander through the centuries leaving their traces in texts, which in turn leave their marks and remember hi/stories into the future' (2–3). Just as written literature has incorporated oral genres, online texts do so too, but here with the added dimension of making possible traditional-style interaction with the readers. One of Nigeria's emerging poetic voices, Yemi Soneye, acknowledges the debt that the digital generation owes to the past. In the first part of his poem *It is Development*, published in the Nigeria-based digital magazine, *Saraba* (owned and run by a collective of young writers), the speaker points out:

> Nothing is recently born.
> All things are not new,
> from primeval times they have been.
> Only oscillations in form,
> we see and feel.
> Or what are communal tales
> told under gleaming trees in the village square to Facebook, Twitter and others?
> Would ancient folders of roads have had reason to race, fly or sail if with a tap, they were at terminal?
>   Calls, SMS, MMS and
> Emails, just as a talking drum, stroked by the chosen, vibrated with
> Arokos, these are the classic couriers.

The speaker is arguably telling us that the new cannot exist without the past; the digital cannot be divorced from the oral and the written. Poetry in online space, although middle-class in concept, is not without precedent and emerging creative works should not be seen as entirely separate from what came before, because African texts in cyberspace bear imprints of the past, including a history of poetic licence as well as various forms of privilege and marginalisation.

The speaker in Shailja Patel's *On New Art* – first published in her 2010's seminal work *Migritude*, before it was cross-posted on the CKW listserv – espouses a similar notion about the intertextual link between the analogue and the digital eras:

> Someday I'll start a museum
> where all Works of Art
> are for touching
>
> > itchy fingers can sink
> > into sculptures stroke
> > grained canvasses trace
> > calligraphy
> > on manuscripts
>
> hands can swell
>
> [ ]
>
> > Art that stays intact
> > will be retired

Patel's speaker lays emphasis on the digital as the latest phase for African poetry, one in which texts are continuously changing with the potential to travel around cyberspace within the blink of an eye. Africans are used to the aesthetics of the bronze sculpture, the wooden mask, the moving, dancing bodies, the spectacle of television and radio. The materiality and the aesthetic of the new art, however, is interactive because it responds to touch. The itchy fingers are digital, if one accepts one of the dictionaries' many definitions of the word 'digital'. The restlessness of the speaker's 'itchy fingers' therefore not only represents the mobility of text and of art in the new media age, it is also a moving away from the rigidity of the print medium. The digital space brings the past and the present together, and African poetic tradition is yet again going through a transformation without shedding its past. This tradition as we know it is becoming digitised, and the speaker is warning that poems that refuse to take their place within the digital landscape are in danger of becoming moribund.

The two poems by Soneye and Patel are also indicating that poems on digital platforms speak to explicit as well as implicit connections between the real (offline) space of Africa and cyberspace. The two worlds should not be seen as separate entities. At the same time, the digital symbolises the new, and we must acknowledge that it is different from the past. What new voices are doing online is therefore a continuation of the historical function of the artist in many African societies, but with a new, digital twist. The terrain of the African text is shifting, as it always does, but the role of the artist as the 'classic courier' who sits in the middle, still remains the same. Additionally, in an attempt to bridge the gap between educated African middle classes and their unconnected fellow citizens, the poet in cyberspace tries to represent the unconnected by harking back to African oral history and by marrying African tradition with the twenty-first century's contemporary culture and values. The work of these two poets reflects the way in which several middle-class African poets have appropriated some of the skills of the old oral poets, many of whom occupied the middle rung of the economic ladder in the precolonial era. Their speakers allude to the fact that the digital space may be the perfect platform for African texts in the same way that the old poets used traditional musical instruments along with dance and chants to convey poetry to the public.

These poems showcase the educated middle-class people's day-to-day engagement with history, and these interactions through poetry often speak to the multiplicity of the text. Hyperlinks (or hyper-textuality) allow readers to link texts from different poets on their Facebook and Twitter page. Poets also often 'tag' other poets when a new poem is posted on social media. Within a few seconds they can share these writings with thousands of people across the globe. Unlike poetry published in print, in cyberspace, not only can poets amend their texts, commentators on social media can also edit or delete their own contributions to online conversations. In addition, while changing poems that have been published in a book is often impossible (and if it is possible the process is long and expensive), text editing online can be done within a few minutes and the amendment can be witnessed in real-time by writers and readers alike.

On 18 August 2015, the poet Afam Akeh published two poems on his Facebook page, *Ancient Water* and *They Talk into The Silence*, which sparked poetical and political debates from other poets (such as Pius Adesanmi and Chuma Nwokolo) and readers alike. These are some of the online comments:

Chijioke Amu-nnadi:	Brilliant, as always.
Pius Adesanmi:	Afam efuna! The return of da master! Where u disappear go since?
Akeem Lasisi:	Oga Afam, these are very beautiful lines. May I use this opportunity to confess that when I was growing up on the lap of the muse, I found your STOLEN MOMENTS one of the most interesting and inspiring collections I came across ...
Chuma Nwokolo:	Dalu[well done]smile emoticon
Saddiq M Dzukogi:	This thread is for Elders. Thrilling!
Asomwan Sonnie Adagbonyin:	Quintessential Afam! Vivid lines, sharp like a butcher's knife cuts on the skin of a deep haunting somnolence. Why do these images steal my heart so?

Sola Olorunyomi:	And in the season of the Idoto celebrations too … poetry returns. Nehru Odeh: These poems remind us of those unforgettable, stolen moments your poetry gave us. Good we now have those moments back with this offering. Welcome back, Afam … and well done.
Niran Okewole:	Deft, luminous, pure class
Chiedu Ezeanah:	'The Chants of the Quintessential Afam Akeh'
Olasunkanmi Ibikunle:	Our Afam is back. What a way to announce your return!
Ifeanyi Edeh:	'… It feeds its folk and feeds on them … the Atlantic opens wide and swallows like a great fish … swallowing more water, mixing rivers in its gut, mashing up their stories.' Beautiful!

The poets and their readers, as discussed above, are speaking in a digital language: using words that combine technology-speak with Nigerian Pidgin English, and indigenous Nigerian languages. Most notably, almost all of the respondents are critically acclaimed poets and writers themselves. They affirm the skill of the poet and the aesthetic quality of his poem. This is one of the ways in which the digital space performs 'quality control' even when there are no professional creative writing editors to serve as gatekeepers.

When the critically-acclaimed Ghanaian poet Kofi Awoonor was killed in the September 2013 attack on Nairobi's Westgate Mall, poems paying tribute posted on Facebook gave birth to a series of poems dedicated to Awoonor. These included Olu Oguibe's *Wake for Awoonor*; Obiwu Iwuanyanwu's *Madding Crowd: For Esiaba Irobi and Kofi Awoonor*; Chuma Nwokolo's *True Infidels* and Rasaq Malik Gbolahan's *Kofi*.

Similar digital tributes were paid to Pius Adesanmi, when he was killed in a plane crash in March 2019. Odes to Adesanmi included poetry sessions streamed live on Facebook from university campuses in Nigeria, Ghana, Kenya, Canada and the United Kingdom. Dirges posted on social media include Tade Aina's *Twirling the beads of grief … For Payo*. Lines from this poem posted on Facebook and the digital network *USA-African Dialogue* include:

> In perennial fatigue, desire and toil we have lived.
> We have forever turned vain voyagers of futile life seas
> Sailing in crafts of vanity piled upon insane vanities and futilities
> We have since learned to salve sorrow, pain and loss
> With natural and artificial highs invented and discovered
> Desperate to reclaim the often fleeting moments of joy

Another dirge dedicated to Adesanmi, from his contemporaries in poetry and academia is Nduka Otiono's untitled poem posted on Facebook, which contains these lines:

> Even as I hear your ghost music,
> O death, O mindless death,
> As I hear your soul music
> I shall not waltz to its strange melody
> Nor hum its macabre rhythm
> Borrowed from the racing fingers of Time!

From these poems, we see a continuation of the centuries old tradition of Africans using poetry to express grief. In the digital age as in the past, poetry becomes a means of articulating sorrows of lives lost, and of celebrating lives well lived. Be it ordinary or monumental events, poetry has always been the tool with which people comprehend changes and which also bring together people from all walks of life. This real-time burst of contributions in cyberspace shows the way in which online poetry enables both poetic and political engagements among many young Nigerians and Kenyans. These texts illustrate how online African literature can provide us with an immediate and intimate sense of real-life events. Barber highlights the role that audiences play in the composition and delivery of texts. She argues that through audiences 'one can observe and interact with' and see 'clues to the nature of the society they are part of' (2007,139).

From the poems that I examined for this chapter, few of the online readers complain that they cannot understand what other people are saying. Poetry and literature in the digital age is now crafting a new language and a new dialect that is comprehensible to digital natives, but which may sound like jargon to those outside the digital landscape. And because of this development, the nature of text, its presentation and interpretations in the online space are open ended, flexible and malleable. Every interpretation, every comment and every response to comments has the potential of becoming a new text or new conversations. And every additional text reflects the possibility that more information can lead to a better world. This is a form of collaboration that digital connectivity enables, and the way in which readers and writers collaborate together on Facebook and other online forums suggests openness and frankness of thoughts. This is arguably what those of us researching the nature of text in the online space mean when we suggest that the digital space lends itself to the expression of democratic ideals more easily than the book.

Richard Cutler surmises that real-time interaction is a distinguishing feature of cyberspace as it provides 'a level of conversational interaction' that no other medium provides (352). Cutler is right: interactions like the one in the Akeh post happen every day on Facebook, Twitter and listservs, and in the process such poems inspire more poems and further conversations in a way that would have been impossible in the book age. Many poems speak to the current state of events and the comments from readers reflect their own take on poems and politics. In literary studies, both the intellectual and the aesthetic matter in our articulation of the poetic. Therefore, if we argue that poetry has a history of class bias, especially in the age of the internet, it is because middle-class online readers see themselves and their societies in these works. They not only have the poet as a 'friend' on Facebook, they understand her world view, and the poems she posts online are like a mirror that reflects the way they see the world. Art is political because it is used to project the world view of a certain class of people over those who may not have access to this art or to the medium through which it is projected. Poetry in cyberspace raises similar emotions among those who are proactive within this space.

As many of the poems posted online by these new voices are political, poetry, in the process, becomes a medium for political debate, since the agenda of some of these emerging voices is to use online poetry as a medium for expressing political outrage directed, for example, at the African ruling classes. These online works and performances are often used as tools to remind fellow Africans of the need for the politics of resistance, for which the internet allows greater capacity, much more so than the printed book. Poetry in cyberspace, therefore, has become one of the new tools through which young people are seeking societal renewal. Howard Rheingold notes that 'the vision of a citizen-designed, citizen-controlled worldwide communications network is a version of technological utopianism that could be called the vision of "the electronic agora"'(14). For many digitally wired, middle-class Kenyans and Nigerians, digital space becomes a democratic space that allows the poet to perform without censorship, and where poetry can be produced and consumed without fear, and without having to leave home or travel any great distance in order to participate. Jürgen Habermas argues that public space is where citizens get together as equals to partake in debates and to contest the power of the interventionist and centralised state. African poetry on social networking sites gives poets and their audiences the opportunity to express ideas and contribute to debates, regardless of age, gender, race, ethnicity and sexual orientation. Thus, we can argue that African text in the digital age speaks to the possibility of a freedom of expression for the digitally wired middle classes and the freedom to be different.

Poetry and its Audience

Just as oral performers incorporate audience responses into their materials and adapt text to the mood of the audience, poets in the online writing space are doing the same by inviting readers to partake in the creative process, in addition to allowing outsiders to review work in progress and to make comments on these new materials.

On *Ederi* listservs, the poet Uche Peter Umez openly invites other poets to intervene on a poem in progress:

> Dear bros and sis, this is open to scalpel and scythe. Happy weekend. Uche
> in my land
> here, love is ash
> hate a flare
> as noxious
> as that of Shell
> clouding
> skies;
>
> here, tyrant's fist
> pounds
> pain into hearts
> sorrow
> grinds souls …
> here, no joy just
> inchoate anger
> against
> pot-bellied few.
> Uche peter Umez

A reader responds thus:

> Uche,
> I grant that the worth of this poem could be revealed some time later. For now, though, I'm hard-pressed to impute value to it. Deriving inspirations from the past comments of some members of this group, I'd like to raise a few questions about 'In my Land.'
>
> What nature of human experience does the speaker intend to convey? What human emotion? What idea? What minute, otherwise, ignored aspect of life does the poet want to disclose to the world? What aspect of history, life or heritage is the piece trying to preserve?
>
> My understanding of an artist is that s/he is like somebody walking with another person in a jungle (the jungle of life?). S/he suddenly stops, calls the other's attention to something: 'Hei, look at this?' When the other looks, will there really be something new to see? Something unique? Something old that could be seen in a new light?

On another open and popular listserv, *Nigerian World Forum*, the poet Chidi Anthony Opara posted a new, somewhat sexually explicit, work titled *Demands of the Goddess* on 18 August 2010. The submission also generated response. One commenter complained that his previous admiration for the poet has been seriously compromised by this latest offering:

> I must openly confess that I have often browsed your lucid poetry and prose that anchor their plots on everyday human chores and experience; the imageries you capture span the individual, the family, the local govts, the state and nation, especially the daily experiences of the mis-ruled and mis-led in our contemporary African societies. In all, I have silently commended your literary genius on its merit and level sophistication …
> Now, I realize that genius sometimes exhibits undisciplined or amoral excesses; and as you know, unrestrained and unregulated habits can be uncomfortably unruly and distastefully repugnant. And that is how I evaluate your present poem, entitled 'Demands of the goddess', in which you painted a picture of the act of sex by humans in the most shameful interaction between a man (Iyiafor the god), the woman (Iyieke the goddess) … What a mess!
> Frankly, without attempting any sanctimonious posture, I am moved to say that this poem is an epitome of genius misplaced and misapplied for shameless vulgarity, breach of public decency, and senseless trash-talk. It is juvenile and distasteful; and my advice is that your children should not inherit a literary legacy that includes this dirt.

In the digital space, poets regularly get advice on those elements of their work that readers and fellow poets believe are worth holding on to, verses that need improving upon and those that need to be discarded totally. And because those commenting on these works of literature are not making their views known face-to-face with the writer in a physically shared space but are doing so virtually, they can be more honest and candid in their comment. While only a few people may get to read and comment on a collection of poetry before it is published in print, in the online space there are no limits on the number of people who can judge the merit of a creative work in progress. This evokes the kind of checks and balances that ancient oral performers had to undergo before their peers and audiences.

What the discussions around Umez's and Opara's poems indicate is that the digital space enables debates and performs quality control on African poetry and fiction, but can also engender the suppression of uncomfortable voices. While comments by readers and fellow poetic voices may allay the fear that by bypassing the traditional book publishing process, poets and writers may be producing mediocre work, one can also argue that some of the comments are tantamount to a form of censorship, especially those that criticise work deemed as sexually suggestive and provocative.

In cyberspace, African poetry is rediscovering orature's art of collaboration between the performer and her audience, which has been missing from books. And with more poets putting their poems on social networking tools such as Facebook and Twitter, we are seeing online African literature reprising real-time collaboration between poets and their audiences.

The Kenyan poet Sitawa Namwalie suggested that *Tears*, a poem she published as Facebook status on 16 April 2020, is a response to the Coronavirus pandemic:

> And then, when I had time to set them free,
> They fell in large round globules and wouldn't stop.

Seeing the comments on the poem, Namwalie changed the ending within an hour of the original post, with a new Facebook update, in which she remarks: 'Hi All, I have now changed the ending of the poem. What do you think?' The new ending now reads:

> I let them fall, cleansing the old Africa,
> It is gone.

Comments by readers underlines the communal spirit of poetry on social media. Ruthie Ruwen stated: 'I love the ending here. Cleansing is what the world needs.' Kerubo Abuya, expressed a similar thought: 'The ending inspires hope. Possibility. Healing. Thank you!' Margaretta Gacheru replied to the revised poem: 'I feel the poem isn't done, not quite complete.' To which Namwalie replied: 'Hi what is missing. I'm listening'. Another respondent, Steve Musundi, made this observation: 'Where is the rest of the poem or must we fill in that, Sitawa? And Namwalie replied: 'Steve this is it. I never prescribed.'

Such works of poetry and the kind of conversation they generate, show the way in which African literary work and creative writers can connect and nurture relationships with prospective readers by effectively using social media and real-time online collaboration tools. Just as oral performers inculcated audience responses into their materials and adapted text to the mood of their audiences, poets in the online writing space are doing the same by inviting readers to participate in the creative process, in addition to allowing outsiders to review work in progress and to comment on these new materials. The audience provides approval for online poetry and the cyberspace serves as a test-bed for work that may later go into print, just as traditional poets and musicians try out their new work before a live audience prior to going to print or the recording studio. The storyteller is using the online writing space to gauge the mood of his potential audience; altering textual expression, tone and temper to meet the situation created in relationship with the online audience. In the process, the final text is dynamic and very malleable. As cybertexts are sometimes not permanent because they can be revised or deleted at any time, they are naturally predisposed to allow continuous smaller scale changes by the poets with inputs from his audience. It is not just the content that is changing but how poetry is perceived in its final textual manifestation that is changing the poetics. Like the oral tradition, online texts may have no firm terrain due to the process of collaboration and intervention between the composer and the reader. The knock-on effect is that, like in orature, the meaning of cybertexts is unfixed and subjected to multiple interpretations.

Publication on these social networking spaces also demands the disclosure of information, such as the inspiration behind a particular piece of creative writing and what the poet wants to achieve with a poem. In addition, while poets in these communities jealously protect their copyright they are also open to the idea of readers having an impact on the final outcome of their work. As a poet, Umez is not afraid of criticism as he thinks this will give his works the compact solidity and durability they need. In many instances, the poems he posts on listserv and on Facebook are praised by his contemporary and readers alike. One can therefore see the emergence of a cyberworld, with regular poet–reader cooperations. One can argue that Umez has benefited from posting his work on social networking spaces and his willingness to engage with the peer review this entails, as a collection of his work, *The Runaway Hero* (2011), was nominated for Nigeria's foremost literary prize, the Nigeria Liquefied Natural Gas Company (NLNG), in 2011.

Poetry as Visual Literacy

Jay Bolter believes that the computer enhances the experience of writing through the power of the images and videos that accompany texts on digital platforms. In the same fashion, African online poets are reintroducing the elements of visual literacy found in many oral performances in online poems. In his YouTube poem, *Sudan. Sudan.*, the Nigerian writer and poet Chuma Nwokolo, combines the elements of sound, music, photographic imagery and video together, in order to convey his message to online audiences. In the process, he brings African oral tradition into the twenty-first century. With a soft melody playing, the video begins on the banks of the Nile River in Khartoum, with a man lying on its concrete embankment in the shade of a tree, followed by photographic images of the poet's trip around Sudan. We do not see the face of the poet but his voice follows the scrolling letters:

> Sudan. Sudan.
> Do you hear me call?
> Your lure has fallen on the souls that answer to your ancient name.
> With breezing net,
> Sudan, you seduce me also.
> Look East!
> Your Sun rises on a horizon of river palms.
> Centuries count for slow minutes beside the longest river in the world.

Sudan becomes a metaphor for Africa's glorious past and its recent troubles. The very essence of this poem can only be captured by the poet's use of photographic imagery, music, cybertext and his own voice. The moving images depict the complexities and diversities of Sudan and Africa. At the same time, they challenge the single story narrative that has become Sudan by invoking the multilayered elements that have been buried in the familiar media portrayal. The images, the spoken words and the cybertext, all play an equal role in conveying the poet's message to the reader. One would be meaningless without the other elements.

> You torch your souls again.
> Meroe burns again …
> Those buried souls have gone
> and flowered hope …

The words scroll and tease as they unravel, the unfolding images and the poet's voice capture Sudan's promises and failures. The subversiveness of vocal, visual and virtual text combined together challenges those who constituted the political and religious authority in Sudan, especially with regard to Darfur. The digital poem enables the digital public (the audience) to see beyond the facade of serenity presented by the allure of the capital of Sudan, Khartoum, and the beauty of the glistening Nile River.

Nwokolo, like the court poet of an old African kingdom, has been licensed by the freedom of cyberspace to question the Sudanese authority about Darfur and the harsh reality of a theocracy/despotic regime. Like the ancient poet, the cyber-poet is using the tools of new media to criticise through the ploy of jokes and humour; he tries to reprise the ability of the poet to question the antics and abuses of African rulers which other citizens may not be able to do for fear of reproach. In this online video, we witness the way in which poetry can be potentially critical of its subject matter and how the artist can manipulate texts in this role as the voice of the society. The online space allows texts like this one to criticise contemporary politics without any fear of censorship or reprisal. They can be described as coded criticisms of Africa's big men and these coded messages are then open to different interpretations by the online audience.

Contemporary Class Concerns

In the previous chapter, I discussed how several new Kenyan voices – poets, intellectuals, and photographers – have come together to start *Koroga*, an online project that marries poetry with photography. *Koroga* wants to change the colonial narratives about Kenya and Africa, which still persist today, by telling the African story from an African perspective.

Koroga epitomises the transnational space that is cyberspace, as well as the innovative way tech-savvy African voices are using new media technologies to show the complexities of Africa beyond the familiar images of the continent. The artists on *Koroga* acknowledge the fact that they are part of the professional middle classes; one of the many themes running through the dozens of works that this project has produced is class consciousness, as the poetry and the images that are being posted on *Koroga* often capture and re-imagine the life of Africans across social classes. For example, Phyllis Muthoni's poem *The Sandwich Bar* (16 September 2011) is supported by a photo taken by Jim Chuchu of an expensive restaurant.

While Chuchu's photography presents us with images of a luxurious building and of immense wealth, Muthoni's poem reveals the insecurity of those within that building. Both the patrons and the workers who serve them feel insecure. The privileged professional middle classes worry about the durability of their wealth, and the workers are reminded about their financial insecurity, dependent on the amount of money spent by the privileged. African modernity and class privilege both come with insecurity and instability. Just as the condition of class is unstable, so is the condition of the image-text.

Marziya Mohammedali's poem *Sparks*, which is posted on *Koroga*'s page, (20 September 2011), is supported by another photograph taken by Jim Chuchu. However, this time, the image is of a working-class man, who is busy working on an electricity project. The speaker informs us:

> Cautious and careful,
> He climbs into place.
> He feels the energy thrum
> Under his fingertips,
> The crackle and hum,
> Of some life force, enticing …
>
> One second. Just one second.
> And the life force turns deadly.
> He twists from the pulsing embrace,
> Slips to the safety of the ground.

In these two posts, we see the contrast in the life of working-class Kenyans and that of the professional middle classes. One speaker is concerned about the aesthetic make-up of a restaurant and the effect these designs have on the life of those who patronise the place. While the other speaker illustrates the daily grind of life – that of a man who must risk his life in order to feed his family.

In *Koroga*, the role of the artist as the reporter is not conferred on the poet alone, but the photographer is also our artistic reporter. Literature in the online space thus becomes the new tool for Africa's self-documentation. In these poems and photographs, we see the reverberations between meaning-making and visual performance at the same time. The online as a space for creative writing delineates the fragility of African modernity and of these two social classes – the middle class and the working class. The photographs and the written texts – image-texts – work together to reveal the complexities of African modernity. Cyberspace gives many young middle-class Africans the chance to escape the old colonial-framed narratives about the continent and the people who live in it. As aptly argued by its publishers, what *Koroga* has done is to present an image of Africa that may not be published by foreign publishers, who may be uncomfortable with a complex story of class on the continent.

The texts and images in *Koroga* also contain a substantial amount of verisimilitude as writers and photographers become reporters fixated with mapping out social realism in the digital space. Articulating the nature of African poetry, Adam Schwartzman argues that poems 'do not appeal to readers in empty spaces'. For Schwartzman, they are an essential tool of 'social interactions', through which lived experiences are articulated (3). Cyberspace allows poetry to represent themes such as class consciousness and some of the real-life characters that populate this space. Online literature, therefore, can serve as reliable evidence of some of the changes and challenges facing contemporary Africa, since these are themes reflected in the statements and behaviour of characters in new narratives (poetic as well as fictional), and in the implicit or stated positions of emerging literary voices as middle-class and as cultural ambassadors. Poetical works in cyberspace show that we need to rethink the way citizens engage with one another, and that literary theory needs to take into consideration the way in which literature depicts those small-scale, everyday political engagements, sometimes based on social status rather than on citizenship conferred by the modern state.

Class Consciousness in Online Fictions   3

In an interview with the British journalist Stephen Moss, published on *The Guardian* website, Chimamanda Ngozi Adichie recounts a conversation with an American professor at the university where she was a postgraduate student, who refused to believe in the veracity of her first novel *Purple Hibiscus* (2003):

> I was told by a professor at John Hopkins University that he didn't believe my first book ... because it was too familiar to him. In other words, I was writing about middle-class Africans who had cars and who weren't starving to death, and therefore to him it wasn't authentically African ... People forget that Africa is a place in which class exists ... it's as if Africans are not allowed to have class, that somehow authenticity is synonymous with poverty and demands your pity and your sympathy.

In this interview, Adichie's story about the Johns Hopkins' professor attests to continuing stereotypes about Africa and Africans, even in elite university circles in the global North. In part, this seems symptomatic of a homogenising tendency, as expressed by that professor, which refuses to recognise class differences in African countries, or that some Africans occupy an environment increasingly recognisable as middle class. But if we are to investigate modern Nigerian and African identities being shaped and transformed by globalising and localising tendencies, the question of social class cannot be ignored.

I want to explore how African authors are representing themselves within cyberspace both as African people and as individuals with a burgeoning self-identification as middle class. As previously alluded to, I use the term 'middle class' to designate those who possess the accoutrements of a middle class in terms of education and cultural capital. Illustrating from Nigerian examples, I will discuss how some online writings operate to consolidate the notion of a middle-class identity, how this both performs as something indigenously Nigerian and also reaches towards an international middle-class audience.

The issue of class identity offers the opportunity to robustly unpack the complexity of Nigeria and Kenya in the twenty-first century and it highlights the intersection of literary sociability and class consciousness. Members of digital networks, for example, are often people who have known each other for a long time. *Koroga, Kwani!* and *Krazitivity* are literary networks with many members who attended the same university, and at times, the same secondary school. Some *Koroga* artists belong to *Kwani!*, some members of *Krazitivity* are friends with members of *Kwani!* and *Koroga* in digital projects such as the *Jalada* digital magazine. It is therefore worth pointing out that digital literary networks, especially in the context of Nigeria and Kenya, are populated by people, who often socialise together online and offline, and almost all of them can be considered as belonging to the professional middle class.

Class is important because, as argued in the Introduction, we have to theorise access to the digital network in terms of affordability. As mentioned, a report by the AfDB has chosen internet usage as a signifier of a middle-class lifestyle in Africa and internet penetration to analyse the social classes on the continent. Surveys conducted in 2019 suggest that the majority of the people living in Kenya and Nigeria have access to cyberspace. Yet, figures from Internet World Stats imply that there are less than seven million Kenyans on Facebook and Twitter. Moreover, there are less than ten thousand active users on digital literary networks such as Concerned Kenyan Writers group, Generation Kenya and the ICC Witness Project. The people on these networks constitute the minority when we take into consideration that there are almost thirty million Kenyans with internet-enabled devices. The story is the same in Nigeria; according to the figures from Internet World Stats, there are over one hundred million Nigerians with internet-enabled devices, whereas there are fewer than forty million Nigerians on both Facebook and Twitter. On networks such as *Krazitivity, USA-Africa Dialogue* and *Ederi*, the number of active users is not more than twenty thousand. These figures matter because we need to think of the way in which class divide is reflected in literary networks and in fictional and poetic portrayals. Class divide is also important to our conception of the literary publics. Even in 2019, there is still a digital divide between those who are active on social media networks, blogs and listservs, where a lot of literature is being posted daily, and those who are not connected to these networks.

Given this data, I want to draw from Nigerian short stories published online to argue that the digital space in the context of African literature is very much an elitist space because the majority of the people who socialise around online literature are members of the educated middle class. Nanjala Nyabola echoes similar sentiments in relation to digital Kenya. She posits that those who control the conversation in the digital space are mostly members of the professional middle classes, and that 'if the process of information production or dissemination is controlled by a specific class, the society will construct identities aligned to that dominant class' (43).

As I argue in this and subsequent chapters, many writers from Nigeria and Kenya base their work on their environment, and the literature they produce cannot be separated from their background and the background of those who consume their work – the digital reading public. The immediate reaction and emotion that literature stirs also constitutes a reliable space for us to study socialisation in contemporary Africa. The condition from which these creative works emanate is infused with class consciousness. Therefore an analysis of literary outputs published online shows a recognition of the way in which literature written in non-African languages intersects with class. The digital network is an essential part of globalisation, and discourses within globalisation arguably operate to privilege some classes – those at the centre of these discourses – at the expense of others.

Self-fashioning and the Performance of Middle-class Identity

In a 2013 country report for the international consulting firm McKinsey, Reinaldo Fiorini et al. surmise that the Nigerian middle class has increasing spending power and a love of mall culture and digital technologies: 'Social networking leads as the top reason for internet access on mobile phones, but Nigerians are also using their smart phones for a broad range of activities, including reading news, watching music videos, and doing email and instant messaging' (n.pag). This study reflects the lifestyle of middle-class Africans, in terms of their ability to afford luxury goods and to be digital connected to the rest of the world. But it also makes one think about how their lifestyle and worldview are given wider coverage in literature. And since many writers belong to this social group, art devotes greater attention to documenting the lifestyle of its creators, and institutionalising it in the process.

For members of the Nigerian middle class, class is not just about how people position themselves in terms of a particular social level, which is often determined by occupational identity, but also about how identities can be seen in terms of one's shifting relationships and self-distancing from others through conscious and unconscious choices.

Ben Rogaly and Becky Taylor show us that spatial immobility is just as significant as mobility in the making of personal identities. With regard to Nigeria, the people with regular and reliable access to the internet are those with money to pay for it – mostly members of the middle class. Another privileged group of Nigerians who has regular access to the internet is described by Harish Trivedi as 'upper-class elite migrant[s]' (n.pag) travelling through and living and working in the Diaspora as illustrated by the Nigerian author Tolu Ogunlesi (5 July 2010), who writes on his blog:

> Since June 10 I have been travelling through Europe:
> June 10 – Lagos
> June 11 – Berlin
> June 14 – Freiburg

> June 18 – London
> June 20 – Birmingham
> June 22 – London, Edinburgh
> June 24 – London
> June 25 – Madrid
> June 29 – Brussels, Turnhout (Belgium)
> June 30 – Eindhoven
> July 2 – Berlin
> July 4 – Lagos
>
> I have slept in airports, endured strange languages, taken tonnes of photos, and mused about culture and identity and language and history and exile.

Ogunlesi's travel itinerary speaks to the ease with which middle-class Africans move within the global space, when compared with the working classes and the lower class, who are less likely to have the money or the opportunity to see the outside world, at least physically. Online writing depicts the way in which middle-class Africans like Ogunlesi are able to actually partake in middle-class activities without any obvious constraints of race or ethnicity.

In order to further highlight the ways in which cyberspace allows for the making and the asserting of a middle-class identity, one can look at the online musings of the 2005 Caine Prize winner Segun Afolabi who, in the blog post 'The Tufiakwa Syndrome', alludes to the fact that the physical space that is Nigeria and even the diasporic Nigerian space, are overly conservative. In the blog post, he complains about the expectation to conform to societal values and norms:

> And when people do fail to meet up, they become [the] topic of our side talk, something for us to look at with condemning awe. It is remarkable how Nigerian communities even in different parts of the world continue to live by or even create rules, values and moral obligations that sometimes streamlines [sic] them. And this communal action of creating sets of values also take[s] form in young people setting up these expectations around themselves that they must meet in order to gain some kind of respect. (n.pag)

Afolabi was born in Kaduna, Nigeria, grew up in various countries, including the Congo, Canada, East Germany and Indonesia, and was working for the BBC prior to winning the Caine Prize. For cosmopolitan authors like Afolabi, cyberspace presents an opportunity for the making of an authentic identity, one that is Nigerian and enshrined in 'global' middle-class values, of which individuality is an important aspect. Cyberspace also allows twenty-first-century middle-class Africans to interact with and be closer than ever before to people of similar social status from across the world.

Afolabi craves individuality and rejects the communality that is enshrined in traditional Nigerian space. He suggests 'that individuality and nationalism are so opposing, and can be likened to oil and water' (n.pag), and believes that communality and nationality compromise the self. In the online writing space, a young Nigerian can escape all the negativities that come with the physical African space and at the same time free herself from the burden of societal expectations. Afolabi articulates this further:

> Sometimes, I feel that if life in Nigeria was to be likened to a novel, people, that I love and claim to love me, would become antagonistic to me, not for some intrinsic vileness in them, but for the reason that my core contradicts their beliefs and convictions. Yes, this might be the reason why I find the need to use the colloquial 'Tufiakwa' to allude to our reaction to anything different, the reason why I feel torn between being the 'true Nigerian' or being my true self. (n.pag)

The online writing space represents Afolabi in a way that the physical space cannot, as his cosmopolitan lifestyle disconnects him from a geographically constructed Nigerian identity. However, as was discussed in relation to online Nigerian poetry, other writers embrace the communality that the internet can provide for a geographically dispersed community.

The digital space, as analysed in Chapter One on literary networks, can be described as one of those borderlines that Homi Bhabha describes as where the 'global link between colony and metropolis' (304) is enacted. The lived experience of the contemporary African writer is not solely rooted in African poetic and religious traditions, instead the writer tries to mediate between African and European artistic traditions, and in the process, criss-crosses boundaries in many different ways. The twenty-first century African writer can therefore be deemed a cultural translator between the metropolis and the literary periphery. In a somewhat critical review of the term 'cultural translation', Harish Trivedi suggests that what Bhabha means is 'the process and condition of human migrancy' (n.pag) and, it is implied, that migrancy is from the Third to the First World (to use Trivedi's terms). I suggest that migrancy as described by Trivedi is culturally marked by the migrant being in need (of better economic opportunities, of a better education, of political refuge from corruption or violence and so on) creating a particular inequality which might require a migrant to make specific choices about how his or her identity is represented in the host country. However, as the internet neatly obliterates the connection to geographical or temporal locations, Nigerian participants in the online space are not marked by need in this way. In fact, merely being in this space already implies a middle-class identity similar to that of any other participant because of the underlying assumption of ownership of the material goods, education and technological skills necessary to participate.

Class Consciousness and the Writerly Self

To illustrate how the notion of the middle class as a common ground is exploited, I consider a talk given by Chimamanda Ngozi Adichie at a time when she was already well known in the West for her two prize-winning novels *Purple Hibiscus* and *Half of a Yellow Sun*. In 2009, Adichie participated in the programme of talks organised by Technology, Entertainment, Design, commonly known as the TED talks, contributing a lecture entitled 'The Danger of a Single Story'. As TED seeks to bring together people from the three fields indicated in its title in order to promulgate 'Ideas Worth Spreading', the speakers featured – although presenting a conventional lecture, live, to a physically present audience – must also be mindful of the wider virtual and non-synchronous audience who will hear and see them speak when the video of their lecture is published on the TED website. Early in her talk, Adichie tells a story about herself and a houseboy who started working for her family:

> I come from a conventional middle-class family ... and so we had, as was the norm, live-in domestic help who would often come from nearby rural villages; so the year I turned eight we got a new houseboy – his name was Fide. The only thing that my mother told us about him was that his family was very poor. (n.pag)

Adichie thus makes a clear class distinction between her family and other, rural, poor families. The story is apparently told to criticise her eight-year-old self for only seeing their new houseboy as poor (although this is the only information supplied by her mother), a 'single story of poverty' that is exploded during a visit to the boy's family home. Here, Fide's mother 'showed us a beautifully patterned basket made of dyed raffia that his brother had made; I was startled. It had not occurred to me that anyone in his family could actually make something' (n.pag). Adichie's comments do not clarify precisely what the new plural story might be, beyond recognising that it moves her from mere pity. However, the revelation that Fide's brother is a craftsman keeps him firmly relegated to below middle class.

Adichie recounts another personal story: when she first moves to America, assumptions are made by her university room-mate that Adichie will have poor English and no understanding of Western culture or manners, like using a knife and fork. Adichie has to correct this association of herself with a Nigerian of Fide's class, but this is achieved on quite different terms. The room-mate 'asked if she could listen to what she called my "tribal music", and was consequently very disappointed when I produced my tape of Mariah Carey.' (n.pag) This story serves a different function in relation to class. First it exposes her room-mate as ignorant in a comic way, something missing from Adichie's story where she represents herself partly as misled by her mother's prejudices and mature enough to recognise her own error. In turn, by sharing the humour with her audience (visibly white in the video, and arguably middle class through their attendance at such an event) who laugh with her, she positions herself with them as enlightened people who know about the reality of an African middle class that is not 'tribal', nor without access to material goods, education or unaware of global culture. However, as noted earlier, this is perhaps only a semblance of equality as on closer inspection, it appears that Adichie has had to invest in another particular Western discourse about Africa. In moving from pity to respect, in relation to Fide's family, Adichie doesn't reject her idea of them being in 'need', thus sharing the common Western perception of people living in African countries as needy. Instead, she appreciates what any tourist travelling in Africa would: the type of craft sought out and appreciated as authentic and ethnic by tourists. Being a tourist is, of course, a role particularly associated with the affluent Western middle class.

The John D. and Catherine T. MacArthur Foundation, when conferring its 2008 Genius Award on Adichie, noted that 'she is widely appreciated for her stark yet balanced depiction of events in the post-colonial era' (n.pag). In 2016, when Boots made her the face of its No. 7 beauty range, one of the senior executives of the multinational, Kristof Neirynck, told *Vogue* magazine's beauty editor Lisa Niven-Phillips that:

> At No. 7 we believe that when women know their make-up is just right they feel great, they feel ready to show up in the world in the way they want ... Chimamanda was the perfect choice for us, as not only is she an inspirational woman, we share the same philosophy about beauty. (Niven-Phillips par. 6)

One can argue that to the outside world, Adichie is a cultural ambassador not only for Nigeria but also for women in Africa and worldwide. So, how do her online works back up this representational role? One common trend in Adichie's fictions and writings by other literary voices from her generation is the relationship between the middle class and the lower class. Emerging voices may rebuke the stereotypical portrayal of Africa by Westerners, but their own representation of the poor in Africa is equally problematic. Just as some writers from the West often portray Africans as poor, naïve, lower-class characters, in some of these online short stories they are also represented as dirty, ignorant, unwashed, archaic and bucolic. The poor in online fictions are often pictured in childlike postures, forever reliant on the benevolence of the African middle class and at worst, they are a menace to modernity and civilised sensitivity.

In the short story, 'Life During Wartime: Sierra Leone, 1997' published in *The New Yorker* online, Adichie brings the figure of Fide into fiction, and through this figure we are given an insight into the world of middle-class Nigerians and their domestic servants – a middle-class world no different from that of Adichie's. In this short story, Fide, the houseboy from the village is described as someone, who has never seen a refrigerator. He was light-skinned, and his lips were so thick and wide they took up most of his face. He spoke a rural dialect of Igbo that was not Anglicized, like ours, and he chewed rice with his mouth open – you could see the rice, soggy like old cereal, until he swallowed. When he answered the phone, he said, 'Hold on,' as we had taught him to, but then he dropped the receiver back on the cradle. He washed our clothes in metal basins, and pegged them on the line tied from the mango to the guava tree in the back yard. (n.pag)

The division of labour between the lower-class Nigerian and his middle-class boss is clearly represented here, enabling Adichie to reinforce her assertions of class differentiations within Nigerian society. Fide does all the domestic work in the household, while the university lecturer performs the creative role. In 'Life During Wartime: Sierra Leone, 1997', Adichie tries to lay bare the effect of political corruption on those on the lower rung of the economic ladder. She tries to challenge the attitude of the middle classes toward their servants, but at the end of the story, it is Fide who pays the ultimate price by dying in the Sierra Leonean civil war, as a soldier of the peacekeeping Nigerian Army, while the middle-class family's lifestyle goes on uninterrupted by all the instability around it. The mother accepts the houseboy as 'our own Fide' only after his death. Thus, it is through death that the poor manage to lay claim to their humanity.

In attacking both Western portrayals of Africa and Africa's political corruption and widespread poverty, the middle-class writer may have good intentions, but some of the narratives border on an imitation of the way the Western media often portray their own underclass, as well as Western media's representation of people from developing countries. Just as some members of the older generation (Chinua Achebe, Ngũgĩ wa Thiong'o, Bessie Head) used the print media to attack the European imagination, some of the emerging African voices online use this space to overtly attack the 'single story' of African representations outside Africa. For example, voices such as Chika Unigwe, Lola Shoneyin and Richard Ali often attack portrayals of Africans in the West through their Facebook status updates and in much of the online fiction they post on social media networks. Moreover, in the interview with *The Guardian*'s Stephen Moss, Adichie laments that the single story 'simplifies Africa: If you follow the media you'd think that everybody in Africa was starving to death, and that's not the case; so it's important to engage with the other Africa' (n.pag). She finds the coverage by global media powerhouses such as CNN 'exhausting because of its refusal to let Africans do the talking'. Adichie is right in attacking 'the Africa' in the European imagination, for it is the single story that assaults the African consciousness, but she fails to recognise her own investment in a 'single story' of a middle class which, in looking to a Western model, distances itself from poorer people within the same country.

If Adichie's online work captures the current chasm between the urban middle class and the rural poor, Teju Cole's online short story *Modern Girls* gives us an insight into the world that the current generation of middle-class Nigerians was born into – the world of their parents. The narrator is a pupil at an upmarket boarding school, which is based in a rural part of Western Nigeria; the sort of school started by the colonial government to educate the locals who will take over the administration of Nigeria after independence. The small town of Omu, where the Royal College for Girls is situated, serves as a metaphor for class divide. We are told that before the school came into being it 'consisted of a few small farms, a cluster of mud houses with thin roofs, a creek, a chieftain. The people of Omu were mostly Muslims, which meant they were not part of the cultural elite' (par. 2).

For the most part, colonial education was geared at raising Africans who would think and behave like European missionaries; the disdain that some educated Africans had for those elements that denote Africa, such as tradition and Islam, were traits inherited from European educators, and traits which have survived until today. In *Modern Girls*, we see how the middle class has learnt to hate rural people like Nuratu, one of few rural dwellers lucky enough to make it into the Royal College for Girls. The narrator informs us that these students from the village 'had to be good – at least by the standard of their villages and hamlets – but it was often clear that they weren't the usual Royal College material' (par. 3). Their clothes are not only scruffier, but they cannot speak English like the Europeans and instead pronounce 'ch' with a Yoruba-accented 'sh'. Nuratu, the epitome of African tradition and provinciality also 'laughs like a goat', has not mastered Dryden and eats boiled yams like a market woman. The Nuratu that the narrator presents to us seems incapable of cultural development due to her traditional Yoruba upbringing. In short, to use the word of the narrator, she is 'local'. This online fiction reveals the means and ways through which the Nigerian middle class, in its quest for the Western bourgeois lifestyle, has internalised the colonial hatred of those elements that are seen as authentically African.

The educated African fears the return to his supposedly savage past and in the process is determined to 'keep the forest at bay' and has mastered 'Livy and Cicero, learned how to set silverware on a formal table, mastered the expansion of polynomials' (*Modern Girls* par. 9). Thus, Nuratu, in the midst of these middle-class girls, becomes a symbol of backwardness and savagery. And because she does not have a Christian background, it is easy for her middle-class classmates to accuse her of bringing *juju* into the hallowed grounds of Royal College because they believe she lives close to the forest. In examining the state of mind of the middle-class African, these new writers lampoon their fellow middle-class citizens as mimics. But while they expose the hypocrisy and arrogance of the fellow middle classes, their own treatment of lower-class characters is questionable.

Meanwhile, other literary voices in the digital space recognise the potential pitfall of cultural representation. The artist and intellectual Olu Oguibe recognises how this claim of cultural representation by creative artists can become a significant problem in the light of the digital divide between the haves and the have-nots:

> we have also come to acknowledge that a gulf has emerged between those who belong within the network and are thus able to partake of its numerous advantages, and those who are unable to fulfil the conditionality of connectivity … information gathered on the Net becomes our readiest access to other cultures and sections of society as it inveigles us in the lazy preoccupation of going through its own portals of voices and information for our knowledge of the unconnected. (*Connectivity* 175–177)

In reading Oguibe's essay against Cole's fiction, one can argue that rural dwellers, who constitute the unconnected, may be read as the ambassadors of African authenticity in fictional narratives – while having become the bogey people of contemporary African life, including the cyberspace, especially for a middle class that's been trying for years to rescue Africa's 'negative' exotic and naive image from the likes of Nuratu. But while the middle-class African writer preaches Africanism ad nauseam, it is people like Nuratu who remain at the bottom of the African narrative well. Education has become the most potent way through which African tradition and ways of life can be completely devalued. Mrs Allardyce, the British schoolmistress in *Modern Girls,* has no qualms about blaming Nuratu's Africanness and states, 'We have entirely failed to free these girls of the pagan spirit.' Africa has served as the reference point for Western self-definition and in order to do this, Africans' way of life, cultures and behaviour are taken out of context so that they appear unreal, alien and with no historical foundation. Not only is the African devalued, anything Western has essentially imposed itself as the norm and has othered the 'pagan' African way. Since the balance of power tilts toward those who see themselves as representing the norm, it is no surprise that the narrator informs us that one of the Christian girls later rises to become the vice chancellor of the Nigerian Ogun State University. This reflects the consistent effort by middle-class African writers to privilege the Western over the traditional African ways of life, and to show that different destinies await the rich and the poor, thinkers and workers.

Giving the sensitive nature of the dynamics of class, ethnicity and gender in the Nigerian and Kenyan political landscapes, it is important to stress that I have not intentionally singled out certain writers for praise or condemnation. It is not my intention to condemn Yoruba or Igbo or Kikuyu writers because ethnicity is not considered in my selection of the primary texts. My objective is to sensitise readers to the politics of representations, and the roles of identity in the conception, production, distribution and consumption of literary texts. The class consciousness and fashioning that I discussed above illustrate how short stories can be used as cultural practices that mark class distinction and difference. Wai Chee Dimock and Michael T. Gilmore, in their introduction to *Rethinking Class: Literary Studies and Social Formations* (1994), argue that class is not 'a merely privileged analytic category here; it is itself an analysable artefact, itself to be scrutinized, contextualized, critiqued for its commissions and omissions' (2). As identities are constantly constructed in time and space, the digital age and space allow terrain for the asserting and remaking of middle-class identity.

Online forums and social network platforms are becoming spaces where middle-class Africans can assert their presence. This space allows them to escape the blanketing stereotype of poor Africans that the Johns Hopkins University professor seems to allude to in this conversation with Adichie. Online, some of these writers can just be their 'real selves' – Africans of middle-class origin with middle-class world views. This status in the online space is essential for showing that the postcolonial world also has different social layers. Much of the writing and thinking taking place in this digital space arguably reflects transnational conversations and modes of labour that the middle classes tend to indulge in, because the digital space makes for a globalised lifestyle ingrained in materialism. As identity keeps changing in time and space, people like Ogunlesi and Adichie can fit into multiple relationships and several subject positions – as members of the global professional middle class and as Africans with Nigerian passports.

4 Digital Queer: The Queering of African Literature

In the previous chapters, I showed the ways in which class intersects with every facet of the digital network, but in the next four chapters, I am going to analyse this intersection with sexual politics. In this particular chapter, I use the digital writings of mainly Nigerian and Kenyan queer writers to highlight the notion of the queering of African literature. I will compare their aesthetic strategies with that of the first generation of post-independent African writers, with a focus on Wole Soyinka's *The Interpreters* and Ama Ata Aidoo's *Our Sister Killjoy*. I am foregrounding this comparison on the important argument put forward by the Kenyan queer scholar and blogger Keguro Macharia that 'digital Africa cannot be imagined or theorised without placing digital queer Africa, at its heart' (2017, 1). Using Black Looks (*Blacklooks.org*), the queer blog and network set up by the British-Nigerian queer activist Sokari Ekine as his case study, Macharia in 'Digital Queer Africa', his presentation at a workshop I co-organised at Amherst College, USA, in October 2017, surmises that instead of deploying mainly European/Caucasian theorists to understand queer Africa in the digital age, we need to think with queer Africans. This is because digital Africa generates its own theory as bloggers like Ekine 'mapped and created connections across geographies and histories' (1).

Macharia's observation is apt because if we want to articulate the way in which digital African writing challenges and undermines conventional thinking about history, affect, memory and sexual politics, queer Africans are at the forefront of such movements. There are some key points that I want to emphasise in this chapter that Queer Kenya and Queer Nigeria cannot be theorised without approaching them from a continent-wide perspective because queer African writers do not limit their portrayal to a national boundary. In fact, their texts reject all remnants of the project of colonial modernity, of which the twenty-first century's nation-state is a good example. Further I want to highlight that their writings indicate that homophobia in one country affects queer people in other countries, and, therefore, that there is a sense of solidarity in their writings; that queer Africans do not see themselves as powerless and lacking agencies; that being queer is about more than sex and that it is about identity and history; and finally, that there is a robustness and sensitivity in the creative writings of queer writers that is sometimes lacking in the works of non-queer writers.

In the digital age, queer writers and activists feel more at liberty to set their own ideological agendas, and are bringing fresh perspectives to issues such as sexuality, gender, prostitution and class. Queer Africans use personal and fictional narratives to disrupt the narrative of the past with regard to African sexual history, in the process unearth repressed memory and place all variants of human sexuality at the centre of history. The activism of digital African queers is changing the way we understand Africa, and one of the products of this activism is the important book *Queer African Reader* (2013), which Ekine co-edited with the Egyptian queer activist Hakima Abbas. The book, an idea that started on Black Looks, underlines the depth of theory that digital Africa generates.

Tunji Adetunji Osinubi argues that, while digital African writings offer a more diverse insight into queer lives, there is a limited range of queer representation in Nigerian and Kenyan cinema. Traditional media outlets in Kenya and Nigeria – such as television, radio and cinema – mostly cover heterosexual relationships, which is perhaps due to the fact that television and radio stations in both nations are mostly controlled by either the government or by rich private individuals and are often subjected to censorship by their owners. From my examination of television dramas in Nigeria, these broadcasting mediums, because of their omission and misrepresentation of the queer experience, are sites of heteropatriarchy which conform to the notion put forward by many political and religious leaders that homosexuality/queerness is un-African. The traditional travel theatre that preceded the now booming movie industry in much of Africa was mostly based on heteronormative ideals, and most of the productions that came out of the era of the travel theatre (from the late 1940s to early 1990s) contained heterosexual subjects and characters. For example, the plays of Hubert Ogunde and Oyin Adejobi in Nigeria mostly reflected heterosexual identities. Therefore, images from traditional media have defined the roles of men and women within the African space. Until recently, almost all the mediums through which the creative arts are propagated looked at African sexuality through the discourse of polygamy versus monogamy and the modern concept of love versus the traditional view of romance and relationship. Not many studies have taken into account that love and romance existed among the Yoruba in the precolonial era. Women in this era had a choice in the selection of marital and sexual partners. While polygamy was prevalent (which allowed men to have more than one wife), married women could also have lovers through a system known as 'Ale'. The concept of 'Ale', which has been largely ignored in scholarly and media discourses, still exists today in many Yoruba communities. For many Kenyans and Nigerians, these contemporary media outlets, where such old traditions are not at all or certainly not robustly discussed, are spaces where heterosexual identity is defined and reinforced, and they constitute sites that Judith Butler refers to as the 'heterosexual matrix'.

Black Looks Blog

For ten years – from 2004 to 2014 – Black Looks collected important creative writings, essays, art exhibitions, records of seminars and blog posts, from various digital locations. In addition, it invited contributions from guest writers and cross-post contents from other blogs and websites that deal with themes around women and queers of African descent. Through these various digital engagements, Black Looks not only connects Africans on the continent with those of African descent in the Diaspora, it has become a medium that provides a rich portrayal of how those who have been marginalised see, think and act. Even when faced with homophobia and death, Black Look emphasises love and care. An excerpt from the Kenyan queer activist Shailja Patel's poem *Migritude*, cross-posted on Black Looks, illustrates the depth of love that digital African queer entities provide for women and queers alike:

> We have travelled half the world
> with hearts open,
> we've seen everything.
> Always remember who we are,
> where we came from,
> and you'll never do evil

Patel's speaker stresses the journey that queer Africa has made, from being a shadow of history, to being declared alien to that history, to this moment in time when queer Africa is asserting itself as an integral part of the continent's history. Patel's *Migritude* (mashing migrant, attitude and negritude) and the other contributions on Black Looks show that queer Africa is not a figment of the imagination, it is flesh and blood. It is not only a contemporary discourse or a fad; it is then, here, now and the future. This particular poem and the digital platform on which it is published, make us think beyond the news stories of African homophobia to a recognition of everyday lived experiences that go back in time, and which places queer Africa not as a product of colonial modernity but as one that has always been modern, but in a non-occidental kind of way, because it is neither restrictive nor wild but has always been open to imbibing new ideas while celebrating its past.

Macharia in 'Digital Queer Africa', argues that part of the knowledge that digital queer Africans generate is the notion that heteronormativity comes in different forms. These processes speak to the idea of intersection – 'gender, sexuality, desire and personhood' (7). Building on Macharia's theory, I see Sokari Ekine's Black Looks as an embodiment of digital Africa as well as of digital African queers. This is because she used the blog to point us to the multilayeredness of African queer life and history. Black Looks' contributors looked to histories and use memories in their attempts to robustly capture what it means to be a queer person of African descent. Predominant narratives of queer Africa are impacted by patriarchy (Western, African, precolonial, colonial and postcolonial), and these variants of patriarchy affect queer Africans and African women. Writings in the digital space then becomes a tool to contest heteropatriarchal narratives.

For example, *The Memory Snatcher* – a short story by the Kenyan-Somali-British queer writer Diriye Osman published on Black Looks, points us to the implicit workings of postcolonial heteronormativity. Using a queer narrator, the story centres on the life of fictional Kenyan-Somali woman Aunty Beydan, who is also known as 'the Memory Snatcher'. This woman lives in Nairobi, and she is described as follows:

> Before Beydan became a Memory Snatcher she was a Mother. Before she was a Mother she was a Wife and before she was a Wife she was her Father's daughter. Her identity was not hers to keep. Her life was a splintered spine, leaves too loose: an illegible manuscript left languishing on the shelf. (n.pag)

Osman's fiction – like the agenda of Black Looks – highlights the close link between queer African writing and feminist African writing. This is because writers of feminist and queer texts show us that heteronormativity is the source of women's oppression and that of queerphobia. As a teenager, Beydan was politically conscious and drawn to feminist African literature. The narrator tells us that in her teenage years: 'She inhaled Buchi Emecheta's *The Joys of Motherhood,* Tsitsi Dangarembga's *Nervous Conditions,* Nawal El Saadawi's *Memoirs of a Woman Doctor*' (Osman n.pag). These are seminal African feminist texts written by African women who challenge patriarchy through their literature.

Beydan, aka Memory Snatcher, comes from a middle-class family; her father could afford to give her the best education Nairobi and Kenya had to offer, but because she is a woman, her education stopped after she finished secondary school. Beydan is an intelligent woman who 'completed high school with distinction' (Osman n.pag). Beydan is a woman who has her own mind and trains herself to challenge heteronormativity, but her quest to be different is severely suppressed by the men in her life. She is denied a university education and is instead forced into an arranged and an unhappy marriage with an educated man, who fails to appreciate her worth as a human being. Beydan's experience with men in Kenya thus mirrors the patriarchal experience of queer Africans in postcolonial societies. The sensitivity that Osman brings to bear on portraying the character of Beydan arguably comes from his own experience as gay man who constantly challenges heteronormativity. On his blogs and social media pages, Osman paints his face, wears lipsticks and at times he wears women's skirts. Osman's digital media presence and self-fashioning thus subverts heteronormativity and this tendency to be subversive can be seen in Beydan.

Ekine's blog makes a convincing case for us to see the intersection of feminism with queer desire. She views today's homophobia in African countries as synonymous with the suppression of female rights. Queer equality, therefore, intersects with female equality. And these struggles have a direct link to the project of colonialism and colonial modernity. 'The struggle to break free from colonialism was largely a political project,' Ekine argues. She surmises that this in turn had little or no negative impact on 'Western economic interests or hetero-patriarchal structures. Indeed, nationalist movements used the same colonial, militarised masculinities as a foundation for liberation and post-colonialism, thereby maintaining the non-status of African women' (2013, 81).

Ekine's statement can be used in understanding *The Memory Snatcher*: Although she is smart, Beydan occupies a lower status due to her gender. Her husband Rahim is equally well educated and he thinks he is politically conscious because he 'was schooled in Homi Bhabha's theories'. But there is a disconnect between Rahim's academic knowledge and how he behaves in his domestic life. Beydan is neither seen nor heard by Rahim, and so becomes the subaltern of postcolonial Kenya. Her experience of men symbolises the silencing of women who refuse to conform to societal norms. Beydan becomes mentally ill, and she ends up living in the basement of the narrator's parents' home. The men in Beydan's life never bother to ask her if she is sexually attracted to men or if she has high career ambitions. The men in her life do not allow her to take ownership of her body, but being a very determined woman she takes control of her mind and life by becoming insane. The men can have her body, but madness and her retreat into silence ensure she controls her own soul.

As if to hint that Beydan might not be entirely heterosexual, Osman queers her character after she turns mad:

> She looked like a witch:
> red, red hair,
> dark, dark skin,
> skin dry as bark,
> bark bad as bite,
> teeth chipped,
> nails unclipped.

By equating her to a witch, Osman turns Beydan into a feminist symbol and a figure who challenges patriarchy and masculinity. Osman's portrayal of Beydan as a witch is a means to queer her. Witches in many African societies, especially in the precolonial era, are figures who challenge societal norms. In Yoruba culture, for example, a witch is referred to as 'Aje, iya mi Osoronga' – a spiritual mother-figure to all, men and women. A witch in Yoruba culture is also a spiritual figure who strikes fear in people. Osman's depiction of Beydan, to my Yoruba spiritual sensibilities, means that he sees Beydan as a transcendental figure. She occupies a spiritual realm, and she is mentally free from the claws of patriarchy despite being physically chained in a basement. Although Beydan suffers daily violations, insanity becomes her agency and she asserts her selfhood through it. Macharia shows in 'Digital Queer Africa' that even when queer Africans use the digital space to depict everyday violations, they do so with care, and in the process they repudiate 'the spectacular scenes of subjection and violence that devalue black life' (3). In his queering of Beydan, Osman positions the story's narrator – Beydan's niece Aisha – as the symbol of love and care. Aisha sees Beydan's life story as symbolising repressed memories.

Subverting Heteronormativity

In challenging the dominant narratives about the un-Africanness of homosexuality and about homophobia in Africa, Kenyan and Nigerian writers, like their contemporaries across the continent, have adopted a Pan-African approach. Sexual politics is not local, its ramifications criss-cross national boundaries. When the Nigerian parliament tried to introduce a more draconian anti-sodomy law in 2014, Kenya's Binyavanga Wainaina, decided to come out as gay on YouTube during the very week the bill was debated. Wainaina further expressed his displeasure with this poem, *When the Internet Arrived, the Homosexuality Deamon Went Digital*, which he cross-published on Black Looks:

> When the internet arrived, the homosexuality deamon went digital, and was able to climb into optic fibers. Homosexuality deamon learns fast. Full of trickery. Read a lot and decided to convert from simple analogue deamonhood, to an actual ideology. Homosexuality demon is by this time quite African, a middle class one, likes old colonial houses, comfy hotels, really likes imported things.

This poem, written in slam style, speaks to the Victorian attitude of many African middle-class people regarding homosexuality. It tries to historicise the way in which the colonial administration and church officials penetrated the African mind by first controlling the body. The speaker ties colonial officials to the root of the criminalisation of homosexuality in several African countries by arguing that many African leaders and middle classes, who are today condemning homosexuality as un-African, inherited such attitudes from colonial-era schools and churches. This poem speaks to the idea that same-sex desire is not un-African; what is un-African is homophobia, and the people who helped perpetuate homophobia are the middle classes. For writers in the digital age such as Wainaina, the figure of the homosexual African is no longer being used as a body that literature deploys in the project of talking back to the West or in the project of nation building; rather, writers and intellectuals alike in the digital age are pointing to this figure as being part of a continental identity, political discourse and history.

It is important to point out that the passage of the Same-Sex Marriage Prohibition Act in Nigeria was not necessarily the catalyst for the upsurge in queer writings in Nigeria. People like Romeo Oriogun, Unoma Azuah and Jude Dibia were producing queer literature before. Digital platforms such as Black Looks are actually the impetus for queer writing. Black Looks as a site that curates Queer Africa began in June 2004 and ended in August 2014. Black Looks was my own first encounter with digital queer Africa. Through it, I encountered queer thinkers and activists like Diriye Osman, Unoma Azuah, Zanele Muholi, Hakima Abbas, Keguro Macharia, Shailja Patel, Mia Nikasimo, Donald Molosi, David Kato Musile, among many other queer voices. What the law in Nigeria did, however, is to focus world media attention on Nigerian homophobia. Wainaina's response was poignant and notable because it was a Kenyan responding to a situation in Nigeria. This affirms my core argument with regard to digital queer Africa, that African queer voices are people whose activities are not confined to the limited scope within a national boundary. They theorise and give deep insight into queer Africa, across borders, boundaries and historical periods.

Kenya's Shailja Patel's online courtroom drama, *Last Word: Caught in the Act*, published in the digital magazine *The Africa Report*, takes such a Pan-Africanist approach to challenge homophobia. The play is inspired by the persecution of queer people in Uganda and the introduction of an even more stringent bill in parliament to criminalise homosexuals. In the play, the prosecutor, who is also the protagonist, makes a poignant statement before the court as he presents the Ugandan government's case against ten citizens accused of sodomy, by proclaiming that 'I further present Exhibits E, F, G and H, found in defendants' bags. Books promoting homosexuality by William Shakespeare, Wole Soyinka, Dennis Brutus' (n.pag).

Patel's interest in homophobia in Uganda speaks to the need to understand today's queerphobia as being rooted in the experience of colonialism, the tyranny of the postcolonial state, the neocolonial influence of Western churches and politicians on African body politics, as well as the recognition that homophobia crosses national boundaries. Moreover, Patel is not just using Soyinka, Baldwin, Brutus and Appiah as mere backdrops, the protagonist's statement foregrounds the way in which some of the earlier literary works envision the way in which non-entirely-heterosexual bodies are affected by politics. What we witness is both a nod to figures who are gay or who are authors of texts that depict same-sex desire. Most importantly, this statement underlines the intricate link between the process of homosexualisation (confined to just those who identified as gays and lesbians) of African literature in the second half of the twentieth century, and its queering in the twenty-first century. These literary figures represent, for the fictional prosecutor, the corruption of African society from within and outside of the continent. His statement maps the battle over queer Africans' bodies. A close reading of some of the creative works of queer African writers reveals not just a literary recognition of the debt that the digital generation owes to the first generation of modern African writers, but the way in which the 'no gay in Africa' debate has shifted to a more confrontational representation by writers because of the digital space.

I base this comparison on Wole Soyinka's *The Interpreters* (1965) and Ama Ata Aidoo's *Our Sister Killjoy* (1977) to contrast the way in which homosexual subjects within various mappings of nation and Diaspora are being represented in the digital age, and to show the way in which the emerging voices' approach is changing from that of the generations before. An analysis of texts published in print and in cyberspace can provide us with the starting point that one-hundred-percent-non-straight Africans are arguably central to the literary understanding of African politics, because as a response to that politics, literature has to continuously look at shifting sexual meanings and erotic choices. My argument is that what has changed, however, is a growing vocalisation of support for gay rights, within and outside of the literature by emerging voices.

In *Our Sister Killjoy*, the protagonist Sissie recounts the story of a European headmistress in colonial Guinea. The woman came to Africa to devote her life to 'educating and straightening out African girls' (Aidoo 66), and is horrified to find two of her female students in bed together. Shocked that 'sodomy' actually takes place in Africa, the headmistress gasps:

> Good Heavens, girl!
> … Is your mother bush?
> … Is your father bush?
> Then
> Why
> Are
> You
> Bush?

Here, Aidoo affirms the universality of homosexuality: there are lesbians in Europe as there are lesbians in Guinea, this colonial outpost of France. The two pupils, instead of being petrified can only 'giggle' at the headmistress' outburst and ignorance. In this excerpt, lesbianism in the context of Euro-modernity – with the headmistress as an embodiment of the project of colonial modernity – becomes a zone of competing values: Africa versus Europe, which equates to 'bush' versus 'civilised'. In this context, it is lesbianism that is drawing Africa back, and homophobia that becomes the agent of advancement. So-called European civility and civilised behaviour are shown here as not necessarily tantamount to respect for sexual differences.

Like in *Our Sister Killjoy*, a print story from the second half of the twentieth century, in Patel's play in the digital age, gays and lesbians are everywhere, as the prosecutor in *Caught in the Act*, laments:

> It is the gays who drive our poverty and unemployment.
> The gays who created war in Northern Uganda.
> They blocked the peace process.
> They spread HIV.
> They destroy families.
> The gays destroyed our chances in the African Cup of Nations.
> Niger and Benin know how to keep their players undefiled and strong.

The reach of same-sex desire has spread to books, cyberspace and even into the minds of the ruling classes and gays are accused of being responsible for all the ills of society because of their visibility and presence.

What Patel and some of her contemporaries are doing in the twenty-first century is to build on Aidoo's work. Colonial modernity places heterosexuality as 'civilised' and homosexuality as the sexual Other. Aidoo thus helps initiate a smarter reading of African homosexuality in the continent's modern literature because *Our Sister Killjoy* foregrounds the current argument of some members of the internet generation that homosexuality is probably not un-African, but that it is rather homophobia which is alien to precolonial Africa.

Like Aidoo in *Our Sister Killjoy*, Soyinka's *The Interpreters* speculates on homosexuality through the lens of race, capital and politics. In Soyinka's novel, the figure of the homosexual is an African-American, who is one-quarter Black. The character, Joe Golder, lives in Nigeria and he makes references to traces of queerness in Nigerian cultures and history. The fact that Golder is not fully of African descent can be seen as the narrator's attempt to tell us that homosexuality can only come from the West and from bodies that are not authentically African. While this portrayal of Golder as a site of moral corruption that is foreign to Africa, is problematic – because it reinforces the notion that homosexuality is un-African – in *The Interpreters,* Soyinka queers every aspect of Golder in Lagos. For example, the narrator tells us that: 'when Joe Golder was ugly, he went the full range of transformation ... And he was being ugly from pique, self-despising as always ... Kola, even before he began his canvas on the Pantheon, had remarked how well he would translate into one of the gods' (102).

This portrayal of Golder by Soyinka can be read as the precursor to Osman's portrayal of Beydan in *The Memory Snatcher*. It shows that in queer African writings, old texts inspire new texts. This intertextuality is likewise noted in Shailja Patel's referencing of the names of Wole Soyinka and James Baldwin in her earlier online version of her play *Caught in the Act* – which has now been revised on the website of *The Africa Report*. Soyinka in *The Interpreters*, references James Baldwin when the narrator tells us that the character Golder owns a copy of Baldwin's *Another Country*. Ronan Ludot-Vlasak argues that intertextuality in queer representations can be read as affirming literary canons, and at the same time it subverts the canons because it helps to generate new meanings. This argument is important to my reading of Patel's *Caught in the Act*. Both Soyinka and Patel canonise Baldwin in the context of African diasporic literature. Soyinka canonises Baldwin, and Patel canonises Soyinka.

Neville Hoad rightly reads this nod to Baldwin as important to the articulation of the way in which fictional narratives were deployed in the mission of decolonisation. Hoad argues that it shows that African cultures are at the centre of modernity because they are in dialogue 'not only with dominant colonial cultures ... but also with the cultures of diasporic blackness, Garveyism, Pan-Africanism, and Negritude' (45). I take Hoad's argument further by making the case that just as Soyinka acknowledges Baldwin's contribution to Black queer historicism, Patel recognises the importance of both Soyinka and Baldwin to queer African history, and the impetus their works gave to digital queer Africa. Patel's reinvention and regeneration of these figures is a call to revaluate and appreciate the importance of these figures to our understanding of sexual politics on the African continent and its Diaspora. Patel points us to how these figures signpost the world to the marginal position of homosexual African subjects within various mappings of nation and Diaspora.

While *The Interpreters* and *Our Sister Killjoy* problematise the idea of homosexuality being un-African, one notices their narrators' reluctance to embrace every variety of African sexuality. Perhaps because their writers are not queers, the novel's depth of sensitivity to queer emotion is not as deep as those of Patel and Osman's generation, who are queer Africans and who see their works as speaking to the lived experience of queer Africans. Through her reference to Soyinka, Patel reminds us how a reader can subvert a text as she uses online literature to respond to the work of an African canon published in the print format to challenge the premise of representation of queer desire in *The Interpreters*. While Soyinka's novel portrays homosexuality as alien to Africa, Patel's writing challenges this assumption. So what has changed in the portrayal of queer African bodies over the past four to five decades since the publication of *The Interpreters* and *Our Sister Killjoy*?

In a feature interview conducted by *CNN*'s *African Voices*, Adichie gives a pointer to a new agenda of queer representation: 'The reality is there are gay people who are human beings in Nigeria and I want to tell their stories.' The Kenyan writer Stephen Derwent Partington, in an email conversation on the CKW listserv, on 29 November 2010, expresses a similar sentiment:

There is a part of me that feels that arguing for gay rights and acceptance of gayness in Kenya is a brave and still necessary thing in itself; but that a more effective strategy is to argue how it affects us all. My citizenship is threatened when gays are threatened, and the rights of everyone I love, and everyone I share a national space with and don't always like but at least respect; and so, listen to their voices … There is no productive society that can be formed from the voices of the privileged alone; they are the set-upon who will show us all, including those of us who have forgotten what it means to be set-upon, that freedom for all only comes when those wrongly condemned as lepers have taken their full place, and have shown us the horrors of their experience of being condemned.

These statements signify a change in tactic in African literature's long interest in national politics. Writers are suggesting that some fifty years after independence, the postcolonial state is riddled with rampant corruption, and in its bid to maintain its hold on the public, the political class – in coalition with many clerics – are trying to seize the moral high ground by attacking the increasing visibility of African homosexuality in the digital age as a sign of moral corruption. For these writers, the agenda of literature is no longer limited to the exposure of politicians' criminal behaviour, but also challenges the hypocrisy and lies surrounding sexuality by focusing on hidden and marginalised bodies, who continue to haunt African history. This is possible because at the moment, queer fictions and essays can easily and cheaply be published online, where there is no intervention from the big book publishers whose bottom line is financial, is the profit margin – from the number of textbook sales to satisfying African shareholders. In addition, the digital space is largely free of governmental intervention in most African countries.

The agenda of book publishing is different from that of online publishing; writers, editors and publishers are human beings and like every other human endeavour, book publishing has its own politics. Such politics before the advent of the internet suggested that Africans do not 'do' homosexuality, so books on African homosexuality were not expected to sell because they would not meet readers' expectation of African literature, and because various African governments might ban homosexual texts from being used as part of the school curriculum. This politics is articulated in Adichie's *Jumping Monkey Hill*, analysed in Chapter One. That moment in *Jumping Monkey Hill*, when Edward asks, 'How African is it for a person to tell her family that she is homosexual?' suggests that those who set the agenda of book publishing do not see same-sex fiction as being relevant to the African condition. However, in the new media space, there is a growing demand for academic and literary materials on same-sex fictional narratives to be published online. There is a queer African literature group on Facebook and several other African literature groups on Facebook and other social networks seeking same-sex fiction and poetry.

These developments within the online writing space provide a good insight into the thinking and the modus operandi of a new generation of Africans, with the capability to bypass official and unofficial censorship in digital space. In the online writing space, young authors are finding the voice not only to write openly about homosexuality, they are also marketing these works as queer literature. One can ascribe this development not just to the freedom that the digital space provides, but also to the openness with which young people from across the world now talk about their sexuality. By bringing the private into the open, one can argue that these writers/bloggers are envisioning transparency as being ethical. In an article for *Wired* magazine, Facebook's founder Mark Zuckerberg is reported to have articulated the social networking generation's attitude to privacy: that by openly acknowledging who they are and behaving consistently among all their friends, this generation is building a more transparent world, and that young people are becoming more responsible and ready for the consequences of their actions (see David Kirkpatrick).

Another explanation for the change in approach is that both *Our Sister Killjoy* and *The Interpreters* came about as part of the 1960s' Pan-African project of decolonising the Black/African body, while currently emerging fictions and poetry are part of the growing digital African literary works that are questioning the supposedly un-Africanness of homosexuality. With the previous generation's preoccupation with writing back to the West, much of its creative writing privileged African masculinity (read as responsible leadership) over feminism. As Hoad surmises, there was a fixation with liberating the African body from colonial hang-ups, so as to enable the post-independence effort of nation-building through the discourse of Black power and African solidarity. Against this decolonialisation agenda, queer rights and sexual explicitness were arguably considered frivolous. Femi Osofisan argues that up to the present millennium, the gaze of African literature has mostly been fixed on writing back to the West through the creation of heroic figures; fictional characters who are too busy querying the 'white man' and 'constructing a nation out of the debris of colonialism' (65). He goes on to explain that:

> What I'm saying is that the vacancy in our previous literature of the sensual and the erotic, this absence that now seems astonishing to us, had its roots in the conditioning manners of its genesis, and as well in the extant laws of public morality and of creative practice. (65)

In addition, Osofisan argues that many writers had a colonial-style, Victorian-era-type of education, and that literary training at university, until recent years, meant sexual explicitness was avoided in most creative writings. Osofisan accurately articulates this dilemma – even when Aidoo writes about romance in *Our Sister Killjoy*, it is with a Victorian era's style, grace and inhibition: 'So there was a great deal of hand-holding, wet-kissing along ancient cobbled corridors. Pensive stares at the silvery eddies of the river' (41).

Not for Aidoo the graphic details that we see in this excerpt of Patel's queer poems for the digital version of *Outliers* (2008), *This Is How It Feels*:

> when you go down on me
> wind blows fragrant
> through my garden
> from your hungry lips
> earthquake tilts my pelvis
> chalice for your sips
> your tongue a hot wet finger
> separates my labia
> …

These lines would have made *Our Sister Killjoy's* Sissie wince! Not only is lovemaking out in the open, but the love that dared not speak up or come out two decades ago is now erotically provocative, very talkative and likewise political. In digital Africa, queer private moments are no longer private, they have become a tool for political activism. And the reason for this provocative and audacious development is that for those writers who want to represent queer desire, the internet offers the ultimate medium for same-sex erotic writing. For some of these emerging voices in the digital space, queer writings speak the language of rebellion against authority. Osofisan captures this argument when he says: 'It is almost as if the younger writers, later-day Jean Genets, are motivated by a volition for shock and outrage, for deliberate wounding' (69).

Some of these short stories being published online and the agenda of their writers show that African literature in cyberspace can constitute a reliable basis for analysing sexual politics. As argued in the second chapter, new media technologies continue to give writers new avenues to shape, recreate, possess, relive, experience and remember forgotten cultural practices and to create new contemporary cultural values. Patel's poetical explicitness on the theme of sex also offers a reprise of the openness with which some ancient African poems and arts depicted the theme of sex. Osofisan debunks the myth that, historically, Africans do not have an affinity towards the obscene and the sexually explicit texts. He argues that what we are now witnessing in fiction and poetry in the digital age represents the poetic licence that poets in many African societies have been enjoying for many centuries – the licence to explicitly depict the sexual and the profane in oral texts. What Osofisan's argument indicates is that the explicit, as seen in Patel's poem above, can be used to engage with politics. The sexually explicit, in the process, becomes a site for shared awareness of one's history and of one's place in the community. A consciousness of some of the forgotten poetic traditions on explicit sexual texts can be reprised in cyberspace and may be turned into political action.

The African Queer as a Border-Crosser

Another example of this new agenda is seen in the way in which the digital space allows for the outing of Africa's fluid identity. Being Kenyan-Asian and pro-queer, Patel represents the way in which, in this new cultural space, identities are becoming blurred and fluid. The internet speaks many different languages, and it is a site in which different traditions are merging together and thus representing a new African 'metropolitanity' – a melange of ideas and human experience fronted by digitally savvy, educated middle classes.

Patel in cyberspace and in the offline space becomes a border-crosser not only because she represents postcolonial migrancy but also because she intersects the boundary between heterosexuality and queerness. She is the postcolonial figure who has learnt to move seamlessly between various cultural spaces, speaking diverse languages (Kiswahili, Gujarati, English and Kikuyu), and communicating with her audience using different cultural forms (written poetry, drama, YouTube videos, one-person live show, short story, memoirs, essays etc). Himani Bannerji asserts that this politics of identity (which the digital space enhances) allows people a chance of naming themselves. Patel's offline and online relationship with Kenya and the West (where she often travels) speaks to the migratory tendency of many of today's African writers, and the mobility and the hybridity, across multiple online and offline platforms. Patel and her works therefore reflect complex geographies of belonging and alienation, in addition to the problematic politics of recognition and invisibility, synonymous with queers (see Mary Bryson et al.). This is perhaps where the term 'queer' is apt for those Africans who do not fit into the gender binary and identities acceptable to the postcolonial state.

Like most of these emerging African voices, many of the characters and narratives studied in this book are based on the professional middle classes and their lifestyle. For example, the central figures in fictional and true stories that are analysed in this chapter are members of the educated class in Nigeria, Kenya and the rest of the continent. So, as in the texts examined in the previous chapter, the voices of African queerness in cyberspace are predominantly middle class, and their representation in literature has largely mirrored this group. However, these online works are also challenging the agenda of wanton materialism that we often associate with the middle classes in general. Two of Patel's online poems for *Outliers*, *This Is How It Feels* and *Two Girls*, both use sexual pleasure to make a statement against heteronormative capital. We see this in *This Is How It Feels*:

> ...
> let it give
> Pat Robertson
> Dr Laura
> screaming slavering
> wet dream nightmares
> here between my legs
> ...

Here, queer pleasure and same-sex desire in cyberspace can and is meant to be subversive. Queer intimacy is not mere sexual lust; it is militant in its desire. The neoconservative American televangelist Pat Robertson epitomises unbridled capitalism and religious fundamentalism. From this particular angle, some of the emerging online African writings are showing the way in which the new media technologies that tether us to capital and control can also work to resist these tendencies. Through their mobile and active connections, some of these young Africans are creating a public sphere where individuals and groups can express and enlighten, collaborate and organise.

In *This is How It Feels*, the speaker also tells us:

> it's true we really do
> change the world
> by f**king yes
> the revolution
> is our naked bodies
> woman's mouth
> on woman's cunt woman's lips
> in woman's labia woman's tongue

Middle-class text, although an agent of capital, is now rebelling against the physical space's demand on the African person to have a family and be in a relationship with someone of the opposite sex. This poem challenges all forms of patriarchy and the idea that a 'good' woman should not talk about her sexual needs so brazenly, even more so of her desire for another female. The desire intimated by the speaker is not only expressing the pleasure of sex for sex's sake, but that sex can be a revolutionary act and meaningful. In the digital space, lesbian sex also serves as a commentary on the history of subjugation of female nudity. This is because, since the colonial era, African female nudity has been deemed as uncivilised. Nudity as portrayed in this poem is a means to challenging patriarchy. Historically in many societies in East and West Africa, female nudity, especially that of older women, was a tool that women used whenever they wanted to bring about momentous changes in their societies. Additionally, women in many societies the in precolonial era did not cover up the whole of their upper body, and nudity was not sexualised. Patel's poem can therefore be read as a recourse to a history of the African female body as a site of empowerment and freedom.

The Nigerian writer Unoma Azuah is a creative writer and scholar, who is also one of the leading queer activists in the digital landscape. Her poems and fiction have been used in academic discussions on queer identity in Africa such as Chantal Zabus's *Out in Africa: Same-sex Desire in Sub-Saharan Literatures & Cultures* (2019). Her activist profile includes being the editor of the digital publications in which some of Shailja Patel's queer poems are published. Azuah's online poem for the *Sentinel Online* magazine, *Home is Where the Heart Hurts*, captures the anguish of an African Christian lesbian. Her lamentation can be heard in these lines:

> My life is of gazes at metal crosses
> the thorns and blood that was Christ's lot
> I live to partake of the one thorn ripping through
> a clear flesh
> in the communion that is a flash
> in a pan of bread and wine.
> The tolling bell calls
> to sleep, waking, baking, prayers in
> beads of blunted edges
> it calls to vows, reunions, knots and strings of
> dangling hopes.

Within the space that is African Christianity, there is nothing but tears and sorrow for the non-straight Christian. The speaker in the poem longs to partake in the rituals of her religion, but her sexuality becomes a barrier, since heterosexual union is the only recognised lifestyle. The speaker tells us that she is the unacknowledged spectre haunting the church as well as African history:

> There is no name for our game
> its identity is stuffed like torn papers in the cracks of caves
> My lover and I
> are eunuchs on the corridors of echoes
> the sterility of crosses, silence, prayers and mortality.

The church and Africa are spaces where memories are smouldered and killed; where homosexual desire cannot be expressed but must be bottled up and neutered. The queer figure within these spaces is therefore a eunuch parading the corridor of history. The anguish that the lesbian speaker is experiencing is then described as similar to what Jesus Christ went through. Christ as an asexual figure; Christ as the revolutionary fighting history and sexual longing.

And because Christ won the battle of ideas, the lesbian figure tells us that she is going to be defiant:

> After a long trek in the desert of life
> My lover is a festival of meals
> We have devoured love and made lust
> the aroma that hangs in our kitchen.
> I bore my lover like news delivered
> to a keen receiver
> the message and the messenger merge
> in nights of sweat and fear
> it's either the heat of the tropics or
> the steam of love lost and found.

What Azuah writes here would probably not have been accepted by many book publishers in Nigeria and Kenya, who may fear incurring the wrath of the church and the state. Zabus makes the poignant observation that, unlike in the poem, where the queer speaker is outspoken, queer identity is intentionally repressed in Azuah's novel *Sky-High Flames* (2005). The book instead endorses what Zabus refers to as 'the stereotype that lesbianism is just a "passing thing"' (139). The politics and the economics of book publishing arguably put a limit on Azuah's ability to depict the full range of queer desire in *Sky-High Flames*. But in the digital space, Azuah's erotic poems capture a wider range of queer identity. When she publishes online, her poetry like that of Patel, fits into the idea posited by Patel and Anthony Giddens – that sex in cyberspace now speaks the language of revolution. Azuah and Patel show that digital African is a site that queries history and subverts sexual norms. It also provides scholars with the tools to re-examine contemporary attitudes. In this regard, Patel and Azuah, in their online writings, can be read as writers who want to use literature to bring about rapid reform, rather than follow subtle politics, in which queer desire is restrained. The encounter of their speakers and fictional characters with those in authority, and the way in which Patel and Azuah are challenging the church and the political establishment in the real space of Africa, underline the way in which spaces acquire meanings through our interactions with them. What African literature is doing in the digital space is therefore as important as the advocacy work that these writers are doing in the offline space.

All Homosexuals Are Terrorists!

We see that through literature, the internet is becoming the gathering point of desires and dreams for contemporary Africa; an archive of unseen pleasures and pains; a free space for marginalised bodies; and a performative site of contestation and contradiction. Michael W. Ross argues that the interaction on the world wide web is liberating, as under the guise of anonymity users can adopt identities that suit their current need. African literature in the online writing space reflects the way in which the internet provides an escape from social and sexual conventions that human beings may encounter in the physical space. In the process, intimacy and relationship are quickly and easily formed.

Speakers in poetry and characters in fictional narratives are plausibly depicting the life that some real-life queer Africans lead. They arguably symbolise the experience of African queerness and the queering of the African space. The role-playing activities that are becoming available in literature in cyberspace allow real-life queer Africans to explore different aspects of their sexual identity in a way that is impossible in the 'real' world. For example, if fictional queer characters are coming out online or are gathering in a certain online space, real life lesbians may want to explore these avenues and imitate fictional characters. James Weinrich studies queer communities and the online space. He argues that the internet may have benefited this community the most, in that people who are unsure about their sexuality can experiment and experience a new sexuality from a safe distance in different online gay communities before deciding to 'come out' in the real world. This is because in pre-internet years, there were not many openly gay meeting points for queer Africans in the same way as there are in the West. For the fictional Ugandan defendants arrested in a cybercafé in *Caught in the Act*, the internet is playing a critical role as the site of African queer culture and as the space for nurturing libidinal, romantic, social and political investments against state-sponsored homophobia. In addition, with a growing number of blogs, essays, short stories and other online literatures written by Africans for fellow Africans within and outside the continent, many real-life queer Africans can now partake in activities that they can easily identify with, such as the latest gay fashion, literature and other issues of interest that fit into their African identity and tradition. In addition, these digital queers can use the digital space to forge global solidarity against rabid homophobia in the offline space.

Notisha Massaquoi enjoins scholars to look at the connection between the continent's political history and the relationship of all queered bodies to this history. The private, of course, is political, and just as there is a political agenda in *Our Sister Killjoy* and *The Interpreters*, so *Caught in the Act* reflects the agenda of the political class in stoking up homophobia in order to gain favour from the larger public. In this online drama, all the monologues come from the prosecutor, who serves as a metaphor for the male authority figure in postcolonial African politics. He reads out the charges against the defendant as:

> Conspiracy to engage in homosexuality
> Promoting homosexuality
> Promoting-aggravated-homosexuality
> Attempted-aggravated-homosexuality.

From the prosecutor, we hear the rhetoric against homosexuality as he reiterates the point that same-sex desire equals violence. The prosecution of the defendants for exploring homosexual desire on the internet reveals the way in which the persecution of the sexual other is used to serve as an example of the consequence of crossing the line between what the authority deems as the 'normal' and the 'abnormal'. The trial serves as a warning to all dissident figures in Uganda. Cross the line against the government and you will be hunted down, even in cyberspace. The prosecutor also provides a testament to the vital historic link between Christianity and contemporary attitude towards queer Africans, when he intones before the court:

> Your Honour, this case is clear cut.
> Not all dissidents are gay. But all gays are dissidents.
> All sodomites are criminals. But not all criminals are sodomites.
> Not all terrorists are homosexuals. But all homosexuals are terrorists.
> All human rights people are not of Gomorrah. But all sodomites take shelter under the tree of human rights.

The Bible, a text that was central to the colonial project and the Europeanisation of African cultures, is used here by the prosecutor to justify homophobia and to affirm the Ugandan government's view of homosexuality as un-African. Literature is utilised to point out the irony of African homophobia. While Patel's writings depict queer African desire as revolutionary, the prosecutor sees such revolutionary acts as acts of terrorism. In the view of many African political leaders, homosexuality is a radical ideology that challenges the patriarchal hold on politics, and therefore same-sex desire is labelled by politics as an act of terrorism on the postcolonial state, as well as a danger to Africans who are heterosexuals. By linking the defendants' homosexuality to prostitution and paedophilia, the prosecutor as a symbol of patriarchal authority shows us that homosexuals deserve their marginal status, because they are a menace to the society in the eyes of those in position of power, just like terrorist and dissidents are. This is not only reinforcing what is considered the norm but justifies the legal means of excluding and punishing those bodies that are deemed as contradicting the 'traditional' African way of life. The prosecutor's actions demonstrate fully and dangerously that, within the postcolonial state, the struggle over queer rights is fundamentally a struggle about human rights.

Michel Foucault argues that modern social life is influenced by the rise of disciplinary power, which tries to control and regulate (see Anthony Giddens). In his view, modern society has managed to enforce discipline through institutions like the school, the church and the military. In the process, the body becomes docile and obedient to authorities. Foucault sees sexuality in terms of power dynamic and control, while the African cyberspace represents the site where the 'other' or the 'abnormal' can strategically hope to free herself of the societal norm. But while Foucault thinks that the 'emergence' or 'appearance' of the homosexual body or homosexual-like person is central to human histories and the scope of human sexuality, those who see themselves as the norm in both the online and offline spaces, see the homosexual African as a disease, an inauthentic person who is merely an agent of Westernisation.

Ross sees the online writing space as a place for power struggle, for a possible tilting of power in favour of the young, with the dynamic turning against those who have defined sexual normality in the past. While in the offline space, the subject of homosexuality may be a taboo and the expression of same-sex desire a criminal offence, cyberspace allows these Ugandans to rescale, reclaim and reorientate their African and Uganda identity away from the nation-state. As Doering argues, the digital space has the potential of remodelling the concept of citizenship, such that it is no longer determined just by the state but by multiple forms of engagement and belongings. The crackdown that we see in *Caught in the Act* depicts this fear; the powers-that-be are beginning to see the subversive power of the internet. Increased visibility can of course also lead to more opportunities for both virtual abuse and offline physical violence against homosexuals. Therefore, by imposing criminality on homosexuals and by authorising homophobia, the authority may succeed in driving gays and lesbians who have come out in cyberspace, back into the closet.

Given the homophobic laws in the offline space of Uganda, it is no wonder that the ten fictional defendants assume that the safest place for any Ugandan (straight or queer) lies in cyberspace, out of physical reach of the state. But Patel's *Last Word: Caught in the Act* positions the online space as symbolising a double-edged sword for gay Africans; while it can be the ultimate site for homoerotic experience and performances, it also holds a grave danger for both gays and their friends: It transpires that some of the defendants were caught looking at gay pornographic materials on the internet at the cybercafé. The prosecutor argues before the court:

> Defendant Eleven, Your Honour? She is the owner and operator of the brothel, which masquerades as the Cybersweet Café. Acting on information from a concerned citizen, Pastor Gideon Musoke, police conducted a raid on Cybersweet Café on April 2nd, 2010. They found the defendants engaged in the stated illegal activities. No, Your Honour, not actually in the act of committing homosexuality. They were creating, assembling and discussing pornographic materials promoting homosexuality.

The owner of the café providing access to the internet is accused of running a brothel. The viewing of online gay pornographic materials carries the same penalty as taking part in gay sex in real life. For the gay person using cybercafés, the assumption of the internet as a safe place to experiment with or experience true sexuality may no longer be true, since if he is caught, apart from risking being prosecuted himself, he can put the shop owner in trouble.

The prosecutor's statement suggests that by allowing her internet café to be used to access homoerotic materials, the owner of the cybercafé has become an accessory to the crime of sodomy, with both customer and café owner putting themselves in danger. The digital space of the world wide web is not after all a space beyond the control of those who define what is sinful against God and those who determine what is legal under criminal laws. Patel's online drama builds on news media reports of persecution and Uganda's stringent anti-gay bill, and so we see literature in the online space reporting on the fear that surrounds the criminalising of homosexuality in Uganda. As reported in the media, the play indicates that the proposed bill stipulates that anyone connected to a gay person could be charged under the same penal code.

The fictional police informant in this play is a Christian cleric, Pastor Gideon Musoke. The statement he gives to the police describes 'how the defendants corrupted his two-year old son by playing with him at the Cybersweet Café. Since that assault, the boy has exhibited homosexual behaviour. He cries like a girl. He wants to play with his mother's bracelets'. The prosecutor, in building an antigay coalition between the state and the church, speaks in an evangelical tone by telling the court that:

> Global warming is God's fire to burn homosexuals.
> Malaria is God's scourge for their sins – and we are all paying.
> They shall not live among us as homosexuals.
> They shall not live among us.
> They shall not live.

By linking the church to the criminalisation of homosexuality in this online drama, Patel is pointing out the role that Christian groups in particular (from within and outside of the continent) continue to play in Africa through their interference in politics. The fictional Pastor Musoke represents a brand of anti-gay evangelical movements that are growing rapidly across the continent (often American-styled and sometimes American-funded). The defendants in Patel's play therefore represent the persecution of queer bodies by the global conservative Christian alliance and Patel is highlighting the role that Christianity is playing in the on-going demonising of African gays and lesbians. Her work is a response by African literature to Ugandan politics, during the time when the country's parliamentarians were debating a stringent anti-sodomy law. The digital space of the internet and mobile phones allow writers to safely and quickly counter the heteronormative argument that is being put forward by the authorities. Patel also understands that through these anti-sodomy laws, which are currently used to target queer Africans, many politicians and religious leaders are united in their desire to monitor bodies that are deemed rebellious and un-African and she is using her play to create awareness online, to herself resist this control and to encourage others to join her subversion.

Middle-Class, Transnational, Queer, and African

5

When Wole Soyinka created the character of Joe Golder in *The Interpreters*, he probably did not know that Golder would become the precursor to many transnational black queer characters some four decades later, in the age of the internet. One can argue that Soyinka gave some of the currently emerging African voices the literary narrative to build on, because the text helped usher in a new and different model of a queer African genre, in which alienation is collective rather than idiosyncratically personal. Most importantly, from Soyinka's generation to this new generation, the trope of the non-straight African is still regularly navigated through transnational characters that possess the right kind of education, European language skills, and the financial clout to move easily between the countries of Africa and the West. This seems to suggest that homosexuality and queerness exist only in unfixed spaces, of which transnational spaces are an ideal metaphor. Like intercultural spaces, they are interstitial, located 'between fixed identifications' (Bhabha 4), with flexible borders (see also Anthony Cohen). 'Overlapping geographies' result in 'oscillating identities' (Massaquoi 51). Non-straight desire seems to be the exclusivity of middle-class Africans who have had a Western-style education. Sexual deviation appears to go hand-in-hand with the notion of transnationalism, as does sexual freedom. In this way, foreignness is ascribed to queerness. For example, Golder in *The Interpreters* is an African-American lecturer working at a Nigerian university, but his masculinity is often called into question by his intellectual friends because of his supposed queerness. He becomes an object of constant ridicule because of his sexuality, so much so that this African-American in Africa often expresses his frustration by singing the African-American spiritual 'Sometimes I feel like a motherless child'.

Golder's lamentation is similar to the evocation of home and Diaspora that emanates in the poems and fictional narratives that form the case studies for this paper: works that were published in the digital collection *Outliers* (2008). *Outliers* is a ground-breaking Pan-African project that articulates and theorises homoerotic choices from an Afro-diasporic perspective by bringing together writers and thinkers who are based in Africa and North America. The audacious project came about as part of the intellectual discourses that continue to respond to the notion of the un-Africanness of homosexuality by certain sections of the

African Diaspora. As scholarly studies such as those by Isidore Okpewho and Nkiru Nzegwu suggest, more Africans are emigrating to North America than ever since the end of the transatlantic slave trade. The link I want to make here speaks to the intertextual dialogue that Paul Gilroy famously refers to as the 'Black Atlantic' – the centuries-old continuous movement of texts and people between Africa and its Diaspora in the New World. Susan Arndt aptly points out that, whether consciously or unconsciously, texts across different media, genres and generations talk to one another due to the fact that they 'seek to enter into dialogues with their predecessors to conceptualise and shape new futures' (4). The groundwork for the current digital age's quest for gay rights and the currently emerging articulation of what it means to be a queer African has therefore been laid down by works published decades earlier.

In this book, I have consistently theorised on the remarkable uptake of digital technologies on the African continent, which has more mobile phone users than in the whole of Europe and North America together, and how this trend is impacting on the way literature is produced and consumed. I have also analysed the way in which class, sexuality, politics, and literature intersect in the digital age. This chapter, therefore, aims to contribute to understanding the intricate link between the forces of globalisation, class, gender, and sexuality.

The Queer Twin

The notion of queer transnational intertextuality I am arguing for can be seen in Terna Tilley-Gyado's *Spinning with Longing* and in Rudolph Ogoo Okonkwo's *Prisoners of the Sky*. These two short stories, published in *Outliers*, revisit the transatlantic queer discourse which Soyinka initiated in *The Interpreters*. In these two online stories, we get the classic trope of alienation that a queer black body may experience within this transatlantic space. For example, the protagonist in *Spinning with Longing* remarks that as a Nigerian American living in the USA, she 'was never the desired, only ever a witness to other women desiring each other. I didn't understand why I couldn't seem to get a foothold into this world I so much wanted to be part of. I didn't know there was really any other world for girls like me' (Tilley-Gyado 8). For the protagonist, her black queer body in America has a double connotation: Her queerness challenges the homophobia she encounters in America, while her blackness does the same for the racism she meets with. Additionally, her black body conforms neither to mainstream America's ideal of female beauty nor to its white hegemony. A highly educated, young, middle-class woman, the protagonist should have been able to fit right in with the Beltway crowd. Instead, due to America's racism and homophobia, like Golder in *The Interpreters*, she aches for '*home, home, home, home*' (9, italics in original).

After experiencing racism and alienation in America, the protagonist in *Spinning with Longing* goes to Africa, in search of home in Nigeria, with her Nigerian-born mother's warning ringing in her ears: that Africans do not 'believe in homosexuality, bisexuality, whatever. White people brought that thing with them. It is not natural for Africans' (9). In Nigeria, the homophobia that she encounters is fiercer than in America, so that she has to confront the fact that the image of home she has conjured up while being raised in America is idealised and that the reality is not ready for a Black queer. Instead, Nigerian politicians are bent on expanding the anti-sodomy laws inherited from the colonial government half a century earlier. She laments 'the certainty of moral high ground magnified on the faces of those who believe such laws safeguard the souls of the nation' (10). Men 'toast' her (the Nigerian youth slang for flirting), but she can't bring herself to tell them she is a lesbian. Instead, she partakes in compulsory heterosexuality by not publicly querying the societal pretence and pretentiousness that there are no gays and lesbians in Nigeria, and that all grown-up daughters eventually seek men to marry. Her timidity in not outing herself as a queer person in Nigeria means that she perpetuates a culture of silence. As in Soyinka's *The Interpreters*, this particular story problematises the idyllic imagination of homeland in popular diasporic productions (such as reggae songs and some black cinema) because the physical space of Africa does not necessarily match the image that has been conjured up within the Atlantic world seeking a way leading back to Africa.

The protagonist's desire for home and her disappointment in what she witnesses in Nigeria give us a good view of the impact of the colonial legacy on contemporary African thinking. Oyeronke Oyewumi (1997) argues that colonial modernity adversely impacted on African concepts of sexuality and gender by introducing strictly male and female gender categories as well as stratified straight versus non-straight sexual binary, without anything in between or outside of this gender and sexual convention. Through this imposition, Oyewumi argues, the colonial discourses reduced the complex ways in which social ideologies and cultural practices once operated in many African societies. Using Oyewumi's theory, one can argue that non-straight black (African) bodies disrupt ideas of heteronormativity that emerged from the project of colonial modernity. In this (post)colonial dispensation, those who deviate from the norm are seen as just that – deviants.

Similarly, to Sagoe, Golder's journalist friend in *The Interpreters*, who views Golder's behaviour with suspicion because he is gay, the mother of the lesbian protagonist reacts warily to her daughter in *Spinning with Longing*. She warns her: 'What kind of clothes are you taking? You can't just dress any way you want. It's not America. People will notice. Where are you going with these trousers? … You better not chase people's daughters over there oh' (Tilley-Gyado 8). Sagoe, created more than 40 years before the unnamed protagonist of *Spinning with Longing*, expresses his disapproval of Golder when he sees a copy of James Baldwin's novel, *Another Country*, lying on the back seat of Golder's car, by remarking 'Why is this lying on the car seat? So when you give lifts to students you can find an easy opening for exploring?' (1965, 200). While Baldwin as a gay writer represents America's perversion to Sagoe, it is the cotton trousers that become a symbol of queer perversion for the protagonist's mother in *Spinning with Longing*.

What literary representations, from print to online, have shown over the course of more than half a century is that some members of the middle classes, despite the fact that they have studied and lived in America, still see America as a pervasive site of sexual perversion, while Nigeria is seen as the antithesis of this supposedly American decadence. The protagonist evokes W.E.B. Du Bois's double consciousness, when she speaks of herself as not belonging in either of these two transatlantic spaces as 'the queer twin' (Tilley-Gyado 10) talking across two spaces – the old world (Africa) and the New World (America).

Cyberspace is a space that enables an examination of the idea of transculturality. For writers, it allows for not just the fusing of different aesthetic traditions (Nigerian and American as well as African and Western), it also enables a robust display of how young Africans are negotiating national, class, racial and global identities. A topographic twinning that illustrates how 'the anxiety of our era has to do fundamentally with space' (Foucault 1986, 23). Foucault's argument can be used to understand the way in which digital African queer anxiety differs across two different spaces – Africa and North America. In *Spinning with Longing*, the protagonist grapples with being African and queer, being visible and being invisible; one twin able to speak only in America whereas the other 'aches deeply for home' (Tilley-Gyado 10) to be found, or rather not to be found, in Africa.

These twinned conditions of (inter)cultural space become impossible to reconcile. Four decades after Golder cannot find a lover on either side of the Atlantic, the lesbian protagonist in *Spinning with Longing* hints at the end of the story that she finally has a girlfriend in America – after having experienced 'a terrible affair' (8). The fictional events signify the experience that black kinship, shared history, and geographical location do not necessarily result in either stable relationships or stable identities, even, or especially, in the age of Facebook and Twitter. For the protagonist in *Spinning with Longing*, the 'real' Africa becomes an impossibility; similarly, to the case of Joe Golder in *The Interpreters*, notions of 'home', 'freedom', sexual desire and 'mother' all become elusive. Golder sees Nigeria and Africa as home and a place of refuge from America's rabid racism, but in Nigeria, he is marked out as un-African because he is gay and because he is three-quarters white.

While *Spinning with Longing* is trying to show us that racial identity *can* be a practice of queer intimacy, Rudolf Ogoo Okonkwo's online fictional piece for *Outliers, Prisoners of the Sky*, actually makes this happen. It's a story of another young Nigerian-American woman, Nkechi, who is found frolicking by her parents in the back of a limousine with another girl on her high school's senior prom night. To her parents, her homosexuality is a sign of Western corruption, a belief Nkechi finds incredible, given that her parents are university professors in the US. Her father informs her and us that she has 'staged the last stunt of your teen years here in America' (17), and dispatches her straight to the University of Nigeria in Nsukka. It does not take Nkechi long to realise that, contrary to her parents' belief that Nigeria will cure her lesbianism, queers do exist in Africa. Her freshman year's room-mate, Nkem, soon becomes her lover.

Like *Spinning with Longing*, this cyberstory moves the discourse of queerness beyond sexuality by focusing on the construction of home and Diaspora, both in the sense of domestic intimacy (in Nigeria, in the dormitory of the University in Nsukka) and in the sense of transatlantic belonging. When they sent Nkechi to Nigeria, little do her parents know that she will find the love of her life there, Nkem, whom we are told comes from a humble background: 'Her mother was a petty trader and her father was a carpenter in their village of Ideani. She went to Queen's College, Enugu, on a scholarship' (18). Homosexuality thus cuts across class, and Nkem harbours a middle-class queer ambition: she wants to move to America, and waxes lyrical about the prospect of the state of Massachusetts legalising gay marriage. She asks Nkechi, 'Does the gay marriage law passed in Massachusetts mean that you as an American can marry me and then take me to America?' (18).

Of course, that is not meant to be. Nigeria's compulsory heterosexuality means that the only way in which Nkem can realise her American dream is by falsely agreeing to marry Nkechi's US-based cousin. In a dramatic ending, the two women come out by kissing to glares of the public and in full view of their relatives (who have come to welcome the bride to be) at an American airport. While same-sex desire cannot be achieved in Nigeria, America simultaneously becomes a site of tolerance and of perversion. These movements between Africa and North America speak to African and diasporic queers' search for meaning. They force us to think through domestic spaces as sites of colonial and postcolonial queer intimacies.

London with a Hint of Gugulethu

The speaker in Cary Alan Johnson's poem entitled *Outlier* (40–41) expresses the anguish of the black gay man in America, his stance against the essentialising of the queer black body, and the longing of that queer figure for home in Africa, away from the objectification of his body in America:

> I rail against any attempt to see my sexuality, my sex, my sexing as mainstream.
> Normally, I'm abnormal

> [...]
> I am a brother of Samuel Delaney's Time Square Red, Time Square Blue. Tell the truth.
> There were dicks. They were sucked. It was lovely
> I'm a freak of brother from the People's Republic of Brooklyn who has chosen to live my life in Africa (dark, Dark Continent)
> loving brothers loving brothers
> knowing sisters (really knowing/trying).
> Black men loving black men remains a revolutionary act.

Like the two short stories, this poem illustrates how the black queer body becomes a tool of resistance across the Diaspora. The sexuality that is foregrounded becomes multiply dispersed as sexuality/sex/sexing, the latter together with the variability of Red/Blue indicating a moveable enunciative process, one that is intertextually produced in and from the memoir-like essays of Samuel Delany to shape its own 'square', its own critical topography as sexing becomes a spatial thirding. The transnational space spoken of at the beginning turns out to be 'a space of resistance and permanent struggle', so that it becomes 'a meeting point, a hybrid place, where one can move beyond the existing borders. It is also a place of the marginal women and men, where old connections can be disturbed and new ones emerge. A Third-space consciousness is the precondition to building a community of resistance to all forms of hegemonic power' (Soja 56). The African Diaspora in America gave birth to the 'Black is Beautiful' slogan of the 1960s and 1970s, but the black queer body within that diasporic space is not (yet) accepted as beautiful. These creative works make us look at bodies that still remain hidden within African and Afro-diasporic histories and narratives. As stated in the previous chapter, queer African fictions can contribute to our understanding of how various forms of border crossing shape representations of sexuality in African literature.

It is obvious that, for a growing number of young Africans, straight or gay, as well as for many across the continent of Africa, the internet is ensuring that knowledge, once privileged and situated within the confines of higher education, has never been more free, more plentiful, or more available. Information technologies afford connection, mitigate isolation, and even make way for social movements. Eve Sedgwick's writing enables a realisation that capitalism relies on stimulating or creating consumer interest and participation. Through some of these emerging narratives in the online writing space, we are seeing how the internet, as a product of capitalism, has also become a tool for generating contemporary queer identity in Nigeria and Kenya. More precisely, it is the middle-class gays' preoccupation with living and negotiating what Rosemary Coombe refers to as 'the everyday life of consumer capitalism and the way in which affluent gays and lesbians employ mass culture in quotidian practices' (16) that the fictional protagonists' lifestyle evokes. While the primary focus of this book is on Kenya and Nigeria, I am using an example from South Africa to signpost us to a crisis in representation of queer Africans. There is a crisis in African literature because we rarely get robust fictional queer characters who are either working class or poor. South Africa provides a good case study in this context because it is the country with the most liberal gay laws on the continent: the first nation in the world to outlaw homophobic behaviour and the fifth in the world to legalise gay marriage, which also makes it the only country on the African continent to legalise same-sex union.

The protagonist in *Shades of the New South Africa*, an online short story by the Oxford University-educated South African writer Eusebius McKaiser, recognises the omission of destitute gay Africans from the continent's mainstream gay culture, as he depicts a would-be lover's unconcern about the plight of young, poor, black men in Cape Town:

> Sifiso seems totally oblivious. These street kids are just part of the familiar landscape of Sea point; to be negotiated but never to be acknowledged ... such honesty may ruin your appetite while sitting at Newscafé enjoying the morning's paper and overlooking the gorgeously blue ocean but for the aesthetic blotch of stray dogs and street kids ... (McKaiser n.pag)

This story signposts us to the way in which materialism and the pursuit of the quotidian are intricately linked with regards to literary depiction of queer Africa. And given the representations in many of these online queer writings, we may indeed assume that material culture has become implicated in the construction of queer identity. Queer performances in some of the online fiction often leave little space for the expression of lower and underclass queer experience, since these groups have already been excluded by the barrier of language (the inability to read and write in European languages on which the internet is mostly based), and many may not be able to afford regular internet access due to subscription cost and bandwidth limitation. McKaiser's depiction of Sifiso points us towards an intersectionality of class and sexuality. Sifiso is marginalised because of his sexuality but he is privileged because he is a middle-class South African, and therefore, his experience of marginality differs from those queer Africans who are even further marginalised by poverty. Additionally, the material capital that Sifiso possesses insulates him from the experience of those who are simultaneously gay and poor.

The 'negotiating' that the protagonist undertakes speaks of a joint, inseparable experience between a utopia and the distancing gaze at the 'aesthetic blotch': a mirror in which, as Foucault puts it, 'I discover my absence from the place where I am,' making me visible in seeing myself 'where I am absent' (1986, 24). The conceptualisation of a queer project is, after all, 'a utopian story' of courage, power, and resistance (Massaquoi 52), but it hardly accounts for the mirror function. State control of the media across the African continent has been widely discussed and studied by scholars (examples include Ebenezer Obadare, Nadine Dolby and George Ogola). Online African literature is showing us that we also need to focus our attention on the potential level of control that access to the new media space gives to the educated class, and how those who are in the new information network may unconsciously use the medium to their sole advantage – so much so that the unconnected may not be heard at all. Cultural and economic power thus matters in our articulation of the way in which same-sex and queer desire are being represented. Our attention should not just be on the state and on business corporations; we should also focus on powerful stakeholders beyond these entities. Some of the emerging African queer texts are showing us how the lower classes can easily be excluded and displaced from global cultural consciousness, and how this invisibility has been carried over into the online writing space: much of the new queer fiction in this medium speaks to the middle-class African queer experience, while fictional characters of lower economic status are seldom portrayed. The lifestyle of transnational young African writers who are easily at home in Lagos, London and Los Angeles is now being transplanted into fictional gay characters.

The gay protagonist in *Shades of the New South Africa* attests to this phenomenon:

> So there I am in Joburg in Cape Town. Celebrating thirty years of survival. The crazy world refuses to stop and acknowledge my tenacity. I am invisible in a space littered with twig-figured girls and boys with bulging muscle, as sexy as Popeye after a can of spinach, about to rescue his beloved twig-figurine, Olive. They are all draped in Diesel, Levi's, CK and other funk-indicating labels I cannot pronounce, let alone spell. They dance and giggle and strut around the dance floor, moving skilfully to local house beats, the imported cosmopolitan sounds of London mixed with a hint of Gugulethu, to mask the victory of cultural imperialism. This is the new resistance politics. I inhale the sweet, horny smells of booze and cigarettes and sweat and hormones and youth and promise and life … the intoxicating aroma of the new south Africa [sic]. I sit in a corner, making love to a bottle of Castle while scanning the room. For sex. For escapism. I choose my strategy. I try hard to look 'upwardly mobile' … yet chilled. The popular look seems to say "I'm-an-assistant-MD-but-have-loxion-kulca-flowing-through-my-soul". I realise I am screwed. (Or rather I won't be.) I'm not darkie enough to ooze even an ounce of loxion kulca through my coloured veins. I'm not rich enough to ooze assistant-MD. I'm not scrawny enough to masquerade the lie of 'youthful innocence'. How did I sneak past the doorman? It must have been my coconut twang, I guess – but that brand seems so last year, as stale as the "I-spent-a-gap-year-in-London" gag. (McKaiser n.pag)

The protagonist depicts the pretension of affluence with 'funk-indicating labels', gay men and women who affect a foreign 'twang' and like to display their collection of foreign clothes and other luxuries so as to be accepted into the gay scene. The speaker's 'invisible' quality reveals a positional identity as it (once again) 'enables me to see myself there where I am absent' (Foucault 1986, 24). The London-Gugulethu mix is less an intercultural space than one of class division, a world that is far removed from the South African townships and a million miles away from most villages in Nigeria and Kenya. But this world is real to many middle-class writers. In this new century, as in the last, class remains a very important factor in literature's representation of queer African life, because what literature is imitating is the fact that class embodies the experience of most African writers, with a middle-class queer experience that is manifesting itself overwhelmingly in the new media space to create its form of 'cultural imperialism' – which is paradoxically indistinguishable from 'resistance politics'. Stevi Jackson points out: 'Morality and taste are implicated in the maintenance of class boundaries' (17). As capital has bestowed on middle-class writers the opportunity of modern education and the affordability of the internet, the social relationships that these fictional queer characters form online somewhat resemble the literary networks that writers themselves belong to in cyberspace.

Rarely do we see fictional narratives or poems that capture the experience of African homosexuals who live in rural areas, or who are struggling to make ends meet in urban areas. Instead, fictional gay characters, like real-life writers, are often affluent, educated and socially mobile. A global middle-class identity is thus projected as the norm for non-straight Africans, in a continent in which many are indigent. Digital capital is becoming the cultural capital. It contributes to creating 'counter-sites, a kind of effectively enacted utopia in which the real sites, all the other real sites that can be found within the culture, are simultaneously represented, contested, and inverted' (Foucault 1986, 24).

The protagonist in *Shades of the New South Africa* expresses frustration at the limited pool of lovers, and tells us that he is used to 'being spoiled by choice gay hangouts on Christopher Street in New York and Old Compton Street in London' (McKaiser n.pag). We hear his complaint because he has the financial capability to enter the gay metropolises, as both the character and the writer who created him come from the same world – that of the professional African middle class. Furthermore, these short stories in the new media space confirm Robert Cover's assertion that the relationship between capital and labour is linked to both same-sex desire and homophobia. Through these fictions, we see the way that capitalism leads to social exclusion for many Africans, in this case lower-class queers, who cannot afford travel to gay hangouts, pay for internet dating or nightclubbing and who, due to lack of capital, are therefore excluded from many queer activities. The media space functions as a Foucaultian mirror between a utopia and the heterotopia that thrives on its distance from and its marginalising energy against queer existence among the lower classes.

Cyberspace is a construct of both reality and fiction. As Michelle Kendrick argues, it 'foregrounds the ways in which technology intervenes in our subjectivity' (143). The urban gay lifestyle is no different from the lifestyle that middle-class straight characters lead in the fictional narratives being produced by some of Africa's notable transnational literary figures such as Chimamanda Adichie and Teju Cole – they are immersed in smartphones, bling, popular music and digital connectivity. Just as these writers spend much of their time in the metropolitan spaces of Lagos and New York, so do the fictional characters they give us. The world of the fictional African queer characters used in this chapter appears to be that of CNN, the music of the American R&B singer R. Kelly, physically fit gay lovers, and luxurious hotel rooms in Abuja and Cape Town – expensive cities both of them. And since affordability equals accessibility, a subscription to Gaydar.com and high-end drinks in a trendy Cape Town gay bar may well be beyond the reach of many gays and lesbians who are less well off. The affluent lifestyle in conjunction with the expensive mobile phones that these fictional characters often carry as emblems in these online short stories represents the way in which many middle-class Africans are part of the global capitalist system, as people who possess cultural and economic capital. These elements symbolise the transnational and globalised identity of many queer members of this social group as well.

Coming Out in the Digital Age

The idea of 'coming out' in the twenty-first century in an African context can arguably best be understood if we look into, read and theorise the digital age. Online writings are suggesting that many young gay Africans choose to 'come out' through the internet, because it is safer and allows for more anonymity compared to the offline space. Coming out is to risk being subjected to violence. In the physical space, 'corrective rape' is used by some African men to 'cure' woman who come out as lesbians (see, for example, Pumza Fihlani). Literature in the online space indicates men can also be victims of corrective rape. In the online short story *Two-Step Skip* by the Nigerian author Crispin Oduobuk-Mfon Abasi, written for *Outliers*, the sexual violation of the male, gay narrator becomes a means of punishing that which is seen as un-African.

The protagonist in *Two-Step Skip* is a young up-and-coming Nigerian journalist. Trying to avoid the danger and the social stigma of looking for a male lover in the physical space of Abuja, Nigeria, he decides to try internet dating. Through the popular gay dating website, Gaydar.com, he meets a man, who he secretly meets for the first time in a hotel suite. Through this story we see another way in which the online space can pose a danger for a gay person. That danger is manifested in the fact that the protagonist is lured from the safe environment of cyberspace into the physical space by a man who is using a fake name, 'Dave', and who ends up raping the narrator. As will be subsequently discussed, the rape of the narrator shows us how otherness is lived, embodied, represented, experienced and transgressed in contemporary Africa. Relishing the prospect that internet dating will be more liberating and safer than meeting men in the physical space, the protagonist enthuses: 'why should I bring the mysterious too close? There's a degree of safety in arms-length. So when I'm done, I do a little happy two-step skip; once again a child out to buy sweets and chewing gum and looking forward to savouring their sugary sweetness' (Abasi 11).

The protagonist's experience symbolises the loneliness of being gay or lesbian in Nigeria. It also echoes the lamentation of 'Sometimes I feel like a motherless child,' which Joe Golder utters in Wole Soyinka's *The Interpreters*. And just as in the era when *The Interpreters* was written, the world inhabited by gay and lesbian characters in many of these new online fictions is one of alienation. Alienation is derived from the Latin *alius* meaning 'another' and *dienatus* meaning 'estranged'. According to Kolawole Ogungbesan, Hegel sees alienations as 'a characteristic feature of the modern man, his sense of inward estrangements, of more or less conscious awareness that the inner being, the "real," is alienated from the "me," the person as an object in society' (206).

Like his rapist, the protagonist is a closeted gay man, and he tells us that:

> Several people I know, including my girl and co-workers, question my sexuality sometimes because, braided hair and ladylike clothes apart, I'm one of those men born with very noticeable feminine traits. My colleagues often tease me about my voice and gestures. I've even overheard some call me *Dan Daudu*, the northern derogatory term for a gay sex worker. Okay, so I too have sometimes wondered about myself. It's why I registered with Gaydar. In meeting Dave, I've come for an evening of intelligent conversation on art, politics, and, well, okay, gay issues as well. I guess at some level it can be said that I'm exploring. Perhaps even experimenting, though this truly is a mysterious world to me. (Abasi 13)

We see gay characters constantly described as un-African because of their sexuality, and in the process we see estrangement, unease and friction in the physical space, which is driving them to cyberspace in the first place. The protagonist chats up men online, but he is forced to meet them secretly in the physical space. He tries to not incur the wrath of the contemporary society's homophobia and informs us 'That way, I two-step skip the security system' (12). Desire is expressed openly in the online space, and experienced secretly – as a shadow – in the offline space. The people in the narrator's life suspect his homosexuality but have chosen not to take this possibility seriously; instead they jokingly tag him a 'Dan Daudu'. Thus, the Nigerian society is also in the closet. Maintaining the front of having a girlfriend in the offline space while seeking a boyfriend in the digital space not only speaks to a crossing of boundaries, but to the 'down low' phenomenon, which Keith Boykin suggests is common with African-American gay men, who sleep with men (who they often meet online) while officially dating a female partner because of their community's homophobia. This is a Nigerian version of the 'down low'.

When, in the story, Dave remarks that the narrator speaks and looks like a girl, the narrator confirms his desire to be a girl. He tells us that 'I'd shown him my pictures on the net and had explained that I wished more than anything else that I'd been born a girl' (Abasi 13). He tells us about the look people give him when he acts like a woman as 'That look I get every day. The one which says, He must be gay!' (11). Here the internet also serves as a site for gender desire. At the root of the narrator's desire to fit into the contemporary gender normative in his online dating profile is the offline heteronormativity, a result of colonial modernity. It demands that a man must sound and act like a man, otherwise he can neither be considered a man nor a woman. People who do not fit into this man–woman binary can become a spectre, an invisible being which history refuses to place or acknowledge.

Two-Step Skip's 'coming out' narrative speaks to the role which the internet can play in the discovery of the 'real' self for many young Africans who have access to the internet via mobile phones. Both the protagonist and his rapist use Gaydar.com because of the promise that online dating holds for those gays and lesbians who can afford online dating subscriptions. The digital space is arguably becoming *the* space for gay and lesbian Africans to meet fellow Africans for either sex or a secret relationship. The protagonist's view of online dating as a site of queer enlightenment and experimentation confirms Mary Bryson's argument that cyberspace can be 'a powerful tool for learning to be, or perhaps more specifically, to do, queer' (85).

The chat room of Gaydar.com is a site for the outing of the queer self and this corroborates the argument that gender is an act of performance (see Annie Hau-nung Chan). The social interaction between the protagonist and Dave alludes to the fact that the internet chat is a prelude to dating, which is an essential element of the twenty-first century narrative discourse. It depicts how the 'self' connects with like-minded people in this new media age. Clifford Geertz points out that internet chat rooms make for 'metasocial commentary … a story they tell themselves about themselves" (quoted in Islam 82). For the characters in *Two-Step Skip*, a chatroom such as Gaydar.com not only enables real-time interactions between queer Africans, it is also a space for self-discovery and self-presentation as members can explore their queer side, which society's homophobia has suppressed. In *Two-Step Skip*, the narrator makes a point that 'there's a degree of safety in arms-length' (Abasi 11), so the chatroom in this story is space for African queers to keep their coming out strictly to the confines of online space. Being able to express their fear and experience of victimisation in chatrooms such as Gaydar.com, reflects the liberty queer Africans think a chatroom affords. A chatroom can then be seen as a community whose modes of operation differ greatly from that of an offline community, and as an online community, communication is not just between two people – as in Instant Messaging (IM) services – a chatroom may have several members communicating simultaneously in real time. Each member has a username and a profile, which they use to tell others who they are and what exactly they are looking for. Such self-presentation may be based on the truth and trust, such as in the case of the protagonist, while others may present falsehoods to unsuspecting members of a chatroom, such as in the case of Dave.

Dave has not experienced gay sex before, and he is a self-loathing gay character. His twin brother, who Dave, in online chats with the protagonist, has described as 'the most enviable man alive for being successful with women' (13), turns out to be gay, and he is the object of Dave's homophobic rage. Dave's self-loathing is born out of his cowardice – his lack of courage to proclaim his sexuality in the physical space. Because of the heteronormative patriarchy of the 'real' world, he instead restricts himself to avowing his queer desire in cyberspace. Dave thus represents the authoritative and hypocritical figure in the 'real' world, who while publicly condemning homosexuality as corrupting social mores, is secretly a closeted homosexual. His anger, which results in sexual violence, is arguably the consequence of pent-up shame and sorrow.

Monica T. Whitty encourages researchers interested in cyber-flirting to look at how online daters choose to reconstruct the body in cyberspace. In the online space, the narrator tells us, Dave 'is usually chatty and funny, eager to share anecdotes about his work and family', but in the physical space he is 'bland', 'inane', and 'unsophisticated' (13). Dave's screen persona or avatar represents a certain image of his homosexual self in the virtual world. Monica T. Whitty and Tom Buchanan argue that the name that online daters choose is an important factor in drawing people to their profiles as screen names are assumed by other punters as the initial window into one's online and offline personality. Although some Nigerians have Western names in real life, 'Dave' is a generic Western name that is supposed to sound neutral and worldly, and it bears no affiliation to any ethnic groups in Nigeria, except to suggest that the bearer is likely to be a Christian. Dave is thus a reassuring screen name that the would-be rapist adopts online in order to lure in his victim. An analysis of the figure of Dave is pivotal in order to understand the reality in which the queer African body is being consistently violated in silence, with no one to offer support and no possibility of legal recourse or justice. *Two-Step Skip* resembles a true-life story, 'Scammers Targeting Gay Men in Ghana,' told by Sokari Ekine, the publisher of the queer blog Black Looks, about gay-baiting. She reveals that the emerging gay websites in Kenya and Ghana 'are being used to trap' gays by men posting fake dating profiles, who lure the 'real' gay men from online chat rooms to isolated offline spaces with promises of sex. The article tells us that the gay men 'are then either blackmailed or assaulted by the "fake gays"'(n.pag). The charming Dave who initially chatted with the protagonist on Gaydar.com is arguably the 'real' Dave, while Dave the rapist, in the offline space of Abuja, is a by-product of society's imposition, of the community that demands wife, children and toughness from a man. As he rapes the protagonist, Dave mocks the protagonist's effeminate build and clothing: 'You're just like a woman! Look at your face! See your red lips. Did you use lipstick?' (14). Through this combination of ridicule and sexual violence, Dave is trying to prove to the 'real' world that he is the opposite of the weak 'un-African' gay men who inhabits the digital space. Dave's mocking testifies to a postcolonial Africa's physical, affective and ideological concept of manhood. The sexual violence visited on the protagonist symbolises the fight-back by the heteronormative society against the coming out of queerness. While the rape of women (lesbian and straight) in wars and in domestic environments has been well documented around the world, the rape of gay men such as the fictional protagonist in *Two-Step Skip* stands as a reminder of the unreported sexual violence visited on gay men every day, not just on the continent of Africa, but on every continent across the globe. In the digital age, as Sokari Ekine shows on Black Looks, these men are likely to have met their rapists and may have forged a relationship with them through internet dating. Many religious leaders in Africa have voiced support for sexual violence against homosexuals (see Neville Hoad) and they encourage rape as a tool to try and keep societal order. The queer African body as represented by the protagonist in *Two-Step Skip*, in both the online and offline spaces, is a site for religious and neocolonial violence. It is an example of how many young African writers are using the experience of queer characters to portray the collective dangers posed by individuals who take it on themselves to execute the views of society and those in positions of authority. Dave in his rapist rage embodies the heterosexual middle class and an educated African male's determination to remain in control of Africa's destiny, and he carries out this agenda by forcing himself on the protagonist.

After he fights his rapist into a comatose state, the protagonist walks back into the real world as a queer Nigerian with spectral status, as an unreal man. Traumatised but still forced into silence by the heteromasculinity of the outside world, he will be able to tell his story only in cyberspace. Again, we see the queer person as the 'loner', the person who has no shoulder to cry on in the physical space and who remains a spectre haunting the postcolonial history. The protagonist's experience in that hotel room symbolises a re-enforcement of the culture of silence that currently surrounds queer bodies and identities in the physical space. Abrahams points out that such silence does not benefit the queer community, since people are getting raped whether they remain silent or speak out. The internet and the digital space provide the queer figure with the chance to emerge from the shadow of African history. Cyberspace is not only becoming a space for affirming African queer identity but also the space for the outing of repressed memories for marginalised bodies. From here queer activists, along with writers and theorists of different sexual persuasions, can go on to tell the queer story in both the virtual and physical spaces of Africa.

Queer African Bodies and Global Capital

African literature in the digital writing space gives us an insight into the way global market forces operate within the continent. The short stories and poems on African homosexuality show us is that there is a connection between the capitalist metropolis, national capitalism and African queer culture in the twenty-first century, notably enhanced by the new tools of globalisation of which the internet is an important part. In cyberspace, the queer African body simultaneously reveals and signifies the obscenity of materialism and exploitation.

Some of the new online writings suggest that there might not be a space for queer expression within this capitalist desire. The protagonist in *Two-Step Skip* tells us that he risks becoming a persona non grata within his wealthy circle of friends and clientele if it is confirmed that he is gay. In a more radical reading, the rape of the narrator in *Two-Step Skip* is a metaphor for the continuous exploitation of Africans by global capital. Robert Cover argues that queerness is often affected by the agenda of 'late capitalism'. Through Dave, we see how emerging queer texts are suggesting that by supporting violence against the homosexual person, those in position of power in Africa are carrying out a capitalist agenda, one that seeks orderliness and the rule of law as being conducive to national growth and development. Homosexual bodies signify the unpredictability of the African market to foreign investors. African thinkers such as Keguro Macharia and Wambui Mwangi ('Koroga: Another African Story') and Binyavanga Wainaina ('How to Write About Africa') have shown that to some foreign businesses, Africa is a hypermasculine continent, where heteronormativity helps to foster a good atmosphere for business. If this is the case, to violently abuse queer Africans, as highlighted in these online fictional narratives, is to make a statement against crisis and chaos, thus telling the outside world that Africa is open and ready for business. As many of these new cybertexts reveal, capitalism weakens the communal spirit of Africa, as the twenty-first century African middle classes have to spread across the globe in order to attain material wealth. At the same time, as discussed earlier, African queer transnationalists seem to fully buy into the allure of 'funk-indicating labels', exclusive gay hangouts, paying in pain and hard cash for fashionably skinny and muscled bodies and the latest high-end cell phones.

From *Skipping with Longing* to *Two-Step Skip*, and to *Prisoners of the Sky*, works published with finance from US-based organisations (IRN-Africa and City University of New York), the interconnectedness between different literary spaces, especially between the metropolitan centres of Africa and

North America, has helped advance the cause of gay rights movements in postcolonial Africa. Yet literature depicting transnational figures also shows the challenges faced by people whom many would deem privileged due to the economic and cultural power they have access to. Literature helps to undermine the stance of many African national leaders and their followers who wrongly perceive homosexuality as being un-African, by bringing to the fore nuanced representations of queerness and same-sex desire in an African context. Transnational characters who criss-cross these fictional spaces reveal the experience that homophobia is not just an African dilemma but is very much alive in North America, especially for black queers. For these characters, the experience of being different or queer is not mitigated by their being members of the global middle classes, as they are not fully accepted in either Africa or North America. Despite experiencing marginalisation and discrimination, the fictional narratives themselves are engaged in marginalising and discriminatory stereotyping: The narratives seem to completely ignore the phenomenon that there are working-class Africans who are gays, lesbians, transgender and queers. Much of the depiction online and in print centres solely on middle-class characters who have the ability to travel between countries in Africa and the West, speak European languages and possess the capital to indulge their expensive tastes. At the same time, even affluence cannot shield gays from the violence that is being inflicted on the queer body in Africa, and online literature shows how capitalism and heteronormativity intersect in the exploitation and abuse of gay desire.

6 'Ashewo no be job': The Figure of the Modern Girl in the Digital Age

> The text is home to thoughts
> and its context the rudder
> steering readers from flaws.
> The text is voice inscribed in cold print,
> Readers with mental tools can decode
> Signs, symbols, & codes within.
> Texts respond to texts, linking
> writers with a past not seen.
> The inter-text, hidden between the lines
> only the alert can bring to live.
> (Koleade Odutola xvii)

Much of the creative work that came out of the first half of the last century looked at alienation and disaffection, which fictional narrators and readers of literature regularly blamed on growing urbanisation and the negative effect of modernity on young people, especially young women. Nowadays, several short stories that are being published in the digital space are still preoccupied with the life of urban dwellers and the mannerisms of those who are identified with that space. In the twenty-first century, members of the digital public who are commenting on these stories are as fascinated by the subject as were previous generations. When examining urban settings, I am referring to the lived practices and representations through which a variety of spaces are constituted within the scope of cities such as Lagos and Nairobi. In this chapter, I use creative writings, published over the course of a century across print and digital mediums, to historicise the interest – of writers and readers alike – in the trope of the modern girl. If we analyse some of the creative writings online, we see a continuation of the tradition where texts and images report on intimacy. From the precolonial era to the colonial period and to the digital era, the African body, as a sexual being, has always been at the centre of political discourses, through artistic interventions. The artworks of societies such as the ancient Benin and Yoruba (Oyo) kingdoms underlined the intersection of sexuality with religion and politics, especially among the ruling classes of that era. Several verses in Odu-Ifa (the Yoruba main theological text) are poems that are sexually explicit, with some graphically depicting the pleasure of sex. Carvings and statues in many ruling houses include imagery of nudity and the erotic. During the Atlantic slave trade, bodily imaginations about African sexuality in literary texts and other artistic endeavours were at the centre of the dehumanisation of enslaved Africans, and such imaginations fuelled colonial discourses. Sylvia Tamale, in 'Researching and Theorizing Sexualities in Africa', recounts the story of the English explorer Sir Richard Burton, who in his travel memoirs published in the 1860s described the women of present day's Benin Republic as 'hideous', having a 'muscular development of the frame … femininity could be detected only by the bosom', and 'taken in adultery or too shrewish to live with their husbands' (23).

My starting point is that, over the course of a century, discourses around the figure of the modern girl are about sexual deviancy and that middle-class writers and middle-class readers are central to these narratives. I argue that terms like 'Ashewo' in Nigeria (Yoruba for money-changer) and 'Malaya' in Kenya lump together women who do not conform to contemporary sexual norms. A woman referred to as Ashewo could be a medical doctor who likes sex or who is sexually confident, while at the same time, a sex worker is also categorised as Ashewo. In 1929, the narrator in I.B. Thomas's *Itan Igbesi Aiye Emi Ṣẹgilọla Ẹleyinju, Ẹlẹgbẹrun Oko L'Aiye*, towards the end of his narrative uses the term 'Ashewo' to interpret the figure of Ṣẹgilọla. Eighty years later, the narrator in *Ashewos Anonymous*, a short story posted on Facebook by the Nigerian writer and journalist Terna Tilley-Gyado, uses the same word to describe their version of modern women. I use this conflation to analyse the sexual market and how the figure of the Ashewo challenges some of the dominant assumptions relating to the libidinal economy.

While many new texts in the digital space can be seen as representing an alternative to the mainstream media discourse on sexual intimacies, other new texts moralise and perpetuate the accepted decorum on sexuality. In these stories, we meet a figure familiar to many city dwellers and cultural anthropologists alike, a character who has become a regular staple of many fictional narratives. She has a history that dates back almost a century in Africa, and she is the sexualised modern urban 'girl' or 'good time' woman. I want to show that even in the digital age, African intimacy can be analysed and understood through the figure of the modern girl, because she represents the conflict between traditional and contemporary notions of courtship, romance and sexual relationships.

Writings about women who do not conform to prevailing sexual decorum often reveal anxieties over the impact of modernity on society. When some writers write about women and sex, we often see an amalgamation of African and Western anxieties over the African female body; one in which the body is, on the one hand, seen as a site of (communal) purity, and on the other hand, is envisioned as a potential site of sins that came about through increasing globalisation. Both perceptions reflected in creative writings capture how colonial modernity subjugated African women's sexuality. The mostly male colonialists and missionaries made African women into symbols of African savagery and moral corruption. Drawing from historical accounts in Kenya, Nanjala Nyabola argues that for the colonialist 'the idea of managing African sexuality itself stems from a racist colonial fear of the same' (133). Marc Epprecht offers similar argument when he suggests that writings by Westerners during the colonial era portrayed African women as being sexually rampant and that the colonialists characterised this promiscuity as pathological and dangerous. Both Nyabola and Epprecht show that to the educated male Africans who took over political power after independence, women who exhibit sexual desire are seen as exhibiting moral corruption brought about by colonial modernity, and such African women are portrayed as trying to behave like European women. Born out of these two positions is the confusion over what constitutes African sexuality.

Given these developments, fictional narratives and poetry show us Africans being conflicted between what they perceive as the African way of life and what they see as a Western lifestyle. Ada Uzoamaka Azodo and Maureen Ngozi Eke put these dilemmas into two categories: 'historical shifts and shifts in popular culture' (18). The shifts that Azodo and Eke point to underline my argument that for more than a century, people in societies across the continent have been facing competing and multiple perspectives on life which often oscillate between the Occidental (European), the Oriental (mostly Arab-Islamic) and the African traditions. Literature, like the contemporary society it tries to represent, has been trying to resolve this dilemma through the figure of the modern girl. Within this struggle, literature shows us that the modern girl encompasses two bodies in the postcolonial contemporary – that of the libidinous woman and the embodiment of romantic love. By looking at the figure of the modern girl, we see how members of a new generation of writers, like the generations before them, are navigating between these discordant messages.

Ashewos Anonymous, continues African literature's long fascination with this representative of the contemporary African woman. The narrator tells the story of six Lagos women from different social class backgrounds, who meet regularly in 'a small conference room at the Eko Le Meriden'. The women, we are informed, are the six remaining members of a support group for women who are addicted to sex. The narrator familiarises his readers with the fictional subjects in a satirical tone, by portraying the women as the girls-next-door gone 'bad' simply due to their 'unhealthy' interest in sex. He paints a vivid picture of their meeting as that of members of a self-help group who sit around to discuss their problems 'in a semi-circle'. Suffice it to point out that through his characterisation the writer refuses to distinguish between a sex worker and a woman with a healthy sex life. These are some of the comments by readers of the story:

Ekide Ekrika Nwanze:	It is so true, it hurts! Sadly, the biz of 'Ashewo' has been 'rebranded'. They drive the posh cars, live in big houses, they are the bigz (sic) gals, the movers and shakers of the big cities, they even get political appointments!! Sad, very sad. God help us. Nice piece, very humorous too, I didn't want it to stop.
Mayowa Adeyemi:	very interesting with an hidden lesson to learn for anybody that wants to learn. and like play (sic) it is part of the reality of our time.
Hadiza Rasheed-Jada:	hilarious, maybe ur part 2 shud depict the uni [university] students that belong to the wider AA [*Ashewos Anonymous*].

For the narrator and the Facebook readers who comment on the story, women across different social classes partake in the libidinal economy that is Ashewo, and regardless of the social-economic background, Ashewo are women who either like sex and men too much, or are sex workers. These instances are often conflated in Nigerian society. The term 'Ashewo' is one that has been ascribed to prostitutes and sexualised women alike in modern Nigeria. In Kenya, like most of East Africa, the term 'Malaya' is often used to describe a prostitute. Both are terminologies that arguably came out of colonial modernity discourse. 'Ashewo' means 'money-changer' in Yoruba, and the monetary aspect of it likely refers to the exchanging of currency – coins and notes that came with the British. The figure of the modern woman and the discourse surrounding her are likely to have come out of this colonial encounter, especially the sex trade along the West African coast and have become ingrained in contemporary perceptions. David Bennett points out that in England the word 'purse' might have connoted 'either scrotum or vagina and "spending" either seminal or vaginal fluid since the late sixteenth century' (4). This connection with monetary exchange within Euro-modernity then helped to transform both the female sex worker and a woman who likes sex a lot into 'Ashewo'. For example, in *Ashewos Anonymous*, the character Funke Okunrinoletemilorun, who is the founder of the society, is described by the narrator as 'a young lady with genuine sexual neuroses. At the last count she had slept with no less than 127 men, not including the okada driver that would drop her later that evening' (n.pag). At the same time, other female characters in the story, who are sex workers, are also referred to as 'Ashewo'. What the narrator in *Ashewos Anonymous* therefore shows is that for the contemporary society, sex is only normal when it is not enjoyed and when it is not for sale. Any sexual acts outside of these scenarios then fall into the 'Ashewo' category. For the narrator and most of the readers who commented on the story on Facebook, there is no mitigation for these fictional women, even though we are told that some of them are in dire need of money. Poverty and the possibility of bankruptcy are not mitigating circumstances that warrant sympathy for the women.

The sentiments expressed by the readers of *Ashewos Anonymous* are similar to those expressed by their Kenyan counterparts with regard to another short story based on a fictional young woman in Nairobi. *Her Friend's Father*, by the Kenyan writer and journalist Pauline Odhiambo, was published on the Kenyan-based *Storymoja* blog. The story centres on a twenty-year-old woman from Nairobi, who is having an affair with her best friend's father, and who uses the money the man gives her to buy accessories that include a mobile phone and luxuries that she could not otherwise afford. Some of the responses to the story include:

Marcia Wachira:	I love the flow and the story telling. It's almost like having a conversation with the writer. I vote 10 because i can't wait to read part two if possible. In today's society making money is top of the list and not everyone opts for a nine to five job. Good job Pauline for portraying the modern ho and disgusting old men in today's light. 10/10.
Rain Kenya:	Well written story, that depicts what happens every day! i read it all at one go, with other browser windows open! (you most definitely understand the allure of a new chat message on Facebook, can distract one's attention don't you?) I give it a 9!
Yvonne:	I found this a sad story, but very well told - very candid and a great opening paragraph. I'm not sure who was manipulating who in the story but I doubt that we can fix what seems to be a modern day form of prostitution which isn't going away any time soon.
Hmutugi:	Real life during these real times ... all u gotta do is be very careful.
Cheptiony Mutai:	The introduction of this story is very catchy. It's creatively written. Your story is real. It happens every day, and brings to light the strange behaviours of Kenyan men. I am one of them, and for sure we Kenyan men don't know what we want. And hence, we

	end up being manipulated… It's sad. Pauline, I would advise you to come up with a book, exposing how Kenyan men are being exploited by college girls. I am a writer and dream of writing a book explaining the same. Men, when will begin identifying what we want? Let's be ourselves. Cheers Pauline! Keep up the good work.
Monica:	The story is so real i almost felt it. I truly uphold the writer for the works. We need to read what we can relate to at times. Part 2 should surely follow couz we need to know the repercussions.
Ivory Punk:	True, she is just twenty - the things she spends the money on are a bit too trivial considering what she is giving up. Kuonjeshana [compromise] ladybird.

Responses to fictional narratives posted online, such as the above stories, possess their own literariness. This is because the comments are an extension of the fiction. The fictional narrative may reflect what the readers may have encountered and experienced in real life, but in turn, the comments from readers constitute a further reading of the fiction. Comments on online posts fit into the realm of fiction, because we cannot determine or confirm the true identity of the responders, even when a name resembles that of a 'real' person. If identity can be fictionalised, so can the view expressed by the commentator. Does the opinion of a someone responding reflect their true feelings about the fiction or are they just following the online crowd? If the views expressed by the readers of agreeing with the writer are a true reflection of their world view, we can argue that the online fiction cements preconceived perceptions, and comments affirm the text's aesthetic value while also 'writing to' the text. Each comment and the comments put together constitute a basis for further close reading. The response of the commenter Monica, on how 'the story is so real I almost felt it,' signifies the way in which the fictional becomes 'real' because in the mind of the reader it is no longer a 'made-up' story but one that is experienced.

The social commentary, then, does not have to be in a didactic style; the stories retain their purpose to entertain, but the reader maintains a right to moralise about the women's actions. From the comments, one can see that both male and female readers lay the blame of sexual exploits on the female protagonist, while the male character is mainly viewed as the victim of the 'devious' modern woman. The reactions of readers to the protagonist as the figure of the modern girl echo the reaction of the readers who comment on Tilley-Gyardo's Facebook story. Odhiambo, the author, although a woman herself, does not see the need to come to the side of her female protagonist nor does she offer an alternative perspective to that of the digital public. Her response is: 'Thanks for your encouraging comments everyone. Marcia, Part 2 might be in the offing.' The writer is, therefore, not an objective by-stander. The protagonist's portrayal by the writer and her readers' reaction to her show that people's online comments are a reflection of what they have seen or read offline. What people read or see online may also influence their offline behaviour and the way they react to daily experiences in the physical space. Although they are not necessarily equal, the digital life and the analogue life resemble each other. In the digital space, the writer and her readers write on the female body in a more critical manner than the male body. In these two stories, a distinction is not made by readers between middle-class and working/poor women who are portrayed in fictions as sexual deviants. Instead, many of the online readers who comment on the stories see their role as intervening on behalf of society and reaffirm the need to fight moral corruption in both online and offline spaces. The editors of *Storymoja* blog invite writers to submit fictions for publication, and readers to rate each submission. Odhiambo's *Her Father's Friend* is one of the many stories the editors received and published. Since writing and reading in online communities demand the ability to read and understand in African and European languages, as well as fluency in the language of 'emoji' and GIFs that people use as part of communicating emotions online, one can venture that many of the readers and writers in African digital communities such as *Storymoja* and Facebook, belong to the educated middle and upper classes. And as argued previously in this book, literary networks of mostly middle-class Africans (editors, publisher, writers and readers) emerged out of this sociability, and often members of these digital networks see it as part of their duties to comment on women's erotic desire. The opportunity to write back in real-time to the writer in the digital space gives the reader the chance to exhibit their knowledge of their society and its traditions. And when it comes to sexual deviancy, some constitute themselves as moral authorities because they assume they know the correct way that women and men should conduct themselves.

The protagonist in Odhiambo's short story comes from a lower middle-class family; she wants the latest mobile phones, and wants to patronise trendy cafés and shopping malls but she does not have the financial capability to afford the lifestyle of Nairobi's middle and upper classes. She has friends who come from rich and well-to-do homes and she wants to lead a lifestyle similar to theirs. She realises the power of her sexuality and she is using this power for monetary needs. But some of the readers, like those of *Ashewos Anonymous*, see the protagonist as compromised, a modern whore, a blight on society. From these comments from Kenyan and Nigerian readers, we can see how a piece of fiction can serve both as source material for social anthropology in the sense that it gives more of an insight into readers' views than into the lives of women like the protagonist. Additionally, it is also a means of documenting what people have read and seen in cyberspace. For members of the digital public therefore, such short stories connect cyberspace with the material world.

Between Literature and Journalism

Online narratives about sexuality in modern Nigeria and Kenya, especially about female sexuality – as commented upon by the reading public – show the connection between what journalism reports and how modern writers mediate such reports. In my work, I noticed that several writers who have used literature to comment on modern women and sexual deviancy, also have journalistic experience. In his analysis of online commentaries on African digital forums, Koleade Odutola surmises that what people read in the news media (online and print) is an important part of how they remember and conceive their history and culture, as well as how they associate with others online. Given Odutola's digital ethnographical study, it comes as little surprise that writers who use literature to comment on female sexuality are often journalists who are conversant with gossip about sexually confident women. They understand the intricate link between what journalists produce and how people make meaning out of media outputs, and we see literature as building upon what journalism has produced. It is important to stress that I recognise that literature can offer its own unique take on female sexual desire, which is different from that of the news media. In addition to being creative writers, both Terna Tilley-Gyado and Pauline Odhiambo are journalists and media practitioners who have large followings on social media. Their career paths mimic those of some of the writers from the previous generations. This intersection between journalism and creative writing is important to our understanding of the way in which the figure of the modern girl has been constructed and maintained over the course of a century. Furthermore, the writer did not just stumble upon the figure of the modern girl as a sexual deviant; at the heart of this portrayal is the figure of the writer as a voice of political and moral authority. Just as I.B. Thomas and Cyprian Ekwensi were held in high esteem by their readers, so are today's writers seen as the voice of the people. And as new fictions echo fictions from the decades before, we see some of today's writers occupying the sexual moral high ground that was once occupied by the previous generations of writers-cum-journalists.

Between the 1920s and the 1940s, Isaac Babalola Thomas was a popular Lagos-based journalist, who also became well known as the author of the fictional character of the modern girl Sẹgilọla in his story *Itan Igbesi Aiye Emi Sẹgilọla Ẹleyinju, Ẹlẹgbẹrun Ọkọ L'Aiye* (1929). Thomas initially published the story of Sẹgilọla in the popular Lagos newspaper *Akede Eko*, of which he was an editor.

The collection later metamorphosed into the first novel written in Yoruba. Just as some members of the online public are commenting on works of literature being published in the digital space, the public of the last century used the print medium to comment on modern women and their representations in literature. As a response to the fictional figure of Sẹgilọla, many readers wrote to I.B. Thomas to express their condemnation of modern women, among them the following:

> Nwọn ha le l'ojuti, ki nwọn ma hu oniruru iwakiwa ni'le ọkọ wọn, ki ale mẹta, mẹrin lode maṣe tẹ wọn l'ọrun, nwọn ha le loju ti ki oni gbese ma wọ ti rẹ ni ile wọn, tabi ojuti a wa, nwọn a ma mu Sarotu *Cigarettes* ati *Cigar* l'oju gbogbo enia Apejọ, nwọn a ma mu Ọti bi ẹni mu Omi, nwọn a ma sọrọ alufanṣa lẹnu, nwọn a ma wipe ọkọ mẹwa ki nṣe baba mẹwa, o ni lati tun ma lọ fọ iyere na l'odo mirantiti iyere yio fi mọ; nwọn gbagbe pe iyere ti nwọn fọ ni odo kini, ikeji, ikẹta, ikẹrin ti ko mọ, ti nwọn ko ba dẹhin, ijọkan-jọkan ni odo yio gbe ati awọn ati iyere wọn lọ bamubamu. (*Akede Eko* 15 August 1929)

> (If they have any shame, debt collectors would not be visiting them at home and they would not be smoking cigarettes and cigars in public, or drink alcohol as if it were water. They wouldn't be very loud and proclaim that ten husbands do not equal ten fathers, and that they need to be sexually satisfied by as many men as possible; they have forgotten that taking on one, two, three and four lovers will lead to destruction.)

Cyprian Ekwensi, the creator of another fictional modern girl, Jagua Nana, was also a highly regarded Lagos-based journalist who used many of the real-life characters he encountered in his journalism career in his fictional work, including in *People of the City, Jagua Nana* and *Jagua Nana's Daughter*. Similarly to the public's reaction to Sẹgilọla, many readers also reacted passionately to these fictional characters especially that of Jagua Nana, a Lagos prostitute. They wrote directly to Ekwensi, to condemn those real-life 'Jagua Nanas' they knew across many Nigerian towns and cities (see Ernest Emenyonu).

As in the analogue era, today's fictional narrators try to warn not only males about the danger that the libidinal modern girl may pose, the fictional modern girl is also deployed as an important element of cautionary tales directed at women. In the online short story *Her Friend's Father*, we see that women are equally meant to fear the modern woman. The protagonist is having an 'illicit' sexual relationship with the father of a young woman who she is supposed to be a close confidant of, and because of this betrayal she becomes a figure that men and women alike cannot trust.

Through fictional texts we see the way in which the figure of the modern girl is put to use within modernity and through postcolonial discourses from the print to the internet age. Stephanie Newell's (1996) study of Nigerian market literatures blames such anxiety on male writers and male readers, but unlike the printed works that constitute Newell's research, the internet space is less gender-weighted towards men and represents more equally the voices of male and female readers and writers. By instigating discussions on these fictional characters, the online writing space becomes a site not only for societal gossip but also for defining gendered performances. We can see that almost all of the readers put the blame of sexual immorality and deviancy on the fictional female characters, while male characters are often not only not condemned but seen as victims. Having several lovers is an act that the contemporary society allows men, while 'good' women are not supposed to do likewise. Be it in print or digital, when it comes to modern women in urban spaces, literature becomes a site that pontificates on sexual decorum and its readers and writers pass judgement on what they perceive as moral corruption. In the case of stories posted on social networking sites and blogs, comments by readers of fictions show how many authors and fictional narrators intentionally 'dog-whistle' to the digital public, by surrounding the modern girl with sexual scandals. In this way, literature becomes an additional tool – in print and in new media – with which society admonishes all non-compliant bodies by promoting sexual restraint over sexual recklessness.

Sex and Technology: The Writer/Journalist in Modern African Writings

D.O. Adebayo et al. argue that not only does society and culture influence intimacy, but sexual behaviour in Africa is also impacted upon by technology (745). The printing press and the print culture that came with it, helped to introduce a pseudo-European concept of sexual decorum in both Kenya and Nigeria. In publications such as young Jomo Kenyatta's *Muigwithania*, and I.B. Thomas's *Akede Eko*, writers and journalists often used the most patriarchal elements of African and European cultures in their commentaries on sexual decorum and morality. The message that print culture in Kenya and Nigeria regularly conveyed to its readers and society at large was that good young women (and men) do not indulge in sexual activities beyond procreation. Sexual pleasure was deemed as frivolous, un-African and at the same time portrayed as being a barrier to Africans reaching a Western standard of technological advancement. At the beginning of the last century, these publications, and the print culture that they created, helped define the modern African girl as sexualised and corrupt. In the current digital age, some of the new online fiction suggests that this stereotype remains tenacious. However, by providing immediate ways in which to debate female sexuality, the internet can allow the writer and his or her readers to interact in challenging the stereotypes. Readers and writers can comment and respond rapidly, and publicly, so that a debate or even an online community can form quickly out of these discussions in a way that was not possible in the print age.

As pointed out in the introductory chapter, literature in Africa arguably positions the author as an intentional subject. There is the frequent connection between life and art, in addition to the notion that texts and their productions are hard-wired elements of human cognition. The privilege of being connected to real-life human characters, to the pulse of urban life, gives African writers the opportunity to utilise the tool of verisimilitude in their creative work. These interactions also mean that writers often have access to the latest societal gossip, which often finds its ways into literature. In the Facebook fiction *Ashewos Anonymous*, Eko Le Meridien, the hotel in which the women regular meet, is a real-life place that often features in the print and in online news. Other young writers likewise tend to include familiar places and familiar elements of contemporary life such as popular music and celebrities, in some of the short stories on African intimacy.

By building on their own familiarity with real life spaces and mimicking real life scandals, a new generation of writers uses fictional narratives – as well as the immediacy of the digital space such as Google Maps and internet location apps – to intentionally map fictions back to real life. Verisimilitude as a literary device used by some emerging voices writing on social media and blog platforms can be traced back to the early twentieth century when writers of that era used it as a technique to comment on the figure of the modern girl. Thus, when it comes to female sexuality, some the fictional narratives of the digital age are not necessarily ideologically different from earlier, print-based writings – literature and journalism – where place, and its associated political and cultural specificities, predominated. For example, in the prologue to the fictional text of *Itan Igbesi Aiye Emi Ṣegilọla Ẹlẹyinju, Ẹlẹgbẹrun Ọkọ L'Aiye*, the narrator tells us that the fictional character physically walked into the office where the writer works as an editor.

> Obinrin yi funrarẹ ni o f'ẹsẹ ara rẹ tọ wa wa l'aṣalẹ ọjọ Saturday kan ninu Office wa ni No. 47, Bamgboṣe Street, Lagos, ti alagba obinrin na si fi ẹmi-ẹdun ọkan rẹ bẹ wa pe inu on yio dun pupọ bi awa be le gba ọjẹgẹ fun on lati ma kọ itan igbesi aiye on sinu iwe irohin wa 'Akede Eko'. (I.B. Thomas 2)

> (This woman, of her own accord walked into our office on No. 47, Bamgboṣe Street, Lagos, and begged us that she would be very pleased if we would allow her to publish her life story in our publication 'Akede Eko'.)

Through the fictional narrator, Thomas blurs the line between reality and fiction, he positions the narrative in real time and places the protagonist in locations readers can identify in real life (see Karin Barber 1997). In addition, the protagonist tells us that she knows most of the important men living in Lagos at the time, and that if her identity were revealed her own scandalous sexual exploits would tarnish their good image. The observational skill of the writer as a reporter is thus effectively deployed to construct the image of the libidinal modern woman as a believable real-life character, who is scandalous and tainted; a woman who might be the 'girl next door' but whose presence jeopardises the communal well-being. Thomas not only wrote a 'novel' warning readers about the antics of his protagonist, he also took it upon himself to comment on the sexual antics of real life and fictional modern women, in addition to encouraging his readers to write letters of condemnation against modern women's supposed sexual waywardness. My own research into the story of Sẹgilọla at the National Archives of Nigeria in Ibadan, revealed that through these discussions in *Akede Eko* newspaper, the writer used his position to embark on a crusade against the modern girl, and he arguably saw himself as saving Lagos and Nigerian society from the destructive impact of the behaviour of this fictional character.

In *Jagua Nana*, Ekwensi uses the same energy that he employed in his journalistic career on the body of the libidinal protagonist. Like I.B. Thomas some thirty years before, Ekwensi also sees his role as a journalist-cum-fictional-writer, saving the society from modernity's decadence, and he takes that role very seriously. As the literary critic Ernest Emenyonu points out:

> Ekwensi knows his city (Lagos) very well. He also knows to the most minute detail the idiosyncrasies of the characters he has chosen who are symptomatic of the moral depravities of the city ... The author's didacticism and sense of retribution are very much in evidence in every action in the novel. Often he oversteps his role of mirroring society to that of standing in judgement over it. He is both the plaintiff and the jury and the only clause in his Magna Charta is that 'the wages of sin is death.' (42–43).

Emenyonu's observation is relevant in today's digital writing. The retribution that Ekwensi visited on the modern girl is echoed in the two online short stories by Tilley-Gyado and Odhiambo. Like Ekwensi and Thomas before them, both of these new voices place the figure of the modern girl in a city setting, and the city as a symbol of modernity, a site of corruption. These fictional female characters – Sẹgilọla, Jagua Nana, the young woman in *Her Father's Friend*, and the female characters in *Ashewos Anonymous* – are urban women and they embody sex and the city.

Michael W. Ross argues that 'sexuality in the unfolding age of the virtual age is also a discourse about human interaction at the closing of the mechanical age' (342). For both print and new media writers, fictional characters such as Sẹgilọla, Jagua Nana and Funke (the fictional founder of the self-help group *Ashewos Anonymous*) are not emerging out of a vacuum; these fictional figures reveal the energies that propel modernity, first in the colonial years and now in the postcolonial era. By using fictional figures to represent this danger, these narratives are trying to use literature as a harness to pull back the society from the abyss of its obsession with all aspects of modern life.

Literary representation of modern women highlights the way in which fiction reports on deviants, and how it has the potential to create and manipulate history in the process. Punishment and societal revenge can be argued to be the ultimate trope of fictional narratives, especially those dealing with libidinal modern women. Therefore, just as the protagonist in *Itan Igbesi Aiye Emi Ṣegilọla Ẹlẹyinju, Ẹlẹgbẹrun Ọkọ L'Aiye* is afflicted with a terminal illness and the writer accepts that her impending demise is a well-deserved comeuppance, so does the narrator in *Ashewos Anonymous* inform us that the founder of the Ashewos Anonymous group dies 'less than a year after the inaugural meeting from an AIDS related illness'. By dying painfully, these two fictional women across two different literary eras, pay the ultimate price for their sexual rebellion, and their afflictions serve as a warning to readers. From these and other stories, one can argue that fictional narratives that position modern women as libidinal women strike a chord with readers because these stories successfully paint a picture of devious, often money-hungry, as well as sex-hungry women, who are a threat to not just the institution of marriage but a threat to public health, safety and communal harmony. Thus the modern girl inhabits a diseased body, which tells us that she and other women like her are a potential danger to everybody. Yet again, the death of a deviant body symbolises not just comeuppance but society punishing rebellion and winning the moral battle.

A Different View of the Modern Girl

The fictions I analysed above reflect a long history of modern texts and their readers commenting on African women who are seen as sexual deviants – one through which the figure of the modern girl and that of the female sex worker are portrayed as one. However, there is a growing body of works by writers using the figure of the sex worker and modern women more generally to highlight how previous portrayals wrongly made women the perpetrators. Like much of the creative writings published within digital literary networks, the creative works being analysed in this section speak to a moving away from the grand narratives of postcoloniality, as Berger notes, towards an ideological agenda that highlights social issues more significant to an African readership.

Online, these works appear to reflect the news cycles, building on academic and journalistic investigations. In fact, there is often no clear separation between fiction writers, reporters and social commentators, roles that are frequently embodied in a single online persona. Take, for example, the writings of Chika Unigwe. In her short story *Dreams*, the female character,

Uche, is forced into prostitution to care for her children after the death of her husband. Although the medical cause of death is heart failure, Uche's mother-in-law, Mama Obi, consults a 'prophet' who explains the unexpected demise in spiritual terms, placing blame on the 'evil' wife. This allows Mama Obi to invoke traditional practices to take away her young grandson to raise herself, and to evict Uche from her home along with her twin daughters. Comments on the *Nigerian Village Square* website make links between this story, social reality and the need for social change to protect women:

> With cases as such very popular (happened to someone I know […]), I think it'd be such a great idea if the Government made laws (and enforced them) that protects the Uches from the hands of Mama Obis who try to separate them from that which is rightfully theirs. Such women should not have to have to prostitute to make ends meet. (Anike n.pag)

Unigwe regularly gives interviews in new media forums such as *The Guardian* (UK), *The Independent* (UK), *The New York Times* (USA) as well as several African online forums, where she discusses some of the characters in her fictional narratives and how these characters represent real-life women that she came across when she was doing background research for her creative work reiterating those connections between reality and fiction.

A story like *Dreams* deviates ideologically from much of the earlier creative work that came out of Africa, which considered the negative effect of modernity on young women in particular, and which regularly considered how women, corrupted by the urban environment, needed to be redeemed through a return to traditional roles or to rural locations. These short stories published in the new media space are equally preoccupied with the life of female urban dwellers, but position themselves differently in ideological terms. Their writers explore the social and cultural circumstances which shape women's experiences in the city, and much of this investigates how women's bodies are exploited, as in *Dreams* or, in a slightly different way, in Sefi Atta's online fiction *Glory*. Here, the narrator tells us about desperate young Nigerian women hanging out in Lagos hotels, looking for a way out to Europe. Atta references not only the uses to which women's bodies are put, but also the risks of human trafficking faced by African women desperate to improve their circumstances:

> The hotel was full of prostitutes, packed with them, and they were dressed in western attire. They could easily pass for proper elite. What gave them away were the crooked-legged walks they acquired from parading up and down the diplomatic district. Glory called them *va bene*, not *ashawo*, as everyone else called them. So many of them ended up in Rome. (par. 11)

Chimamanda Ngozi Adichie's story *Birdsong* tackles a different part of the continuum by writing about a young woman whose lover is a married man. This relationship is akin to prostitution in its reality of exchange – the woman gets gifts from the man in exchange for sex. Adichie's story attracted many comments which debated the sexual theme of the story: some suggested that she was sex-obsessed, or trivialising sex, but one commentator takes a feminist position to suggest that Adichie 'describes sex and sexuality from a unique, dignified and wholly female perspective'. Adichie does not condemn her female character, nor pity her, but shows her gradual recognition that she is in a relationship where only her body is valued. Her status is clear to the wider society, for example when she visits a restaurant with the lover:

> 'Good evening, sah,' the waiter said when we were seated. 'You are welcome, sah.'
> 'Have you noticed that they never greet me?' I asked my lover.
> 'Well …,' he said, and adjusted his glasses.
> The waiter came back […] and I waited until he had opened the bottle of red wine before I asked, 'Why don't you greet me?'
> The waiter glanced at my lover, as though seeking guidance, and this infuriated me even more. 'Am I invisible? I am the one who asked you a question. Why do all of you waiters and gatemen and drivers in this Lagos refuse to greet me? Do you not see me?' (par. 66–70)

Her new awareness that her sex defines her, spills into her work place, too, when she questions why it is always her, or her female co-worker, who have to cut up and distribute the birthday cakes the men bring in. Using fiction to highlight sexism is not new, but because this is published online, the story's debate is carried into its reading in overt ways through readers' comments. If we agree with those reader-response theories that insist meaning lies with the reader, here we have a practical manifestation of that process enabled by the publishing platforms on the internet.

'Birdsong' points to a new and growing type of sexual relationship taking place in Nigeria and Kenya, where young female professionals often willingly accept romantic involvement with their companies' clients for several reasons, which may include promotion within their organisation, extra income for material goods, or in order to secure a contract or commission. Rebecca Surtees surmises that in the global South, some urban women who are attractive and well educated, enter such sexual relationships as part of the unwritten rules in emerging economies. Surtees suggests that this phenomenon goes against 'mainstream sexual discourse to which the middle class, in particular, adhere' (n.pag). This short story depicts urban sexual culture in Africa, and suggests that some young African women have a more liberal attitude to sex and morality than their societies may want to admit. Unlike other urban women, who might take a lover so that he takes care of her material needs, because the relationship brings business to her company, or so she is in her boss's good books and can advance her career, the sexual marketability of the 'Birdsong' protagonist as well as that of her lover is based on the fact that both are educated and high earners. The protagonist is able to attract a high-class married man, whom she describes as 'courtly, his life lived in well-oiled sequences', because of her education and middle-class status, and these two elements combined equal market value and potential. She knows that her lover's wife is in America and does not enter the relationship without having made an informed decision. 'Birdsong' shows us that modern women do not necessarily lack the resources to handle this moral crisis, the tools they use simply do not depend on the moralising and didactic messages that some politicians, journalists and religious clerics send to the public. Instead, they rationalise and employ a different moral discourse to justify their involvement with men. What this chapter has been demonstrating is how desire continues to remain at the very heart of the postcolonial bodies. Sexual desire represents the unfolding condition of the postcolonial state; complex and fractured in so many ways. Desire is competing with the demand of market forces and human longings that are affected and impacted upon by material, spiritual and other emotional needs. The digital short stories in this chapter constitute sites of desire. Their reading gives us an insight into the modern sexual culture and the role that institutional actors and stakeholders – online platforms, social media commentators, politicians and religious organisations – play in this culture.

The Erotic in New Writing from Nigeria   7

When examined through the scope of technology, new writings that focus on the erotic and the sexually explicit often reveal surprising results about repressed history and the impact of Euro-modernity on what many now consider as taboos. As discussed previously, for about two centuries in the Nigerian context, various forms of media technology have been intervening in the articulation of the sexual. From the early days of colonialism in the nineteenth century, Christian missionaries and colonial officials invested capital in schools and in printing presses, which they used to enforce a Victorian-style puritanism. The age of the printing press – from Irohin Yoruba to Random House – therefore positions African and Nigerian writing at the intersection of race, class and sex.

In the context of Nigerian literature, what can be deduced from much of the creative writing in the age of the book is that fictional characters such as Segilọla and Jagua Nana, discussed in the previous chapter, did not come out of a vacuum; they reveal the discourses that helped problematise the idea of the modern and the notion of the traditional. During the heyday of colonialism, to be modern translated to embracing the Victorian era's Christian attitude towards sex as represented in works such as I.B. Thomas' *Itan Igbesi Aiye Emi Segilọla Ẹleyinju, Ẹlegbẹrun Ọkọ L'Aiye*. The erotic, as represented in fictional narratives, is therefore an important way for us to see the confusion of what history and modernity represent for many Nigerians and Africans.

This legacy is not lost on the eminent Nigerian poet, dramatist and scholar Femi Osofisan, who, in a contribution to *Outliers*, a digital project on African sexuality, makes a case for literary studies' closer engagement with the erotic as a means of analysing sexual history in Nigeria in particular, and Africa in general. His essay discusses the way in which different generations of Nigerian and African writers have dealt with sexual explicitness and the erotic. Osofisan argues that attitudes towards the overtly sexual have shifted remarkably in the twenty-first century, as a new generation of writers is now producing works that are less restrained when it comes to the portrayal of the erotic. This is in comparison to his (Osofisan's) generation of writers. Osofisan surmises:

> Up at least till the turn of the new millennium, you will observe, the exploration of romantic love or of sex as a theme was remarkably rare in the output of our writers. Virtually no literary work dared venture, except in the deflected language of metaphor and refringent echo, into the contentious area of carnal experience. From Tutuola to Okpewho; Achebe to Iyayi; Soyinka to Sowande; Clark to Onwueme – we are talking of over four decades of writing – *there is no instance of a memorable kiss* … The consensus among our pioneer authors, and their immediate successors, seemed to have been that heroes could not be engaged in the epic battle of rescuing our land and our people from all kinds of malevolent forces, and of constructing a nation out of the debris of colonialism, and still indulge in amatory liaisons, except in moments of careless and irresponsible decadence. That is why women appear in these works, for the most part, only in the margin, largely unheard. (64)

Osofisan goes on to say that, thanks to the age of the new media,

> the old notions of privacy, the consensual secretiveness and 'holiness' that used to be attached to such matters as love and sex have long been axed and discarded as antiquated relic. Bashfulness, decency and self-respect have become casualties in the new ethos of the so-called 'free society', where the reigning creed is to 'tell it all'. (70)

What Osofisan is alluding to here is the increasing number of erotic writings, mostly led by feminist writers who are using the opportunities provided by the digital era to address a history of anxiety over sexually explicit materials and their effects on women. This is an anxiety – as argued throughout this book – that is linked to notions of modernity, especially those of the colonial project of modernity. By colonial modernity, I am referring to the period from which colonial rule started to take root across West Africa from the mid-nineteenth century to the early 1960s. Furthermore, one can argue that the current anxiety over the erotic in public spheres is not just linked to but started during the colonial era. This is important because this chapter will show that some members of a new generation of modern Nigerian writers use creative writings to point out that part of the legacies of colonialism is the erroneous assumption that, traditionally, Africans do not talk about sex in the open or that the erotic and the profane are not important parts of the arts.

The Aesthetics of the Erotic

The aesthetics of the erotic lies in its vivid imagery of sex; be it sexual intercourse, thoughts or simulations. Because of its bluntness in the context of what it so graphically depicts, the erotic is political given that in many parts of the world – including Nigeria and Kenya – the display of the overtly sexual is often censored. Music with sexually explicit lyrics and profanity normally come with parental guidance warnings. When it comes to the erotic, what applies in the music industry also applies in the film industry. Communities in Nigeria and Kenya still regard the erotic and nudity as deviant sexuality. For example, there have been cases of attacks on women wearing miniskirts. #Mydressmychoice started on Twitter as a middle-class Nairobi woman's response to attacks on women wearing miniskirts. As a response, Kenyans who hold a more conservative world view on female sexuality launched a counter digital movement #Nudityisnotmychoice (see Nanjala Nyabola). Similar incidents with regard to nudity also happened in Nigeria. If 'nudity' is political, so is sex. Therefore, one can argue that talks about sex are political, but not talking about sex also reveals a political agenda.

This chapter is interested in the implicit messages that one can garner from texts that have ambition that goes beyond titillation; they are not pornography because the sex is not just for sex's sake as the works being analysed query the current rendition of Nigeria and Africa's sexual history. The erotic is also a means of addressing related issues such as class and gender, as well as the place of technology in fulfilling desire. The erotic, Audre Lorde reminds us, has been misnamed by patriarchy in societies across the globe, as a means of control, especially the control of women. Lorde said:

> For this reason, we have turned away from the exploration and consideration of the erotic as a source of power and information, confusing it with the pornographic. But pornography is a direct denial of the power of the erotic, for it represents the suppression of true feeling. Pornography emphasizes sensation without feeling. (88)

Lorde signposts us to the fact that the erotic is at the fulcrum of power and control. She sees pornography as the direct opposite of the erotic, because the former is produced by men to dehumanise women for men's pleasure. While showing how pornography is another extension of patriarchy, Lorde steers us to the fact that there is nothing abnormal – especially for women – about having sexual desires and fulfilling them, and what is abnormal is the suppression of a woman's sexual desire. Nyabola points out that African women's voices are often stifled in the offline space, and that the digital space is giving women the means to challenge contemporary perceptions and ideas. In the spirit of Lorde's work, several emerging literary voices are not using metaphors and coded language in their portrayal of the overtly sexual. By being frank and blunt in their depictions, writers give voice to what has been unsaid or deemed taboo, and in the process, the erotic is providing an opportunity to challenge all forms of patriarchal authority. These writers are also aware that digital technology is allowing many Africans new means of meeting people for relationships and sexual pleasure, as online dating is becoming popular. Young people on Facebook and on online forums often talk about the way in which they make sexual connections online which may or may not be consummated offline. The explicit is the truth, and the explicit is ethical.

Writers who are active on social media are well aware of the choices young people are making with regards to sex. Joy Isi Bewaji is a Lagos-based writer and digital entrepreneur. She is very popular on Facebook and Twitter, especially among young urban social media users. Almost every day, she uses the digital space to educate young women about their sexual rights. She also runs the popular blog Happenings.com.ng. One of the online projects she recently completed is *Story of my Vagina* (Twitter hashtag #Storyofmyvagina). The project brings together writers who create poems, fiction and personal stories, aimed at enlightening young women about the power of the female anatomy.

A short story, *#Storyofmyvagina: Old Things*, written by Bewaji under the nom de plume Uche Okonkwo, focuses on a young woman on her wedding night whose husband discovers his bride is not a virgin. The husband, who has been saving himself for this particular evening, feels threatened because the name of a former lover is tattooed on the inner thighs of his new wife. The story highlights the fragility of patriarchy, especially when a man encounters a woman with more sexual conquests.

Another writer, Temitola Olofinlua, captures the very essence of #Storyofmyvagina with her prose-poetry *#Storyofmyvagina: Who's Afraid of the Vagina?*

> Condoms. Pills. Orgasms. Choices. Sex.
> Girl, this bridge between your legs, can unite or destroy. It can have people grovelling at its feet, a servant to a master, for a chance to pass through. Or just to peep through its keyhole. Use the power wisely. Think through your choices … *Who is afraid of the vagina?* Show yourself. Do not hide behind the heavy cloak of shame. Come out from behind the veil of fear. Do not hide behind the mask of ignorance.
> Here is why. Ignorance about the vagina could be detrimental. If you are ever going to remove the veil, at least it is important to know yourself. Know your vagina. Do not be ashamed of it.

Ucheoma Onwutuebe contributes a personal story entitled *#Storyofmyvagina: Lessons from My Mother*. In the story, she recounts how talking about sex with her mother empowered her and how the erotic speaks the language of freedom:

> 'V-A-G-I-N-A,' call it after me. Liberating. The world has not fallen apart. Neither is it filled with more sin waiting to be cleansed. It is not a word to be said in hushed tones. Saying it loud will not make you 'dirty', neither does it mean that you are … Even amid pleasure, we clench our teeth and shut our eyes, afraid to mumble our pleasure when being stroked right because … *how dare you talk about it?*

For these female writers, honesty comes with sexual explicitness. They challenge the privatisation of the erotic. Women should not be embarrassed to publicly admit they enjoy sex. Their views of the sexually explicit – in an age when vivid sexual images abound online – speak to Lorde's view of the erotic as intersecting with gender and power. This argument is germane because when women write or talk about the erotic, they are seizing power from men who largely control the porn industry. Furthermore, women are marginalised when they are not allowed to talk about the erotic in the offline space, and when women themselves are reluctant to admit to the pleasure that can be derived from sex. By not talking about the erotic, women can become vulnerable to sexual abuse, and in the wider context can be marginalised in political discourses. Moreover, literature and conversations that do not shy away from being sexually explicit, especially when it comes to women, empower through the sex education they provide. These works also speak the language of sexual revolution and disrupt old concepts of Nigerian and African female sexuality. Using the word 'vagina' may make many uncomfortable in the offline world of Lagos, Kano and Port Harcourt, but writers and commentators do not have to censor themselves in the online space. #Storyofmyvagina disrupts the masculine notion of sexual intercourse as being something men control. It puts women in charge of their bodies, desires and sexual pleasure. The hashtag also echoes another, more popular hashtag movement in Kenya #Mydressmychoice, which started in 2014, when a young woman was assaulted at a bus stop in Nairobi for wearing a miniskirt. Like the Nigerian vagina hashtag, #Mydressmychoice asserts Kenyan women's rights over their body and sexuality.

#Storyofmyvagina is travelling across different social media platforms, from Twitter to Facebook and to Instagram, and it garners followers in the process. The project has since branched off into a book, and was also made into a play staged at a theatre in Lagos. These movements and renditions across the digital and analogue platforms underline the way in which many African writers and readers interact with literature and other art forms in the twenty-first century. Each platform complements the other and readers have the freedom to make new meanings of the messages behind the texts. For example, readers on Facebook seem so intimate with Bewaji's writing style, that they recognise her erotic fiction even when she writes under an alias, and fans of her erotic work use excerpts from the short stories on her website, as part of their tweets. Since individual writers for #Storyofmyvagina also often reposts their erotic work on different digital sites, these writers are able to reach new audiences, to test and rework their craft, while also tailoring the creative writing to a specific audience on each platform. What is presented on Twitter, for example, may be shorter and more succinct than what is offered on Facebook, where there is no limit on the word count. On Instagram, the narratives of #Storyofmyvagina come with colourful images, but with shorter text, because Instagram is more image-friendly than Twitter. It is also worth pointing out that the theatre rendition of #Storyofmyvagina is more extensive, because the theatre production incorporates and unifies the creative ideas generated by several writers.

Moreover, because it is a hashtag, #Storyofmyvagina becomes a digital tool – a metadata – that provides an insight into the way in which technology impacts sex and desire. Anyone searching internet platforms specifically for female empowerment and 'vagina' is likely to see this particular hashtag. On Twitter, female readers and followers of #Storyofmyvagina who are based outside of Nigeria have also commented on how inspiring they find these erotic fictions and essays. This international appeal speaks to the possibility of erotic stories published on digital platforms not merely as an effective tool for educating women on how sexual and erotic discourses affect their lives, but also as sheer pleasure and enjoyment for women. Erotic literature across multiple digital platforms also provides an avenue to spread feminist ideals to women who may be reluctant to buy erotic material in shops. The writers of #Storyofmyvagina believe that a woman's sexual freedom determines her life choices including jobs, contraception, freedom of expression and her place in society. By placing the erotic at the fore of online literature, they are inspiring women to see women who do not apologise for being true to themselves; who dare to be bold and who want to be successful. Therefore, what is published online is a test run for offline feminist campaigns. Through these and other measures, one can argue that the mostly female writers of #Storyofmyvagina hope to change not just Nigeria's online communities but also Nigerian society in general.

The erotic is becoming a means of querying current attitudes and a way to reprise the erotic aspect of Nigerian history that has become subjugated by the project of colonial modernity. In an interview with the blogger and writer Anike aka Cosmic Yoruba, the writer Kiru Taye makes a case for the erotic as a means of bringing the more liberal parts of precolonial Nigerian history to the fore:

> Absolutely. I'm hoping to convert the thinking of a lot of people including Africans about our ancient practices, especially with regard to relationships and sex. A lot of African behaviour was altered with the introduction of Christianity and some things that are seen as taboo today were not in the past. (n.pag)

In the quest to reprise forgotten practices and attitudes, Taye sees erotic fiction in cyberspace as a way to rethink history and to educate readers about the past. She attributes contemporary perceptions of the erotic as reflecting the impact of colonial modernity on modern Nigerian writing. Taye's argument should be read alongside the Osofisan quote at the beginning of this chapter because it makes the link that the erotic was suppressed in much of the work published by mainstream publishers due to the influence of Christianity and Islam on society. The arrival of Islam and then Christianity as well as colonialism, arguably marked a change in the way in which Nigerians talked and still talk about sex. This is because, in Judeo-Christian and Islamic traditions, the sacred and the overtly sexual (including the profane) are often viewed as the antithesis of each other. What Lorde points out is the trend in which the spiritual and the erotic are seen as separate entities. In the Christian tradition, especially since the days of the Roman Catholic church, talking about sex in the open is considered unholy, and what is unholy is deemed barbaric. Chastity, especially for women, became the norm and sex was seen as mainly a tool for procreation. Suppressing people's sexual urges was part of the teachings of church and mosque. Those teachings are the origin of the idea that the erotic is dirty and that sexual frivolity endangers public health. As a model, it was adopted by subsequent political and religious entities across Europe and applied to control their own societies.

Satya P. Mohanty aptly surmises that we cannot robustly capture the nature of colonial modernity in the non-West, without referencing oral traditions. Mohanty calls for 'a project of historical retrieval and imaginative philosophical reconstruction' (3). Many of the texts that emanated from precolonial Nigerian communities are oral, and an analysis of some of these traditions reveals that there was a space for the sexual and the spiritual to interact with one another in many of the societies in what is now known as Nigeria. A good example is to be found in the Ifa religious poetry of the Yoruba people; in the section known as Eji Ogbe, Ifa references the intricate link between the sacred and the profane:

> Ogoteere ni oruko ta npe oko; Ehinwọran ni oruko ta npe obo. Ewọ, oko gbọdọ bo'bo ja. T'oko ba ba obo jo, yio jẹ gba.
>
> (Ogoteere is the other name for the penis; Ehinwọran is another name for the vagina. The penis must never fight the vagina. It is a taboo.)

At the annual Oke-Ibadan Festival, in Ibadan, Nigeria, one of the beloved, favourite songs goes:

> O tin do mi la'tan 'na ko ma je ki sun o. Oke 'Badan wo irun obo mi meta l'oku.
>
> (He has been having sexual intercourse with me since last night and would not let me sleep, Oke'Badan please look at my vagina, I am only left with three strands of pubic hair.)

The Igbo people of Nigeria are also not afraid to talk openly about sex. There is a saying in Igbo: 'A penis that sleeps on duty will slip into the trouble of boiling water in the mortar of his woman.' The Igbo people use the term 'ila otu' to describe oral sex. Among the Yoruba and the Igbo people, talking about sex is not solely meant for light-hearted moments but also for articulating serious moments. In these cultures, sex is pleasurable and what is pleasurable is also important. However, the project of colonial modernity and the politics of print publication that came with it, curtailed the freedom of writers to write openly about sexuality, and it still affects the way in which many Nigerians in the contemporary era approach the discourse of sex. Colonialism, of which Christianity is an integral part, introduced a Victorian attitude to sex to many communities in Nigeria, one in which women are not expected to express overt sexual needs, and in which men in polite company were expected to talk about sex in coded language. Even today, much of what is being published in novels, short stories and news publication avoids direct sexual connotations. In many television and video-film productions, sexually active female characters are often portrayed as carriers of diseases and as a danger to their communities, and the comeuppance for these women is often regret, agony or even death.

Thighs Fell Apart: Eroticising an African Classic

Kiru Taye has made erotic fiction her speciality. In collaborative projects with the popular blog *Brittle Paper*, Taye provides an erotic rendition of two modern literary canonical texts in print – Chinua Achebe's *Things Fall Apart* and Chimamanda Ngozi Adichie's *Americanah*. In a series of short stories entitled *Thighs Fell Apart*, Taye rewrites the encounter between Okonkwo and Ekwefi before the latter becomes Okonkwo's second wife. In her rendition, the two characters are having an extramarital affair, and during the course of this affair, sex and the danger of being discovered thrills both of them. In this narrative, as in some of her works, Taye paints a graphic image of steamy sexual encounters, in which a woman is not ashamed of indulging in sexual pleasure. In the story, Ekwefi sneaks out of her marital home into Okonkwo's bedroom for sexual gratification. The narrator does not hold back:

> He roamed her body with his hands, tweaking and rubbing her breasts, which grew heavier, and nipples that got tighter. They moved lower to caress her stomach and waist. Overcome by rippling sensations, she couldn't tell where she ended and where Okonkwo began. When he lifted his head, she was gasping for breath.
> 'I need you, please.' (n.pag)

Remediation is the process through which digital media become (and produce) a new cultural form by reimagining and reworking works produced by previous media such as print, photography, recorded music, painting etc. Taye's remediation and the reimagining of Achebe's seminal work pushes sexual and fictional boundaries. It not only creates a new sexual 'reality' in cyberspace it also frees Achebe's fictional characters from sexual restrains. If we revisit Osofisan's argument about the absence of sex in much of early modern Nigerian literature, one can argue that Taye's writing symbolises the distinction between the sexual boldness in online literature and the rather timid depictions that abound in much of the creative writing published in print by the first generation of contemporary Nigerian writers. One can sense the freedom in Taye's writing as her characters shed all sexual inhibitions. Umuofia as portrayed by Achebe symbolises Africa's struggle with the colonial project of modernity and Christianisation; Taye's

Umuofia is a story that focuses only on sexual pleasure in a community that has become sexually restrained. Ekwefi's sexual longing in *Thighs Fell Apart* would have arguably made Achebe's Okonkwo faint.

James Yeku provides a good reading of *Thighs Fell Apart*. He argues that by eroticising a canonical African text 'Taye articulates a paradigm of erotic fantasy not too familiar in canonical African literature' (2). Yeku demonstrates how Taye makes the text available to the digital natives as well as those familiar with the original text. He shows that Taye's objective is not merely to excite but that her rendition of a canon offers us what he aptly describes as a revisit of some of the discourses surrounding patriarchy in the context of Nigeria. In this story, the digital reworks and reimagines the analogue. Yeku's argument is germane; while Achebe's Okonkwo is a figure whom one can imagine sees sexual pleasure as frivolous when compared to such masculine tasks as defending one's honour, Taye's Okonkwo not only enjoys dominating others outside of the bedroom, but that domination also extends to the bedroom. This Okonkwo, as reimagined and remediated in the twenty-first century, is an attentive lover who is sensitive to the feelings of women. In *Thighs Fell Apart*, the character of Ekwefi thinks Okonkwo, whose '[e]very touch, every movement of his body against hers drove her to the peak of her sexual pleasure', is a better lover than her husband Maduka. And as Okonkwo brags that he is determined to make her his latest wife, we are told that 'his voice was low and deep, and she detected some emotion in there too'.

Taye's narrative shows Okonkwo as a modern man, and it highlights the complexity of Nigerian sexuality, because the African men she created in *Thighs Fell Apart* are simultaneously powerful and thoughtful. Brawn and brain go together, inside and outside of the bedroom. To the fans of Taye's work, online literature offers them the chance to embrace their erotic and sexual selves. The digital space allows Taye to create a world that readers consider more real than the offline space, because of the perceived honesty and frankness in Taye's narratives. Through erotic fiction, readers can imagine a new (sexual) horizon; they can even begin to imagine new possibilities of sexual empowerment. Readers' responses to *Thighs Fell Apart* reflect my argument, which is that erotic fiction shows that the online is becoming a space that frees the imagination of the writer and her readers. Comments include:

> Catherine 2014/02/15 at 5:19 am: OMG!!! Can u really do this? I loved the book by Chinua Achebe and i must say that I have never for once pictured Okonkwo as someone who could kiss his woman talk more of give heads... it's too hot in here, I really need to cool off #fanning self# Brb
>
> Alba 2014/02/17 at 9:59 am: Steamy! Catherine, I agree, Okonkwo never struck me as a man who would be oooooo, sooooo .... gosh, I'm out of breath.

Mariam Sule 2015/02/03 at 11:58 am: This is so sizzling hot and powerful. I wish my emojis would show because i clapped over a million times.

What these comments indicate is that not only does erotic literature in the digital space bring about instant and real-time interactions between writers and their readers, but it is also a source of inspiration to many digitally wired Nigerians because the erotic gives readers the courage to freely express their sexual selves. Through erotic fiction, many readers, like the commentators above, are encountering stories that speak to their repressed desire or to their hidden personal experience. Literature is also being reimagined not only from editors who commission erotic fictions, but also from the discussions emanating from poetry and fiction. Because of this, new ideas about sexuality are evolving and old assumptions are being challenged if not discarded. This will arguably filter through to the physical space and have an impact on the way in which people see themselves and approach discourses surrounding sexuality, which allows us to see the transformative power of the erotic in the digital age.

Mechanised Sexuality

Amrohini Sahay sees cyberspace as the 'trope for a new cybercultural imaginary' (543), the standard-bearer for a new aesthetic – technoculture. The digital age is the era in which the 'machine' and culture are fused together. Machines are not just meant to make life easier, some are also meant to provide us with a wider range of pleasure and in the process bring us to the state of ecstasy. Sahay utilises Donna Haraway's cyborg in asking us to imagine a 'hybrid of machine and organism … narrated in a tone that blurs and blends a "New Age" experimentalism' (547). In the digital age, some writers and poets are moving literature from the prosaic narrative that characterises much of the representation of the sexual in Nigerian literature in the print format to an aesthetic that gives room for a robust imagination of the sexual, and in the process they reprise some of the explicitness of the arts in precolonial societies. Art is playful, uninhibited, and rebellious. As Osofisan surmises at the start of this chapter, writing about sex in this era is no longer satisfied with just the 'missionary' position but wants every variation of it portrayed. Moreover, not only are new technologies enriching the life of digitally connected Nigerians, they are also transforming how people experience sex. Dele Meiji's poem *Mourning Lover*, published by the online literary magazine *Jalada*, provides a new portrayal of sexual pleasure – one that can be derived from masturbation.

Through poetry, Meiji shows there are different ways of having sex and that they are not necessarily human-with-human all of the time. He uses this human-with-machine sexual encounter to probe a new generation of (educated, middle-class) Nigerians' need for pleasure and fulfilment. Technology makes our life enjoyable but it may not always provide fulfilment. From this poem's articulation of sexual frustration in the age of digital technology, one can deduce that when it comes to the question of fulfilment, technology and sex do intersect. People want to be in control of every facet of their own life, and sexuality is part of that quest. The mechanised sex toy seems to fit the digital age perfectly, as it allows people to take control of their own sexual experience. Just as the dildo fits in with the quest for privacy and control, the digital age also allows for anonymity and control. The speaker could be a man or woman performing a sexual act with a dildo, but we cannot tell from this poem. This depicts the fact that in the twenty-first century, gender is immaterial when it comes to human interaction with the machine. The internet and the mechanised sex toy are unisex, new symbols of desire and its fulfilment. Both sexes crave the joy that sex can bring. In this particular poem, the poet, who is a man, does not specify the gender of the speaker but leaves us to fill in the blank. What this poem does, therefore, is to further articulate the emotion surrounding the way in which modern technologies intervene in our subjectivity in a digital age, and how the anonymity of the digital age allows us to use technology to experiment with our gender and sexual preferences. Sexuality and gender performance, this poem indicates, are in a state of flux. The poem itself vividly portrays the sexual relationship between the human and the machine, and in a way illustrates the way in which the machine allows us to experiment with our sexuality within the privacy of our home.

Poetry can highlight our new dependence on technologies as we start to push for new experiences. Attitudes to sex and sexual fulfilment are no longer influenced by only old traditions and contemporary religious practices, but new technologies are also a major factor in the way a growing number of people in Nigeria experience sex. The machine may not be capable of speaking back to us but it does not judge us either, the way the society judged the protagonist in Thomas's *Itan Igbesi Aiye Emi Sẹgilọla Ẹlẹyinju, Ẹlẹgbẹrun Ọkọ L'Aiye*. Not once does the speaker crave the human touch but he or she longs for the sexual bliss that the machine brings. Michelle Kendrick argues that online literature often turns our anxieties 'regarding technology into romanticized notions of a reconfigured subjectivity' (n.pag). Technology allows for the realisation of one's true sexual self but, as Kendrick surmises, it can also lead to confusion and anxiety over what could be considered as the true sexual self. Towards the end of the poem, the speaker admits that the dildo is 'just a fantasy'. The machine will not, after all, provide a lasting fulfilment for our sexual urges; its enjoyment is fleeting. Ecstasy stops once the batteries run out. But there is a sense of control over one's sexuality as long as we can afford new batteries. This poem illustrates how modern technologies – from computers to sex toys – provide many Nigerians who can afford them, new ways of sexually defining who they are.

The Erotic and the Spiritual

In the digital age, the erotic provides an avenue to discuss the way in which the flesh and the spiritual relate to each other. With Christian evangelism spreading widely across Nigeria's urban and rural areas, especially in the southern part of the country, writers are depicting the role that sex plays in contemporary churches and mosques.

Like Kiru Taye, whose fiction was discussed above, Obinna Udenwe is a writer commissioned by the publisher of *Brittlepaper.com* to write a 'Nigerian Church Erotica', that will respond to the current trend of Christian evangelism in Nigeria. *Holy Sex* is a seven-part series of different narrators but with the one principal character known as Pastor Samuel. Episode 1, published on 18 May 2015, opens with the statement 'Your pastor secretes holy milk. That is the story being whispered by everyone in the church – choristers, ushers, and the women' (n.pag), thus setting the tone that churches in twenty-first century Nigeria are the ultimate sites of the erotic. The narrator also points out to us how the spiritual, the erotic, aesthetic and the digital intersect. In church, Pastor Samuel uses iPads and huge projector screens to deliver sermons and the congregation uses mobile devices to record them. The narrator tells us: 'For every trendy woman in town, there are three things in vogue: Blackberry Z10, Saving Grace Inc and pinging dresses – in that order.'

The Nigerian church of the twenty-first century is one that is fully embedded in digital material culture, one in which sex, class and wealth intersect. At the same time, *Holy Sex* also reprises the centuries-old religious traditions in many Nigerian communities that I referenced earlier in this chapter, in which the sexual and the spiritual sit side by side. There is a lot of sex taking place in Pastor Samuel's church. He is handsome and charismatic. He preys on innocent women but at the same time some female members of his congregation who are educated and well-off also lust after him. While women are at the centre of Udenwe's erotic writing, it is the patriarchal Pastor Samuel who seems to have it all – a beautiful wife and beautiful mistresses who are more than happy to have sex with him despite the fact that there are rumours that he has fathered several children through these liaisons. Feona Attwood suggests that global Anglophone writings on digital platforms are unwittingly recycling old sexist stereotypes of weak women, but at the same time, Attwood admits that fictional female characters (which I am extending to African literature in a digital age, including the women in *Holy Sex*) 'embody transgressive female sexualities' (7).

Attwood's hypothesis is apt here, not all the female characters in *Holy Sex* are blind to Pastor Samuel's patriarchal antics. Some use their liaison with the pastor as a recreational means to a new sexual adventure and as an escape from a busy work and private life. Nigerian women are not always victims of patriarchal male figures, they are also willing participants in sexual liaisons and they may even use their sexuality as a means of subverting patriarchy. The Nigerian church erotica therefore depicts the complexity of Nigerian and African female sexuality. Readers who comment on these stories point out that they paint a true picture of some of Nigeria's evangelical churches. Others seeking to live out their own sexual fantasy urge the writer to push the sexual boundaries further. Commenting on Episode 4, a reader, Jude (8 June 2015), says:

> The stories get better and more interesting by the day, I love the author's simple ways of capturing the voice of the characters and the depth of the narration. This made me wonder about what people could do to achieve that which they desire.

Commenting on Episode 3, another reader, Victhur (6 June 2015), says:

> Awesome read! I would appreciate the writer pushing it further in subsequent editions. Something like the Pastor's beautiful wife who seduced the young handsome pianist or the female worship leader who is having a lesbian affair with the Pastor's wife. So much 'Holy Sex' going on in churches. Bravo.

The comments by readers underline the tangibility of the digital space as the defining cultural medium of this millennium. They also show that the erotic is tangible and important because people see themselves as sexual beings and they see meanings in erotic fiction. Once again, they make the connection with some of the sexual scandals that have become the staple of the Nigerian media in recent years. Art and life mirror and affirm each other. What is published as cybertext is just as relevant as texts published in book or magazine form. The gaining importance of the erotic is also buttressed by the fact that *Holy Sex* was awarded the best short story in the 2015 edition of the Nigerian Writers Awards.

Social Media and the Aesthetics of the Quotidian

8

In *Blogging Queer Kenya*, Keguro Macharia directs us to the emerging aesthetics of ordinariness in the Kenyan digital space.

> In their narratives, younger writers have moved away from the allegorical mode privileged by Ngũgĩ wa Thiong'o, Kenya's best known writer, and are now focused on quotidian details, without taking on the burden of representing revolutionary peasants, the urban working class, or betrayed freedom fighters. These characters are not absent from contemporary fiction; instead, they are no longer the privileged subjects of representation.

Macharia's statement is apt: all too often, African narratives come with stereotypes of magic realism and the extraordinary, what Wainaina in 'How To Write About Africa' describes as 'naked warriors, loyal servants, diviners and seers, ancient wise men living in hermitic splendour' (n.pag). These stereotypes are best represented by the images of Africa so familiar from Hollywood films filled with colonial fantasies and from pseudo-documentary newsreels of blood thirsty dictators like *The Last King of Scotland*; by photographic images of the exotic continent that have become the staple of the National Geographic magazine; by Nollywood films filled with magical powers and Christian miracles. Even in the twenty-first century, the images of Africa that many Westerners see in Billboards, print and broadcast media are often that of starving children who need to be rescued by charitable organisations. Equally problematic, however, is the Harlem Renaissance's romantic depiction of the continent – represented in Countee Cullen's famous poem 'Heritage' – as a Utopia, with exotic culture and people.

The rise of the everyday in African writings speaks to an aesthetic strategy that is no longer preoccupied with responding to the aforementioned imaginary about Africa, but one that reflects what Evan Mwangi uses as the title of his book – *Africa writes back to self* (2009). I make this argument based on the hypothesis that the first generation of contemporary Nigerian and Kenyan writers focuses on making a space for African literature in the world's republic of letters. Equally important, writers of that generation also see their responsibilities as fighting the 'culture war' on behalf of Africans who have long been represented as savages in some canonical Western texts. In fulfilling their duty, the older generation of writers resort to using various literary strategies in their narratives, such as the creation of heroic figures who fought the colonialists, for example in Ngũgĩ and Micere Githae Mugo's *The Trial of Dedan Kimathi* (1976), and the deployment of larger than life figures in asserting African humanity such as the character of Okonkwo in Chinua Achebe's *Things Fall Apart* (1958).

Since the turn of the current millennium, a renewed scholarly interest in the aesthetic of the quotidian has emerged, in which researchers build on the works of modernist thinkers such as Henry Lefebvre and Erving Goffman. While the everyday has for a while been the site of analysis in Western literary studies such as Siobhan Phillips's *The Poetics of the Everyday: Creative Repetition in Modern American Verse* (2009), and Anne Jamison's *Poetics en Passant: Redefining the Relationship Between Victorian and Modern Poetry* (2009), the quotidian is a relatively-new area of interest in African literary studies. In the twenty-first century, the emerging aesthetic seeks to move literature away from the topical issues and the big ideas that characterised much of the portrayal in the first wave of post-independent writing from Kenya and Nigeria, into making the ordinary the basis for understanding African societies. Social media platforms are the sites where we can daily see Nigerian and Kenyan writers at work – where we get an insight into their world view, and see how they seek to influence national discourses – since most writers, poets and politicians from Kenya and Nigeria now have a social media presence. While they have not stopped writing about powerful protagonists, they are using the quotidian as the foundation for capturing African humanity. And as we approach the third decade of the twenty-first century, writers are not fixated on trying to disabuse the outside world of a Conradian perception of Africa. Instead, a mode of writing that is grounded in the ordinary and the everyday is emerging on social media. The quotidian disrupts past distortions and simplifications, by placing ordinary Africans doing ordinary things at the very core of creative writing.

For writers, the everyday online experience is as real as the dailiness of the physical space. They unabashedly assert their middle-class selves in that space; mixing poetry, fiction and their own personal stories together. Their thoughts are conveyed to thousands of followers through literature and through personal updates on social media. Their readers share their own stories with these writers in return. When Wainaina came out as gay in 2014, he did it on social media; when he suffered a stroke a year later, he announced it on Facebook. Wainaina symbolises the way in which the personal, the everyday and the literary feed on each other. The late Wainaina wrote passionately about the quotidian experience of being middle-class and the joy and disillusionment of this identity. Often, in his writing he bares his soul, putting the personal right in the open before his followers. His writing is often fragmented, like a jazz musician jamming and improvising. Or perhaps the fragmentation reflects his transnational and nomadic existence: Johannesburg today, Lagos tomorrow and New York two days after that. Perhaps it symbolises the disjointed nature of everyday social media conversations. Such activities are at the centre of twenty-first-century modernity because digital modernity feeds on being continuously present on social media, on the amount of likes a post gathers, on tweets and retweets. A key determinant of a one's cultural value in this digital era is the amount of attention one's posts garner among the digital public. Ours is the age of the quotidian, because the everyday is the foundation upon which the likes of Facebook and Instagram are built and on which they thrive. And in an increasingly networked world, as social media is now an everyday tool for many Nigerians and Kenyans, it is no surprise that the quotidian has found a home in the creative writings being published on social media platforms, because everyday action is being consciously and unconsciously reflected in works of literature.

With over one billion people using social media networks every day, the quotidian matters because platforms such as Facebook, Twitter and Instagram are sites that archive everyday human experience. For many Africans, the mobile phone is an everyday, ubiquitous functional tool that people use to access social media as part of everyday engagement with literature and the world. Those who partake in these digital conversations that take place every second of every day, are doing so as participants in digital modernity. The idea of modernity tethers us to newness and progress. In the age of the book, the project of colonial modernity created Kenyans and Nigerians who read and wrote – modern people. Yoruba language poets of the Ewi genre, for example, used the words 'ọlaju' and 'alakọwe' to describe modernity and those who were considered modern because they were educated. Interestingly enough, 'ọlaju' directly translates as 'opening of the eye' and the word 'alakọwe' was used to describe the Ifa oracle long before the arrival of print culture in West Africa (see also Adeleke Adeeko). In the twenty-first century, the notion of digital modernity speaks to the view that those who are on social media every day are people versed in a new 'lingua franca', different from what was used in the analogue age. They socialise not only through the written words, but also express themselves through emoticons, emojis, GIFs, images and instant videos. The mobile phone, the written texts, the images and videos that Africans use for digital communication all possess aesthetic value. So apart from the text, the commonplace also merits critical engagement in terms of material culture and its importance to the performance of modernity in the digital age.

Digital modernity means the ability to be instantly and constantly interactive. Millions of Kenyans and Nigerians post their daily routines online; from pictures of their children going to school, to asking for cooking recipes. Their essential selves are on display on social media: people are not just talking about politics, they play, make meaningless banter, flirt, mourn and laugh on Facebook and Instagram. This means that modernity in the twenty-first century revolves around digital everydayness. The quotidian has also become a tool of self-fashioning, with people posting images of themselves and writing about their daily existence. Every day, Nigerian and Kenyan politicians are on social media in their attempts to sell themselves as women and men of the people. Election campaigns are as competitive on social media platforms as they are in the physical space of Kenya and Nigeria. African pop stars are equally active on Facebook as the politicians. And ordinary people want to be part of social media's everyday experience. Like everybody else, writers and creative artists, as well as their readers and followers, are participants in this culture of self-fashioning. Creative artists often post notifications as well as videos and photos of book launches, readings, art exhibitions, appearances on television and radio stations, on social media. Literature on social media sites foregrounds the way in which the everyday intersects with arts, class and politics.

Quotidian Objects

In the field of philosophy, scholars such as Thomas Leddy theorise on whether or not ordinary things have aesthetic attributes. Leddy's focus is on the materiality of the everyday, and how the ordinary can be made extraordinary by acquiring an 'aura'. Leddy uses household objects such as furniture and kitchen utensils as examples of materials that can be made extraordinary. These materials, Leddy suggests, acquire their aesthetic qualities, an 'aura', because of the sentiment attached to them. But Jane Forsey takes a different view of the quotidian object. For Forsey, the notion of an aesthetic of the ordinary should not be seen as subjective or based on the sentiment a particular person attaches to an object, instead there must be a collective agreement that an object is aesthetically pleasing, based on the fact that the said object has been appraised by others as having certain qualities that make it extraordinary. In calling for an aesthetic of the ordinary, Forsey argues that: 'functional excellence, contextually specific knowledge, actual qualities of the thing in question, its quotidian use, and the in-principle communicability of our judgements with others, then we have the makings of an aesthetic of the ordinary as it is ordinarily experienced' (244).

I believe that in the context of Kenyan and Nigerian literature in the digital age, both the arguments put forward by Leddy and Forsey are germane: creative artists make the commonplace sublime when poetry and fictional narratives are foregrounded in everyday objects, sights and sounds, because objects invoke sentiments, judgement and attachments which we communicate to others. Here I want to return to *Koroga*, the digital postcard project that marries poetry with photography. As discussed previously, *Koroga* brings together individual artists and the community to define African aesthetics and to narrate the complexity of Africa in the digital space. Even when addressing 'bigger' themes, such as class, politics and sexuality, every bit of *Koroga* is foregrounded in the quotidian object: a clay pot, electrical wires, coffee mugs, chairs by the seaside. *Koroga* underlines the importance of the commonplace, the ordinary and the everyday to our understanding of African creativity and their projects embody the idea of ordinary objects acquiring an aura that speaks to their communicability.

Digital Comfort by Michael Onsando and Marziya Mohammedali is an example reflecting the everydayness of digital relationships, in which virtual hugs – with the use of GIFs and emoji – have replaced physical hugs. Affections are increasingly expressed in noughts and crosses representing hugs and kisses rather than in deeds or words. The poem in this *Koroga* project is equally foregrounded by ordinary symbols of communications – a pole and the cables it carries. The pole and cables, are of course, symbols of analogue and digital communication. The pole and the cables are ordinary objects used to historicise modernity: first, the landline telephone, telex and the telegram messages were objects of modern communication, replacing the town-criers, postal coaches and pigeons as carriers of messages. Now in the digital age, cables, especially fibre-optic cables, have become the backbone of digital communication.

The second example, entitled *(Re)member*, is a poetography by Michael Onsando and Jerry Riley. The main image for this project is a tyre. The tyre is yet another commonplace object that one encounters every day on the continent. What the poem suggests, however, is that what creative artists are doing in the digital age reprises the works of the creative artists who came before them. Everyday objects remind us that nothing is totally new; we are just reinventing the wheel. By using the quotidian as its foundation, *Koroga* follows a long African tradition in which quotidian objects, images and sound fire up great works of art. The poems of the Gikuyu people of Kenya, the songs and poetry of Fulani-Hausa people and those of the Yoruba people of Nigeria are animated by the sounds of birds in the morning, the pit-pat of rains on roofs and the colour of the sky. There is no art without the ordinary and the commonplace.

The Quotidian and Transformative

The Nigerian writer Chuma Nwokolo embodies the intersection of the analogue world and the digital. Nwokolo made his name as a novelist in the 1980s during the heyday of the popular middlebrow series Macmillan Pacesetter. Over the course of four decades, he has published widely and worked with literary networks across the continent, and has made appearances in several workshops, book fairs and writers retreats in every region of Africa. Nwokolo is also a digital pioneer in the context of literature. He is the publisher of *Africanwriting.com*, one of the very first online magazines to specialise in African literature. He has a large following on social media and he is a leading member of digital literary networks that include

Chimurenga, *Krazitivity* and *Ederi*. His YouTube video *Sudan.Sudan.* was one of the first digital poems to gain critical attention on social media. Nwokolo belongs to several Nigerian literary listservs and has collaborated in several digital projects such as *Jalada Africa* and South Africa's *Chimurenga Chronic*.

Nwokolo's literary output on social media pages – mainly flash fictions, poems and short essays – suggests he has a strong belief in the power of literature to change societies. Some of his works in the digital space seek to use literature as a tool of everyday reawakening, with the hope of raising people's consciousness with regard to the Nigerian and the African condition. With Nwokolo's writing as the starting point, what I want to do in this section is to examine the robust ways in which writers use social media platforms to depict the complexity of ordinariness and the everyday.

In a flash fiction (fictional work of extreme brevity but offering character and plot development) that was published on his Facebook page as a Facebook Note, *The Inhuman Race*, Nwokolo's narrator starts with a scene so ordinary that one could mistakenly think that the story is an attempt at comedy:

> They surprised her on the anniversary, just when she thought they had forgotten, brought a basket of fruits just before midnight when the last of the friends returned from his shift at the factory.

In this story about a working-class protagonist who lost a leg after a terror attack, Nwokolo uses commonplace scenes of working-class people peeling oranges whilst filling a room with 'laughter of common people with the uncommon gift of coping' to lead us to the everyday tragedy that surrounds his fictional characters. The story only has four paragraphs, but it deftly uses the quotidian to point its readers to the tragic and the transcendent that can lurk in the ordinary. As she is presented with a prosthetic leg, the protagonist sees beyond her own personal scar to the humanity of those who almost killed her. 'They are sitting like us right now,' she wept, 'building more bombs.' Nwokolo deploys the ordinary in this story to bring out the idea that the good and the bad are two sides of the same coin. Everybody, perhaps, possesses the capability to commit heinous crimes. Some of those who carry out evil deeds live among their victims, and like their victims, they are often poor and lead a precarious everyday existence.

The story elicited passionate responses from readers. Despite not naming a place, or time, or the ethnic composition of its fictional group of characters, Nwokolo's social media followers are able to use this particular fiction to see the everyday tragedy that a section of the Nigerian social classes is going through under Boko Haram, whose overwhelming majority of victims are poor. This is a comment by a reader:

Social Media and the Aesthetics of the Quotidian   149

Basil Okafor: 'The bitter truth! They are ever so busy upgrading their instruments of death and plotting the next attack. Inhuman race indeed.'

Okafor's comment signifies how the everyday constitutes a starting point for thinking about life-changing moments, and how these momentous periods start and dwell in the domain of the routine. A quotidian aesthetic points us to what happens when the abnormal becomes the norm. It sensitises us to the long-lasting impacts of small-scale, everyday political developments, and how these occurrences constitute the building block of a moment in time.

In an even shorter fiction of just two paragraphs, called *Present Tense,* Nwokolo uses the quotidian to draw in the readers – inviting them to use their imaginations in building the story. The fiction centres around a married middle-class woman who is watching the evening news on the television with her husband, while their children do their school homework. For a very brief period, she lets her mind wander from her domestic bliss to her pre-marital years when she dated a man whose name she cannot recall but who 'had groomed his beard upward until he had some wisps of hair between his lips ... She remembered sitting across from him, still dressed in her suit from her day in the bank, and thinking with sudden conviction that this was too playful a man to father her children.'

In the and second, and last, paragraph, we are told that the woman has a moment of remorse, which only lasts a few seconds; a very fleeting moment, which however, Nwokolo's readers find enthralling. Is it remorse that the character, a married woman, is thinking about a former lover, whom she can hardly recollect? Or is it remorse that she cannot vividly remember an old love? Or the remorse of not being married to him instead of the man she is sitting next to?

Both the woman's previous lover and her spouse are members of the professional middle class, and they are characters that Nwokolo's Facebook fans easily relate to. The narrative prompts this response from a reader:

Chima A. Ejiofor: So many possibilities from this short passage. It leaves you imagining things.

This response brings about the following conversation between the writer and the reader:

Chuma Nwokolo: Collaborative fiction: ensnares the reader into the imaginative enterprise.

Chima A. Ejiofor: Literature as a community enterprise, then?

Chuma Nwokolo: Was always ever so: especially so with call and response orature, but even so with literature ...

The dialogue between the writer and the reader highlights how writers on digital platforms link their craft to the artistic practices of the precolonial era, a factor that I return to throughout this book. Nwokolo recognises the everydayness of the arts that predates his era, and how the close interaction between the digital public and the digital writer resembles that of centuries ago. Artistic practices in the African context have always been a community enterprise. In this conversation, the everyday becomes the site of collaboration between the writer and his readers. Additionally, this particular flash fiction and the conversations that come out of it underline the way in which people on social media find meanings in ordinary satisfactions – a well-paid job, a good husband, children and a happy home. The everydayness of the flash fiction alongside Nwokolo's regular interaction with readers on social media fosters an appreciation of common sense that the fictional female character shows in *Present Tense*. For the female protagonist, real happiness lies in domestic bliss and the pleasure that she finds in everyday rituals.

Quotidian Love

Ella Chikezie is a member of the new generation of writers born in the digital era that is very much at home on Facebook, Instagram and Twitter. In addition to being an active blogger, Chikezie posts her creative writings across different digital sites, sometimes simultaneously, at other times, a piece of work is only published on one platform. Chikezie's works cover every aspect of everyday experience, but it is in her love and domestic poems that the quotidian often comes alive. In an untitled poem, posted on Instagram on 16 February 2019, which is also cross-posted on her blog, Chikezie wants people to discuss their experience of quotidian love:

> Our love isn't fairytale
> those type with happily ever after
> It isn't candle light dinners
> and scented love letters
> It isn't moonlight kisses
> and shiny red roses.
> It isn't a stroll in the park
> or pillow fights after dark
>
> …
>
> And when it got hard sometimes
> It was you choosing to stay
> It was you choosing to pray
> It was us choosing us everyday

Figure 2 *Our love isn't fairytale* by Ella Chikezie. An image-poem posted on Instagram by the poet.

This particular poem, which she dedicates to her followers, as a Valentine's Day gift, places love at the centre of the everyday experience. For Chikezie, there is beauty, ugliness, ecstasy, anguish and truth to be found in quotidian love, and these experiences are on display every minute of every day on social media. Chikezie uses this poem to invite her readers to post poems that speak to the everyday effect – the emotion of having someone constantly standing by one's side. By linking the Instagram version of the poem to the version posted on her blog, Ella provides her followers with a more substantial space to discuss the symbolism of love in their lives. She places this love poem alongside the love poems of the Chilean poet Pablo Neruda and the Nigerian poet Chijoke Amu-Nnadi. Not only does she invite an aesthetic comparison from her online followers, she also shows that quotidian love resonates across space and time. She advises her followers:

> If you want to make your girlfriend, wife, boyfriend, husband, or fiancé feel special, sharing a thoughtful reminder of your feelings is a great start. Sending love messages isn't cliché but an expression of your appreciation towards them.

Love, as depicted in Ella's poem, should be expressed daily, and it should not be shown mainly by material symbols of expensive dinners or red roses. This poem, albeit simple, reaches beyond the idealistic poetry of *amour courtois* (courtly love) and some of the narratives that one sees in the Mills & Boons novels of old. For Ella, the simple and the commonplace are the essential nutrients that love needs in order to grow and for it to be everlasting. The quotidian love is therefore rather more grounded, more realistic and even more transcendental than the idealistic notions of love.

Rasaq Malik Gbolahan is another writer born in the digital age, and like Chikezie's, Gbolahan's poetry covers a wide range of themes. Also like Chikezie, his love poems speak to how people look for love in the ordinary. They show that love could be found in the routine and in simple quests, and that love that emerges from the ordinary can be transcendental. On 8 December 2018, Gbolahan posted this ode to love on Facebook, which is a version of his poem *Your Love* published four years earlier on *The New Black Magazine* website:

> Your love stands like a minaret
> in my heart
> I will climb atop to call
> your name
> me – the muezzin, the bilal
> in the city of poets

the bearer of your fragile memory.

II
Your love erects like a streetlight
in my heart tonight
as I walk down the road
to where we serenade
searching for your shadow
your fragrance
and your wholeness
Your love is the door to
the passage of light tonight
Give me the key to bask
in its rays
Be the stream that flows
the kiblah
I will face before
the earth paints my
body with dust.

For the speaker in this poem, everyday love is not only a site of the routine as depicted in the last stanza of Chikezie's poem, it is also spiritually uplifting. The dailiness of love and romance is configured in this poem by the poet's own existence as a devout Muslim. The aesthetic here is foregrounded in the imagery of everydayness; of walking down the street and the spatiality of the ordinary as embodied by the street light, the fragrance and a shadow. On his Facebook page, Gbolahan often posts pictures of his life as a devout Muslim, someone who prays five times a day. In this poem, everyday romantic affect is used to mediate between the spiritually mundane and the secular self. Every day, when Muslims pray, they face the geographical direction of the Kiblah in Mecca, Saudi Arabia. A mosque's minaret usually stands taller than most of the buildings in the community where it is located. Love here is not merely deployed as a metaphor but as a symbol for the high esteem in which the speaker holds his lover. The love the speaker desires is not one that is meant to last for a season, but one that reflects the popular marital vow of 'till death do us part'; love in the rainy and dry season; love when there is no food and when there is a lot to go around. The reference to the mosque speaks to rituals of the ordinary that is equally transforming. Love does not corrupt, it enriches and nurtures the spiritual side of a person. This finite quality of love is based on the aesthetics of everyday spiritual belief that has the power to cement a loving relationship.

The Quotidian of Celebration

In the Yoruba world, the conception of time is underlined by the saying 'Asiko la'ye' or 'time is a moment'. Since the Yoruba world is often foregrounded in duality, the philosophical and the practical notion of time are hard to separate. What is clear is that in Yoruba culture, time is not linear, hence the saying 'obiri la ye yi' which in English loosely translates to 'time is cyclic'. But just because the Yoruba people believe in the cyclicity of time does not mean they think it is reversible. The saying 'Igba ni onigba nlo' means you celebrate a moment and you can relive a moment but at the same time you cannot stop the time. Asiko may mean the present time, but it could also constitute a moment in time – the past, the present and the future. Asiko as a moment in time is also used to refer to an epoch. Within the concept of time, every day constitutes the building block of an era, as days turn into weeks, weeks to months and months to years. The Yoruba people's idea of time is germane in the digital era. On social media sites, dailiness and moments are now a cause for celebration. For example, Facebook now has a dedicated page called 'Memories', where you can 'celebrate' and reflect on the things you have shared with those you are connected to on Facebook. What one would have considered as banal in the analogue age – such as images of being on the bus to work, rants about your boss, or headlines of a news story that you posted on your wall eight years ago – are things to celebrate as *Memories* on Facebook. Another Facebook feature is 'On This Day', which allows you to look back on what you posted on the same day last year, or years before. Other features that celebrate the ordinary include 'Friendversaries' (when you first became friends with someone on Facebook) and 'Memories You May Have Missed'.

The everydayness that social media enables means that poetry can draw on the usage of everydayness in Nigerian and Kenyan poetic tradition. Among the Yoruba people of Nigeria, the poetic genre of Oriki is an oral poetry that taps into the very core of a person's history, as well as the history of the extended family and the community. Every Yoruba family has its unique Oriki, and historically Oriki is recited everyday among family members as a means of greeting, inspiration, encouragement, celebration, and as a means of reminding people of their family and society's history. Oriki is also used to chastise, to mock and to reject. Oriki is different from ordinary conversation including words of encouragement. It is a text that stirs emotion within the subject that it is directed at. Yoruba people use the phrase 'ori mi wu' ('I feel fine') to describe the peak of the (positive) emotion that poetry stirs in a person. Rowland Abiodun argues that understanding the society in which an African artist is born and raised is important to comprehending the art that she produces. Some of these poetic traditions are being reprised on social media by the artistic endeavours of Gbolahan's generation and some members of the older generation of modern African writers. When Wole Soyinka's birthday was trending on social media, Gbolahan posted this Oriki-style poem dedicated to Africa's first Nobel laureate in literature, *FOR OSHOYIMIKA (WOLE SOYINKA) @ 84*:

> III
> Orogbo, the annual feast
> is a ritual you do not forget
> Obi, the tray is here for this
> year's sale
> Let this poem turn into a candlelight
> a candlelight that will burn the forest
> of evils
> Let this offering shake the earth
> till Iroko curses its birth
> Let Asabari forget the name of every
> native
> for I will climb the hill and sketch
> my footprints on the eye of the earth

Soyinka is an extraordinary figure celebrated through this traditional poetry form that is used every day in Yoruba societies. Since social media platforms by their nature are grounded in everyday conversation, the expectation is that poets and writers will elevate the standard of these everyday conversations from mere tittle-tattle to an artistic experience of the quotidian – that is to the level of what we know as text. Although written in English, Gbolahan grounds this poem in a Yoruba milieu, one that is easily recognisable and relatable to those conversant with Yoruba tradition and culture. He makes reference to Soyinka's love of hunting and the ritual that accompanies hunting. Gbolahan also creates a familiarity with his subject by using Soyinka's full name – Oshoyimika – which is only known to those who are close to Soyinka himself. In affirming his and his reader's fondness of Soyinka, Gbolahan references everyday objects and words in the Yoruba world that are also used on special occasions – 'obi' ('kolanut'), 'orogbo', 'Olokun' ('God of the sea'), 'Ogun' ('God of iron and war'). The poem provides a perfect example of how everyday ideas and thoughts based on African languages are framed in a marriage of European and African languages in digital and offline spaces. Languages on social media have a way of kissing and quarrelling. They kiss when they are beautifully woven together and they are aesthetically pleasing to the reader; they quarrel when words and images refuse to come together as meaningful creative projects. Stewart Brown articulates this relationship in the age of the book by using Yoruba and English poetic traditions as case studies. In our social media age, the poetic of the everyday in the digital space becomes the site in which the African and the European converge. This is an example of digital modernity, one in which cultures and languages coalesce, and one in which the written and the audio-visual symbiotically exist.

African poetics are rooted in their symbiotic relationship with lived experience, because across many societies on the continent, there is no binary between art and life, and both elements often imitate each other. Therefore, any study of the poetics in contemporary Africa should not ignore the role that poetics have long played historically across many African societies as essential tools with which people and societies make meaning of their history, life and memory. The historic role of the poet in society may have been restrained in printed works of poetry, simply because of the nature of the book – a materiality that limits the interaction between writers and their readers. Social media platforms, with their real-time audio-visual and textual capabilities, allow poets to better reprise some of the roles that poets have played outside of the printed book in Nigerian societies, in which poetry was an everyday tool used across different economic and social strata. For example, poetry is recited every morning by traditional poets employed by royal households of Nigeria's Yoruba and Hausa-Fulani ruling families and Oriki is recited everyday among ordinary, everyday families.

Borrowing from his Yoruba ancestry, Gbolahan is one of the poets who carry the art of Oriki poetry to the digital age and, in the process, Oriki thus becomes a tool for elevating digital conversations. If Oriki is panegyric because it possesses aesthetic qualities that are lacking in an ordinary conversation, one can argue that on social media there is an emerging aesthetic standard surrounding digital writing, in which readers are separating and elevating the poetic from ordinary conversations that tend to dominate the twenty-four-hour social media circle. Readers' responses to Gbolahan's ode to Soyinka, a legend of the craft, underlines this argument:

Lanase Hussein Kehinde:	This is the language deeper than mere usage of words. RMG, I wish Moren could see this poem, I know he would not hesitate to give you one of his granddaughters with cowries of bead waist, succulent breasts and a silhouette of love.
Richard Mbuthia:	Rasaq Malik Gbolahan you are a fire that rains ice on a burning soul! More power to you. Wole Soyinka is a priced gem.
Waniohi Wa Makokha:	Another masterpiece. Well done and long live the sage.
Ayo Baje:	Deeeeeep! Evocative!! Apt!!!

Going by the names, several of the responses come from readers who are based in Kenya and Nigeria, thus not only affirming the popularity of Soyinka as a literary canon, but also showing an appreciation of the poetic form of praise poetry, a genre that exists in one form or another in many African societies as a tool for contemplating ordinary and monumental periods. What Gbolahan does here is to let his poem be the basis for his readers to appreciate both the subject (Soyinka) and the creator of this poem (Gbolahan). Social media in this instance reprises the communal role that Oriki plays in the analogue world.

Some of the textual qualities that historically make Oriki an ideal tool to articulate the quotidian and the everyday, can also be found in what is being published on social media. This is because, as argued in my article with Helen Cousins, unlike in the world of book publishing, writers can write on their own terms. Since the ordinary in much of book publishing output is not seen as authentically African, poems on social media are being used by writers as a means to subvert the politics of postcolonial publishing. Their works are not shaped by editorial goals, which draw publishing editors, especially those based in the West, to works that mirror news reports in Western journalism. Of equal importance is the fact that there is a real-time interaction between the poet and her readers on social media, as witnessed in the reader response to Gbolahan's Oriki poem.

While Gbolahan's muse in the above poem is a world-famous writer, the poet Dami Ajayi takes us back to the theme of celebrating love with a poem about his friend Raliat's wedding. Writing under the nom de plume of Jollypaps on Instagram, Ajayi, too, borrows from his Yoruba background, especially its musical and poetic tradition in the context of matrimonial unions:

> Wife-in-waiting,
> Camwood adorning her feet
> Her groom with the proverbial blue balls waiting too,
> …
> And that is how affection gains its form like a fetus
> Affection trudges through memory through cornerstones through conduits,
> forgotten and neglected
> Affection finds itself a stool
> in places not foretold
> At Ordinary General Meetings
> Love finds itself and that is enough
> That is enough.

If, as argued by Oyeniyi Okunoye, the Yoruba poetic tradition lends itself to 'constant self-renewal' (46), it is because poetry has the remarkable ability to document everyday life as well as to commemorate special occasions. Those who speak and understand the Yoruba language and culture, and appreciate its importance, find meanings in its rich oral poetic tradition. They adapt oral texts to new cultural and technological developments. In the process, poetry becomes the engine that fuels and powers modernity. The digital is the next stage of

Figure 3 Bride wearing Aso-Oke Gele for her wedding. An image-poem by Dami Àjàyí aka #Jollypaps, posted on Instagram.

modernity, and what Ajayi has done with this poem is to use social media as the medium for the poetic translation of Yoruba poetic code into English, much like a digital transcompiler that takes the source code of a computer program (its engine) and translates it into a different programing language. In order to fully appreciate what Ajayi has done here, one must be fully immersed in both Yoruba poetic tradition as well as its popular culture tradition. When the speaker tells us that Raliat wears 'Camwood' on her feet, the speaker is referencing a famous line from a Yoruba poetic tradition of Ekun-Iyawo or the 'Song/Lament of the Bride' and the tradition of decorating the feet of the bride with Osun or camwood. The part about the groom with the blue balls is a modern Yoruba phrase, 'Oko Iyawo elepon blue', which is often used by musicians to poke fun at the groom. Of great significance is the subject herself: Raliat is a Muslim name and she is dressed in a Yoruba Aso-Oke Gele head tie – an attire worn during special occasions like weddings. The notion of modernity among the Yoruba people is one based on Yoruba people's view of the world as embedded in duality. The past and the present are delineated, as are good and evil. Modernity is also predicated on this duality of the foreign and the local, the modern and the traditional. Everyday performance, be it on social media or in the real-life space of Ibadan or Abeokuta, is based on this world view. The Raliat who wears the traditional clothes is as at home on Instagram as she is in the mosque where her wedding takes place, and where the Yoruba language will mix with a sprinkle of Arabic and English words. The poem by Ajayi, which celebrates Raliat's journey from spinsterhood to marital life, emanates from Yoruba thoughts, and these Yoruba concepts according to Niyi Osundare 'exist in relation to the world, achieving in many areas an ignorable degree of uniqueness' (18). The occasion that warrants the Instagram poem and the accompanying photograph underline how the everyday and the spectacular are intertwined. Poetry in the digital age is therefore an exercise in everyday intertextuality, one in which the past and the present collapse.

The Quotidian, Power Relations and the Other

Although separated by physical geographical boundaries of space, readers want poems that reflect the day-to-day experience of their social status. Karin Barber in *A History of African Popular Culture* theorises the quotidian in Africa as dwelling in the realm of the popular, one in which ordinary folks with little or no political clout negotiate their existence. But the quotidian is more than that; since class, gender, race, ethnicity, and sexuality intricately intersect, poetry, like other artistic endeavours, reflects the quotidian of being poor and being female just as it does being gay and rich. As the Indian sociologist Prasanta Ray aptly points out: 'Every day is an everyday for everybody' (1).

Wambui Kamiru (now Collymore) and Joe Kiragu's postcard *#CroissantRevolution*, is a direct criticism of armchair political activism by some middle- and upper-class Kenyans and Africans – people who only express concern about politics in internet cafés, while the less privileged bear the brunt of the ineffectiveness of the politics of the postcolonial nation. With its glistering coffee cup resting on a saucer in the bright light of a swanky art café and bakery *#CroissantRevolution* poses a stark contrast to Joe Kiragu and Michael Onsando's postcard *The Labourer*.

Both projects speak to the class privilege and the conditions of the social classes in contemporary Kenya and Africa. For the middle-class African, the coffee shop, porcelain cup and saucer are objects of everyday socialisation. To those who are less privileged, these objects reflect their financial impotence. Ugali is detested by the middle class, while it is a staple food for the poor, who have to fight to get even this hot meal. Instead, the middle-class army stirring the *#CroissantRevolution* roots their everyday experience in a European and North American diet, symbolised by the staple of coffee and toast. Not for the labourer to enjoy the leisure of sipping foaming coffee from a clean cup. He works in a dirty environment; he asks for 'Dakika Moja' (one minute) of rest for himself, for his dirty hands and overalls. The cafe is reminiscent of coffee chain franchises that are becoming a trend in cities and towns across the African continent – a capitalist idea that came from the West. Everyday diet and hygiene practices can be linked to class and power: the poor man eats ugali, wholesome African food, albeit with dirty fingers, while the middle class washes their hands clean of the poor and feed on unhealthy toast and caffeine from pristine cups and plates. The labourer accepts the inevitability that he must suffer aches and pains in his day but he offers some form of resistance by demanding at least a minute of rest from his daily grind. For the middle-class person, however, a minute of rest is not a luxury but a given, less than it takes to indulge in a cup of coffee. *#CroissantRevolution* and *The Labourer* and their everyday realities of two different social groups signpost us to how quotidian practices can reflect domination and exploitation.

Ray uses the term 'everyday lifeworlds' to describe the many experiences constituted in the quotidian of life. He argues that everyday lifeworlds are 'spaces for interrogation, contestations and transgressions, as well as for unthinking conformity and painful succumbing to ruling ideas of one's time' (4). Taking a cue from Ray, the everyday can also be seen as the starting point for understanding marginalised people's relationship with political and cultural power. How for example, does a gay person handle the everyday challenges of politicians that tell them that homosexuality is un-African? How does one deal with everyday homophobia that is not limited to physical abuse but also verbal abuses and the look you get when people can sense your difference with respect to your sexuality?

The poetry of Romeo Oriogun provides some answers to these questions. In *Gay Boy Blues & Other Poems*, posted as a link on Facebook on 29 April

2017, we hear the daily experience of fear, suicidal thoughts, sexual longing and love:

> Most times,
> the pills are multi-coloured
> like rainbows after a storm,
> It bends me into a dog
> licking a hand in the spirit of forgiveness.
> This is how I beg my body
> for using it like a slave,
> for opening it to lonely nights in a brothel,
> for making it jump across songs,
> for giving it out like a cheap gift,
> …
> Look at me, I'm shameless like
> the wounds of Christ.

In this poem, as in much of his poetry, Oriogun uses everyday queer experience in Nigeria to make his social media followers understand the experience of being deemed abnormal. The speaker in this poem uses everyday imagery to show how hatred can drive queer Nigerians to the extreme. The queer person is not only the sexual Other; she exists in the realm of the marginalised – the sex worker, the marijuana smoker and others that the society deems unworthy. But away from the violence and the condemnation of queerness that permeate the offline world, social media allows for the full everydayness of being queer. Facebook and Instagram – platforms on which Oriogun is very active – are not tools of escapism or the epitome of the 'unreal'. They elucidate queer experience; real experience as well as longed for experience. His poem's account of being queer and living on the margin problematises what we tend to think as real and fictional. Poetry, especially on social media sites, is the perfect vehicle to convey affects. The experience of being suicidal is real, because the speaker faces homophobia almost every day, and he uses the social media to document and archive his experience.

The symbolism of Christ and the unicorn underlines the quotidian tensions between the spiritual and the mythical; between geo-histories and the contemporary. By referencing 'Christ' and a 'unicorn', Oriogun points us to the way in which queer Africans surmount everyday challenges. The unicorn is an alien in sub-Saharan Africa, as there is no society that I know of that has the myth of the unicorn, the way it exists in Oriental and Occidental mythologies. Oriogun's use of the unicorn can be read as the universality of digital culture, where people can easily borrow ideas and beliefs to suit their everyday requirements. In the digital age, the trope of the unicorn has been used to describe many things; a unicorn is an internet startup that is valued at over one billion US dollars; a unicorn is also an online picture of an attractive person that is available for dating, but the person can never be found in the real world. In the world of digital marketing, a unicorn is a young public relations genius who uses the internet to successfully market brands and is able to edit photographs and videos. The latter description aptly applies to Oriogun and his contemporaries. Oriogun's poetry on Instagram and Facebook captures the way in which social media allows for a true projection of the queer self in a way that may have been impossible in the non-digital space. The digital is real, because it is the site in which the day-to-day experience of queer African life can be showcased through videos and photographs, which can be easily edited to convey a message as intended by the poet. When compared to the freedom which digital technologies open up, it is perhaps the analogue suppressing queer life, represented by the physical space, that is less 'real'.

The Quotidian and Self-Fashioning

Although written in the analogue age, Erving Goffman's observation on how people consciously and unconsciously present themselves in social life to and within a group has some resonance in the digital age:

> Sometimes the individual will be calculating in his activity but be relatively unaware that this is the case. Sometimes he will intentionally and consciously express himself in a particular way, but chiefly because the tradition of his group or social status require this kind of expression and not because of any particular response (other than vague acceptance or approval) that is likely to be evoked from those impressed by the expression. (3)

Goffman envisions social life as a theatre, one in which we perform to others, and those we perform for are also performers, and these two entities constitute the public or the audience. Self-presentation on social media platforms can be seen as a performance and social media as the stage. The selfies and pictures documenting everyday life are at the nucleus of the digital cultural landscape; we often perform to the digital public by projecting an image that will strike a chord with the public. Nowadays, many Africans are accustomed to putting their entire lives online, and in the process they collect 'likes' and some screen approvals. What we present on social media is how we conceive of ourselves, the way we wish we were, which may be different from the way we live in the offline space. It can also be an extension of our offline self, or one which complements our offline self. On Instagram and Facebook, poetry is one of the means of self-fashioning for writers such as Romeo Oriogun. He frequently takes selfies of himself in ordinary places: in restaurants, at the fitness studio or going for a run. Oriogun is a digital native and in the age group that media professionals refer to as Generation Z. He shows us the way in which the quotidian in the digital space constitutes a starting point to imagine the life of Africans, including those who are not one hundred percent heterosexual, and who do not easily fit into a gender category. In pictures, videos and in literature he utilises aspects of life such as playing, working, eating, going to a gym, making love, drinking and every other aspect of dailiness – that we may think of as banal – to constitute a basis for understanding and for investigating. This is because when what we may consider as routine makes its way into the quotidian, poetry becomes an archive that normalises. It undermines the mechanism used to suppress desire while also directing us towards the day-to-day challenges facing those who are maligned for expressing their desire. While the everyday – due to its ritualistic and routine nature – is the natural space to normalise queer desire so that the prevailing view on social relations and human sexuality becomes less queerphobic, for the poetics of the quotidian as exemplified in Oriogun's writings, social media platforms are sites that enable self-affirmation for the queer Nigerian.

The quotidian for Oriogun is foregrounded in the creative writing and the self-portraits (selfies) that he posts every day. Poetry and selfies define his daily existence as a writer in the digital age, and his followers on social media cannot but see the two genres of the arts as essential to the image of a writer in a digital age. In the past, privacy was deemed sacrosanct in the writing trade. The luminaries of modern African literature such as Wole Soyinka, Nadine Gordimer and Ngũgĩ wa Thiong'o guard their personal space and readers only have access to them in public spaces such as book readings, conferences and literary festivals. No one knows who their children are or what they eat for dinner. But such a notion of the personal space as separated from the 'writerly' space is no longer the norm. The everydayness of social media and writers' intentions to display the daily tasks of their creative work alongside that of their private life means more openness with regard to the creative process. It demystifies literature without demystifying the figure of the writer. And just because the writer's private life is nowadays more on display than ever before, does not mean that readers no longer have respect for the creative craft or the writer. The opposite seems to be the case if one considers the hundreds of thousands of people that follow writers like Adichie, Shire, Oriogun and Wainaina on social media sites. People are as interested in these writers' personal life as they are in their literature. From an anecdotal survey on the number of followers some of today's writers attract on social media and the various offline platforms in which people are accessing African literature due to the visibility created by social media sites, it appears that this everyday openness brings African literature to more people than during the pre-internet era, in fact, to more people than ever before.

If social media platforms are sites where digital modernity is performed, it is because people learn new things from it every day. A Pew Research Centre's study by Elisa Shearer suggests that in America, social media surpasses print media as a news source. According to the studies Nyabola used in her important book *Digital Democracy, Analogue Politics: How the Internet Era is Transforming Politics in Kenya* (2018), Nigerians and Kenyans, like their American counterparts, view social media as a believable news source. If, as I have argued previously, arts and life often imitate each other on social media, one can contend that the everyday on social media sites, as exemplified in the quoted Facebook fictions and in the social media activism of the new generation of writers, also constitutes the site of enlightenment and of education for many Kenyans and Nigerians. To these African writers and other creative artists on social media platforms, the embedding of everyday objects in literature and photography, becomes an important means to foster empowerment and knowledge. They use the quotidian to teach the digital public the importance of acknowledging the commonplace and, at the same time, accepting the extraordinary. Both elements are surprisingly intertwined. Every day on social media constitutes a teachable moment and provides a new chance to become aware of the things that we take for granted and the ideas that we dismiss as the Other, which are someone else's everyday reality. Without the ordinary, the commonplace, the quotidian, there is no insight, and there is no art.

Conclusion: Connecting the Dots

In exploring African literature and allied creative works in cyberspace, we get to see the power structures in literature, within both local and global contexts. The discussion on literary networks provides a useful starting point in thinking about the dynamics of power: how it is conceived, how it is used and how it is structured. As scholars like Nyabola and Jagoda remind us: networks are not just useful metaphors for understanding global structures nor are they merely technological infrastructures that drive the information age, the world also operates as a series of interconnected, diverse communities of people. Some, of course, have more visibility than others. Within network thinking, the analysis of literary developments and the application of data from history and current affairs can be used to study what sociability in the context of African literature tells us about marginalisation and power. We can see the people who exerted influence in one way or another on African societies through their engagements with literature in particular, and the arts in general.

In *African Literature in the Digital Age*, we see the way in which some emerging and established voices are using literature that is published online to affirm their identity and literary heritage, by reprising the role of orature in the precolonial era through the use of new media technology. Unlike in the precolonial era, texts can now be stored and transmitted through different digital mediums. And texts are not merely spoken and written words, but they encompass audio-visual elements and are more immediate and interactive. With millions of Africans online on computers and with several millions more on mobile phones, we see how African literature in cyberspace is capitalising on this embrace of digital technologies. The literature that is coming out of the digital space suggests that many writers want a closer interaction between writers and readers of literature in a way that would have been impossible in the book age. Through literature, African cyberspace has become a site where all kinds of discussion and interaction between readers and writers can take place. Poetry and fiction in the online space become gathering points for the digital community to discuss shared history and contemporary experience. But unlike the community of old, the emerging community is virtual; writers, photographers, new media technologists and readers all gather on the internet 'cloud' through various digital mediums and these individuals are based in different locations across the globe. People can log onto cyberspace at different times to access and contribute to the same texts, and texts are susceptible to changes (small or large scale) and so these gatherings complicate ideas of 'space/place' (here) as well as 'space/exploration' (out there). African literature in cyberspace is, at times, a collaborative project between writers, technologists, editors and readers. And this collaborative model of aesthetic production grounded in technological innovation and disseminated virtually engages ongoing transformations in practices and definitions of Africanness. I analysed this collaboration as impacting on the nature of the African text.

While the Pan-Africanist W.E.B. Du Bois famously said that 'the problem of the Twentieth Century is the problem of the colour line,' W.J.T. Mitchell argued that 'the problem of the twenty-first century is the problem of the image' (2). Several African writers and artists see Africa at the core of the image discourse. In Chapter Three, we hear Chimamanda Ngozi Adichie warning against the 'danger of the single story' when it comes to Africa. She uses the example of a real person – an Ivy-League professor who refuses to believe some of her middle class fictional characters – as an embodiment of the way in which many outside of Africa see the continent as a place where everybody is poor and how literature should perpetuate this stereotype. Wainaina's famous online essay for Granta, *How to Write About Africa*, likewise attacks this stereotypical image of Africa: 'Taboo subjects: ordinary domestic scenes, love between Africans (unless a death is involved), references to African writers or intellectuals, mention of school-going children who are not suffering from yaws or Ebola fever or female genital mutilation.'

For several of these writers, the single story about Africa is a legacy of a Conradian world view about a 'dark continent' that is filled with abject poverty and want, and while the internet has provided an opportunity to spread the many facets of Africa in the twenty-first century beyond the familiar stereotypes, the image of Africa (in these writers' view) is nonetheless similar to many verbal and photographic descriptions provided by earlier novelists, journalists and anthropologists. As Macharia and Mwangi argue:

> The image of Africa seems locked in time, occupying what Johannes Fabian terms 'all chronic' time. Fabian's *Time and the Other: How Anthropology Makes Its Object* (2002) is a critique of the ideas that anthropologists are 'here and now', their objects of study are 'there and then', and that the 'other' exists in a time not contemporary with that of the West. (12)

This observation is important; on Facebook, Twitter, blog posts, listservs and in internet chat-rooms, writers regularly use fiction and real-life experiences to disabuse African literature's preoccupation with replying back to many of the negative stereotypes of Africa and Africans that they have encountered in literature and in the media. Social networking platforms open the possibility to address an African digital public, and to provide evidence of Africa's multi-faceted stories as a counter to the single story. I have pointed out that online short stories and poetry as well as writers' social network status updates are part of these cultural mechanisms, in which the conversation – foregrounded on creative writings – is mainly between Africans, although non-Africans can join in.

While it focuses on the freedom that the digital space provides African writers, *African Literature in the Digital Age* also recognises that the online African space is being produced by the global flux of capitalism, in which the unconnected are in danger of being overlooked and misrepresented. Some members of a new generation are preoccupied with using literature to present the African middle classes to the outside world, which is often too willing to believe what Adichie sees as 'the single story' about Africa. This book, therefore, sees an important need to examine African digital literature's obsession with telling the middle-class African story, because some of the fictional narratives can be read as pathologising people who are not educated and who in the process are not part of Africa's cyber-community. We can infer that some of the online short stories that I have examined suggest that some writers are failing to recognise their own investment in a 'single story' of a middle class which, in looking to a Western model, distances itself from poorer people within the same country and continent. In the process, African literature online may be in danger of essentialising the African stories; the stories of middle-class Africans are given more visibility while those of less privileged Africans follow the familiar single-story trope.

The intersectional link between class and sexuality is foregrounded by body politics. Writers and artists alike have continuously used literature and the creative arts to inscribe society's point of view and their own personal agenda on the African body. *African Literature in the Digital Age* directs readers to the way in which marginalised bodies – notably queer Africans and African women – have been inscribed upon by writers, by society and by both the print and new media machine. The human body in literature can arguably be read as a machine and the machine can also be read as performing the role of the human body. As Giles Deleuze and Felix Guattari have pointed out, bodies humanise the machine and the machine in turn incorporates humanity. With regard to techno-bodies, a rough historical map highlights how African literature has responded to the politics surrounding non-straight bodies and to women who do not conform to society's sexual expectations.

From the short stories, poems, photographs and essays that are being posted in cyberspace, we can conclude that some of the emerging voices are using literature in the online space as a way of taking a somewhat provocative stance on taboo subjects, especially with regard to issues like queerness and female sexuality. Reasons for this audacious and welcome development include the fact that some of these writers see the online writing space as representing 'critical and tonal shifts' that allow them to 'intervene into the politics and poetics of what Lauren Berlant terms "stuckness" to posit new and alternative social imaginaries, rich spaces and resources … to inhabit and re-think our collective social and political lives and practices' (see Keguro Macharia and Wambui Mwangi). In addition, African literature in cyberspace has the potential to bypass the state and the religious authorities. On cultural issues such as gender and sexuality, clerics and political leaders wield powerful influence over many Nigerians and Kenyans in the physical space, who, as a result, rarely oppose the discourses expressed by those in position of authority. But literature in the digital space, and the discussions that come about through online writing, provide a counter to conservative and distorted views on African sexuality and history. It provides a voice for repressed identities in all their simple and complicated forms. This is because social media and weblogs are becoming 'real' spaces to discuss matters deemed too provocative, too dissident and too immoral to broach in ordinary and real public spaces.

While the older generations of writers may not have outrightly vocalised their support for the recognition of these bodies or fought for gay rights on the continent, their creative writings have aptly captured the story of these marginalised bodies. An analysis of texts published in print and in cyberspace can provide us with the starting point that non-straight Africans are arguably central to our understanding of African politics, because as a response to that politics, literature has to continuously look at shifting sexual meanings and erotic choices. What has changed in a new media age compared to the printed texts is the growing outspoken support for gay rights, within and outside of literature, by some emerging voices. These writers, while not ignoring the international queer connectedness in cyberspace, are embracing the local uniqueness of same-sex desire in their creative writings and their social media presences. The digital is helping to enable the outing of a submerged African personhood. This is because writers debunk some of the myths surrounding the queer African's body. They also problematise African sexual history in so many ways; so much so that the queer person may after all not be a by-product of colonialism and neocolonialism, but authentically African, with a strong connection to the continent's unfolding history. However, Africa is a complex continent and the internet reflects that complexity by allowing a polyphony of literary voices to speak. Writers and readers do not necessarily look at intimacy from the same angle. It is too easy to romanticise every young African writer and reader, posting on Facebook Notes and 'musing' on African sexuality in the digital space, as a dreamy-eyed radical when it comes to the issues of sexuality and gender. The reality is that the internet can also be a tool for contemporary conservatism.

Furthermore, the emerging creative writings unearth previously unseen patterns of sexual violence. This point cannot be overstressed: while the near ubiquity of mobile phones and internet cafés in Nigeria and Kenya means that acquiring and publishing online information has never been easier, increased access to consuming and producing digital information raises new challenges for those fictional characters who use the internet for sexual experimentation. Shailja Patel's online drama *Last Word: Caught in the Act*, and the short stories of Crispin Oduobuk-Mfon Abasi and Eusebius McKaiser, illustrate the danger that the internet poses for gays and lesbians in Africa, especially when they use the internet to partake in cyber-activities. Such creative writings can be read as 'coming out' fictional narratives made possible by the digital space. They also represent the dangers facing queers within the online and offline space and the fictional digital characters can be read as mirroring the real-life experiences of Africans. However, these stories also reveal that there is an under-representation of poor and working-class queer characters in much of the literature that is being published online. Gay and lesbian characters are very often portrayed as well-to-do urbanites with disposable income and who are able to move seamlessly between African and non-African spaces. The lifestyle of most of these fictional characters is not too different from that of transnational middle-class and highly educated writers of the new media age.

New digital fiction and poetry indicate that literary studies need to pay attention to the ways in which some Africans are using the internet to mobilise and give voices to gays, lesbians and female sex workers, people that contemporary history has ignored. For example, while some members of the older generation of writers see prostitution as a problem created by colonial modernity, some new voices are using literature to reflect on the complexities of the libidinal. Several of these online creative writings suggest that prostitution objectifies African women, but acknowledge that, due to the need to survive in a capitalist postcolonial Africa, many young women see sex work as the quickest way to escape poverty and to gain a foothold in a male-dominated African society. Hence, the libidinal economy that demeans women also, ironically, becomes a tool towards financial security and of empowerment. Writings such as Chika Unigwe's show how African literature in the digital age can represent the true nature of the sex market and how some writers are becoming advocates for marginalised sex workers. In the process, online African literature becomes a potential agent for changing current attitude to sex work and sex workers.

At the same time, online creative writings also emphasise that African women have a sexual culture that is not reliant on prostitution and show us that African women's sexual history is not one of subjugation; women of all backgrounds enjoy sex for sex's sake and the modern girl some writers love to despise is no different from sexually confident women of the precolonial era. New erotic and sexually explicit digital literature claims African women's realities to be as economically productive and libidinally active as men.

By ending with an analysis of the quotidian in the context of literature that is produced and commented upon on social media, this book draws the reader's attention to the near total neglect of the ordinary and the commonplace by

Africanists. The quotidian is often the foundation for much of Africa's artistic endeavours. Everyday objects are the tools with which writers produce fictional narratives and poems: Ujunwa going to the airport in Adichie's *Jumping Monkey Hill*, the speaker in Kamiru's poem *Nightdresses* applying a lipstick and wearing false nails – these are all routine acts that carry poignant messages. Poems and songs are carved out of everyday emotions such as crying, eating and praying. Many of the television and cinematic productions in Kenya and Nigeria speak to the everyday lived experience of Africans. Therefore, the quotidian deserves the same level of seriousness that we attach to the phenomenal, not only because it is the stuff of the popular but also because we cannot fully comprehend African humanity without it. How do we articulate why people laugh, cry, love and work? These are not mere human instincts and basic needs; people put a lot of thought into planning their daily routine. Monumental events in people's life are brought about by everyday actions and thoughts. Social media platforms provide the ideal platform to observe everyday knowledge production. Writers use the digital space to produce literature that comments on socio-political developments. Readers, in turn, build meanings out of these everyday engagements. When Pius Adesanmi died in March 2019, and Binyavanga Wainaina passed away three months later in June, thousands of their followers mourned their deaths on social media and in offline locations. Both men used the digital space to help young Africans understand the implications of everyday socio-cultural and socio-political developments. In their postings, they used everyday language in addition to African proverbs and literature to engage the digital African public. In the process, they created a strong bond between themselves and their followers. Like many writers of their generation, they moved intellectual labour from the lofty heights of the ivory tower and newspapers, to the easily accessible, everyday platforms of Facebook, YouTube and Twitter.

The differences in attitude across generations, the tensions and perhaps disjunctions that *Africa Literature in the Digital Age* has discussed, speak to the complexity of Africa, to the continent's many stories and the different ways in which each individual writer and reader conceptualises their society. They heed Adichie's warning against the danger of the single African story. The Adichie who privileges middle-class characters in her creative writing is also the woman who speaks and writes about the marginalisation that women and the poor experience worldwide. Although I have signposted the readers of this book to the middle-class consciousness of creative writers and their crafts, I have also shown that being middle class has not made them less relevant because they are aware of their class privileges. Many of them are also champions of sexual and gender rights and their stories show that it is not un-African to talk about the pleasure of sex and that class consciousness is in not un-African. What *African Literature in the Digital Age* has tried to do is to unpack the complexity of the African story, to highlight the many African stories and show how online literature is the (cyber)space where technology, class and sexuality intersect. What African literature in the digital age is able to do is to bring these different discourses out into the open and to provide those who are genuinely interested in Africa, its past and present, with new threads to engage and understand the continent.

Bibliography

Abasi, Crispin Oduobuk-Mfon. 'Two-Step Skip'. *Outliers: Theorizing (Homo)Eroticism in Africa: A Collection of Essays and Creative Work on Sexuality in Africa*, IRN-Africa, 2008, pp. 11–16. Pdf file.
Abdul-Jabbar, Omale Allen. 'Little Sailor Boy: A Poem for Mama'. *Africanwriter.com*, 11 April 2016, https://www.africanwriter.com/little-sailor-boy-a-poem-for-mama-by-omale-allen-abdul-jabbar/. Accessed 15 July 2020.
Abimbola, Wande. *Ifa Will Mend Our Broken World: Thoughts on Yoruba Religion and Culture in Africa and the Diaspora*. Aim, 1997.
Abiodun, Rowland. 'African Aesthetics'. *Journal of Aesthetic Education*, vol. 35, no. 4, Winter 2001, pp. 15–23.
Abrahams, Yvette. 'Your Silence Will Not Protect You'. *Outliers: Theorizing (Homo) Eroticism in Africa: A Collection of Essays and Creative Work on Sexuality in Africa*, IRN-Africa, 2008, pp. 30–45. Pdf file.
Achebe, Chinua. *No Longer at Ease*, Heinemann, 1960.
—. *Things Fall Apart*. Heinemann, (1958) 1990.
Adebayo, D.O, I.B. Udegbe, and A.M. Sunmola. 'Gender, Internet Use, and Sexual Behavior Orientation Among Young Nigerians'. *CyberPsychology and Behavior*, vol. 9, no. 6, 2006, pp. 742–752.
Adeeko, Adeleke. *Arts of Being Yoruba: Divination, Allegory, Tragedy, Proverb, Panegyric*. Indiana University Press, 2017.
Adenekan, Shola. 'New Voices, New Media: Class Consciousness, Sex and Politics in Online Nigerian and Kenyan Poetry'. *Postcolonial Text*, vol. 11, no. 1, 2016, pp. 1–21.
—. 'A Review of Koleade Odutola's Diaspora and Imagined Nationality: USA-Africa Dialogue and Cyberframing Nigerian Nationhood'. *Africa*, vol. 84, 2014, pp. 350–351.
—. *Nigerian Colonial History*. National Theatre (UK) programme for the staging of Wole Soyinka's *Death and the King's Horseman*, 2009.
Adenekan, Shola, and Helen Cousins. 'Class Online: Representations of African Middle-Class Identity'. *Postcolonial Text*, vol. 9, no. 3, 2014, pp. 1–15.
Adichie, Chimamanda Ngozi. Instagram post with a YouTube video of Bill Withers singing 'Lean on Me'. *Instagram*, 5 April 2020, https://www.instagram.com/p/B-m84Togh7R/. Accessed 15 July 2020
—. A video clip of the author dancing before the portrait of Andy Warhol on Instagram. Instagram, 28 March 2019, https://www.instagram.com/p/BvkUtgwH7eS/. Accessed 15 July 2020.
—. *Americanah*. Fourth Estate, 2013.
—. 'Birdsong'. *New Yorker Magazine*, 13 September 2010, https://www.newyorker.com/magazine/2010/09/20/birdsong-2. Accessed 15 July 2020.

—. 'The danger of a single story'. *TED,* July 2009, https://www.ted.com/talks/chimamanda_ngozi_adichie_the_danger_of_a_single_story/transcript?language=en. Accessed 15 July 2020.

—. 'Jumping Monkey Hill'. *Granta,* 2 October 2006, https://granta.com/jumping-monkey-hill/. Accessed 15 July 2020

—. *Half of a Yellow Sun.* Knopf/Anchor, 2006.

—. 'Life During Wartime: Sierra Leone, 1997'. *The New Yorker,* 12 June 2006, https://www.newyorker.com/magazine/2006/06/12/sierra-leone-1997. Accessed 15 July 2020.

—. *Purple Hibiscus.* Alongquin Books, 2003.

Afolabi, Segun. 'The Tufiakwa Syndrome'. *Afolabi – Peace of Mind* blog, 7 September 2008, https://afolabi-pieceofmind.blogspot.com/2008/09/tufiakwa-syndrome.html?fbclid=IwAR3QtUJQul6UGUf8YORNAbJ7oExprpjUWn5589jSJvBggRPoxStsWiJnY5Y. Accessed 15 July 2020.

African Development Bank. 'The Middle of the Pyramid: Dynamics of the Middle Class in Africa'. *Africa Development Bank: Market Brief,* 20 April 2011, https://www.afdb.org/en/documents/document/market-brief-the-middle-of-the-pyramid-dynamics-of-the-middle-class-in-africa-23582. Accessed 15 July 2020.

Aidoo, Ama Ata. *Our Sister Killjoy or Reflections From a Black-Eyed Squint.* Longman Group Limited, 1966.

Aigbokhan, Ben. 'Poverty, Growth and Inequality in Nigeria: Executive Summary'. *African Economic Research Consortium,* 2000, https://pdfs.semanticscholar.org/a545/3778c613f3fbef90fbc027a9fd99b1f22ded.pdf. Accessed 15 July 2020.

Aina, Tade. 'Twirling the beads of grief … For Payo'. *USA-Africa Dialogue,* 16 March 2019.

Ajayi, Dami. 'A Poem for Raliat'. Instagram, 3 November 2018, https://www.instagram.com/p/BptxTlvlFfR/. Accessed 15 July 2020.

Ajayi, J.F.A. *Christian Missions in Nigeria 1841–1891: The Making of a New Elite,* Northwestern University Press, 1969.

Akede Eko. Readers' letters for issue for the week 15 August 1929. *Akede Eko,* National Archives of Nigeria, University of Ibadan branch.

Akeh, Afam. 'Ancient Water and They Talk Into the Silence—Two Poems'. Facebook, 18 August 2015, www.facebook/afam.akeh. Accessed 30 July 2019.

Akinyemi, Akintunde. *Yoruba Royal Poetry: A Socio-Historical Exposition and Annotated Translation.* Chancellor College, University of Malawi and Bayreuth University, 2004.

Alexander, Bryant Keith. 'Reflections, Riffs and Remembrances: The Black Queer Studies in the Millennium Conference'. *Callaloo,* vol. 23, no. 4, 2000, pp. 1285–1305.

Ali, Richard. Email conversation. *Ederi* listserv, 31 May 2012.

Amir-Ebrahimi, Masserat. 'Performances in Everyday Life and the Rediscovery of the Self in Iranian Weblogs'. *Bad Jens,* September 2004, http://www.badjens.com/rediscovery.html. Accessed 15 July 2020.

Amutabi, Maurice N. 'Media Boom in Kenya and Celebrity Galore'. *Journal of African Cultural Studies,* vol. 25, no. 1, Special Issue: New Media Entrepreneurs and Changing Styles of Public Communication in Africa (March), 2013, pp. 14–29.

Anike *aka* Cosmic Yoruba. 'Romance novels exploring pre-colonial love and sexuality'. *This is Africa.me*, 2 June 2014, https://thisisafrica.me/lifestyle/romances-explore-pre-colonial-love-sexuality/. Accessed 15 July 2020.
Arndt, Susan. 'Introduction'. *Intertextuality: Dialogues in Motion*, BIGSAS Festival of African Diasporic Literatures, 2013, pp. 1–8.
Atta, Sefi. 'Glory'. *African Writing Online*, vol. 4, no. 1, 2008, http://www.african-writing.com/four/sefiattah.htm. Accessed 15 July 2020.
Attwood, Feona. 'Sexed Up: Theorizing the Sexualization of Culture'. *Sexualities*, vol. 9, no. 1, 2006, pp. 77–94. Pdf file.
Azodo, Ada Uzoamaka, and Maureen Ngozi Eke. 'African Literature: Survey of the Historical and Geographical Scope of Gender and Sexuality in African Literature'. *Gender and Sexuality in African Literature and Film*, edited by Ada Uzoamaka Azodo and Maureen Ngozi Eke, African World Press, 2007, pp. 17–23.
Azuah, Unoma N. *Sky-High Flames*. Publish America, 2005.
—. 'Home is Where the Heart Hurts'. *Sentinel Poetry Online #28*, March 2005. http://www.sentinelpoetry.org.uk/magonline0305/page15.html. Accessed 15 July 2020.
Bannerji, Himani. *Thinking Through: Essays on Feminism, Marxism, and Anti-Racism*. Women's Press, 1995.
Barber, Karin. *A History of African Popular Culture*, Cambridge University Press, 2018.
—. *The Anthropology of Texts, Persons and Publics: Oral and Written Culture in Africa and Beyond*. Cambridge University Press, 2007.
—. 'Literature in Yoruba: Poetry and Prose; Traveling Theater and Modern Drama'. *The Cambridge History of African and Caribbean literature, Volume 1*, edited by F. Abiola Irele and Simon Gikandi, Cambridge University Press, 2004, pp. 357–379.
—. 'Time, Space, and Writing in Three Colonial Yoruba Novels'. *The Yearbook of English Studies*, vol. 27, 1997, pp. 108–129.
—. 'Literacy, Improvisation and the Public in Yoruba Popular Theatre'. *The Pressure of the Text: Orality, Texts and the Telling of Tales*, edited by Stewart Brown, Birmingham University, African Studies Series, no. 4, 1995, pp. 6–28.
—. 'Multiple Discourses in Yoruba Oral Literature'. *Bulletin of the John Rylands University Library of Manchester*, vol. 7, no. 3, Manchester University Library, Autumn 1991, pp. 11–24.
Bassnett, Susan, and Harish Trivedi, editors. *Post-colonial Translation: Theory and Practice*. Routledge, 1999.
Bell, David, and Joanne Hollow, editors. *Ordinary Lifestyles: Popular Media, Consumption and Taste*. Open University Press/McGraw-Hill Education, 2005.
Bennett, David. 'Libidinal Economy, Prostitution and Consumer Culture'. *Textual Practice*, vol. 24, no. 1, 2009, pp. 93–121.
Berger, Roger. 'The Place of (and Place in) the Anglophone African Short Story'. *The Tales We Tell: Perspectives on the Short Story*, edited by Barbara Lounsberry, Susan Lohafer, Mary Rohrberger, Stephen Pett and R.C. Feddersen, Greenwood Press, 1998, pp. 73–81.
Bhabha, Homi K. *The Location of Culture*. Routledge, 1994.
Bolter, J.D. *Writing Space: The Computer, Hypertext, and the History of Writing*. Lawrence Erlbaum, 1991.

Bown, Lalage. 'The Development of African Prose-Writing in English: A Perspective'. *Perspectives on African Literature: Selections from the Proceedings of the Conference on African Literature held at the University of Ife 1968*, edited by Christopher Heywood, Heinemann in Association with University of Ife Press, 1971, pp. 33–48.

Boyd, Danah. 'Viewing American class divisions through Facebook and MySpace'. *Apophenia* blog essay, 24 June 2007, http://www.danah.org/papers/essays/ClassDivisions.html. Accessed 15 July 2020.

Boykin, Keith. *Beyond the Down Low: Sex, Lies, and Denial in Black America*. Carroll & Graff, 2005.

Brown, Stewart, editor. *Kiss & Quarrel: Yoruba/English, Strategies of Mediation*. University of Birmingham, (2000) 2013.

Bryson, Donna. 'A Novel Idea for Spreading Literature in Africa: The Cellphone'. *Christian Science Monitor*, 9 May 2013, https://www.csmonitor.com/World/Africa/2013/0509/A-novel-idea-for-spreading-literature-in-Africa-The-cellphone. Accessed 15 July 2020.

Bryson, Mary. 'Conjuring the quotidian'. *Journal of Gay and Lesbian Issues in Education*, vol. 2, no. 4, 2005, pp. 83–92.

Bryson, Mary, Lori MacIntosh, Sharalyn Jordan, and Hui-Ling Lin. 'Virtually Queer? Homing Devices, Mobility, and Un/Belongings'. *Canadian Journal of Communication*, vol. 31, no. 4, 2006, pp. 791–814.

Bucholz, Sabine, and Mahnfred Jahn. 'Space'. *Routledge Encyclopaedia of Narrative Theory*, edited by David Herman et al., Routledge, 2005, pp. 551–555.

Burke, Martin J. *The Conundrum of Class: Public Discourse on the Social Order in America*. University of Chicago Press, 1995.

Butler, Judith. *Gender: Feminism and the Subversion of Identity*. Routledge, (1990) 1999, available at https://selforganizedseminar.files.wordpress.com/2011/07/butler-gender_trouble.pdf. Accessed 15 July 2020.

Casanova, Pascale. *The World Republic of Letters*. Translated by Malcolm DeBevoise, Harvard University Press, 2007.

Castells, Manuel. *The Rise of the Network Society*. Blackwell Publishers Ltd, (1996) 2000.

—. *The Power of Identity*, Blackwell Publishers Ltd, 2000.

Chan, Annie Hau-nung. 'The Dynamics of Motherhood Performance: Hong Kong's Middle Class Working Mothers On- and Off-Line'. *Sociological Research Online*, vol. 13, no. 4 (4), http://www.socresonline.org.uk/13/4/4.html. Accessed 15 July 2020.

Chikezie, Ella. Untitled Instagram Post. Instagram, 14 February 2019, https://www.instagram.com/ellawritesnaija/. Accessed 15 July 2020.

Chodak, Szymon. 'Social Stratification is Sub-Saharan Africa'. *Canadian Journal of African Studies*, vol. 7, no. 3, Special Issue: Social Stratification in Africa, 1973, pp. 401–417.

CNN African Voices. 'Chimamanda Adichie: Powerful Words'. *African Voices*, 13 July 2019, http://edition.cnn.com/2009/WORLD/africa/07/12/chimamanda.adichie/index.html. Accessed 15 July 2020.

Cohen, Anthony P. *The Symbolic Construction of Community*. Routledge, 1993.

Cole, Jennifer, and Lynn M. Thomas, editors. *Love in Africa*. University of Chicago Press, 2009.

Cole, Teju. 'Modern Girls'. *Qarrtsiluni*, 21 January 2008. https://qarrtsiluni.com/2008/01/21/modern-girls/. Accessed 15 July 2020.
—. *Every Day Is For The Thief.* Cassava Republic, 2007.
Collymore, Wambui W.K., and Joe Kiragu. '#CroissantRevolution'. *Koroga*, 29 July 2013, https://koroga-blog-blog.tumblr.com/image/56773550547. Accessed 15 July 2020.
Collymore, Wambui W.K., and Wambui Mwangi. 'Nightdresses'. *Koroga*, 1 September 2013, http://koroga-blog-blog.tumblr.com/post/59968289620/nightdresses. Accessed 15 July 2020.
Conrad, Joseph. *Heart of Darkness.* William Blackwood and Sons, (1899) 1902.
Confino, Alon. *The Nation as a Local Metaphor: Wurttemberg, Imperial Germany, and National Memory, 1871–1918.* University of North Carolina Press, 1997.
Coombe, Rosemary. 'Publicity Rights and Political Aspiration: Mass Culture, Gender Identity, and Democracy'. *New England Law Review*, vol. 26, 1992, pp. 1221–1280.
Cover, Rob. 'Queer with Class: Absence of the Third World Sweatshop in Lesbian/Gay Discourse and a Rearticulation of Materialist Queer Theory'. *Ariel: A Review of International English Literature*, vol. 30, no. 3, 2003, pp. 29–48.
Cullen, Countee. 'Heritage'. *The Portable Harlem Renaissance Reader*, edited by David Levering Lewis, 1994, pp. 243–244.
Cutler, Richard. 'Technologies, Relations, and Selves'. *Communication and Cyberspace: Social Interaction in an Electronic Environment*, edited by Lance Strate, Ronald Jacobson and Stephanie Gibson, Hampton Press, 1996, pp. 317–333.
Dean, Jodi. *Blog Theory: Feedback and Capture in the Circuits of Drive.* Wiley, 2010.
Deleuze, Giles and Felix Gauttari. *Anti-Oedipus: Capitalism and Schizophrenia.* Minnesota University Press, 1983.
Diabate, Naminata. *Naked Agency: Genital Cursing and Biopolitics in Africa.* Duke University Press, 2020.
Diawara, Manthia. 'Toward a Regional Imaginary of Africa'. *The Cultures of Globalization*, edited by Fredric Jameson and Masao Miyoshi, Duke University Press, 1998, pp. 103–124.
Dimock, Wai Chee, and Michael Gilmore, editors. *Rethinking Class: Literary Studies and Social Formations.* Columbia University Press, 1994.
Doering, Heike. 'Communities and Citizenship: Paths for Engagement'. *Beyond Current Horizons,* December 2008, available at https://issuu.com/gfbertini/docs/communities_and_citizenship_-_paths_for_engagement. Accessed 15 July 2020.
Dolby, Nadine. 'Popular Culture and Public Space in Africa: The Possibilities of Cultural Citizenship'. *African Studies Review*, vol. 49, no. 3, 2006, pp. 31–47.
Du Bois, William Edward Burghardt. *The problem of the 20th century is the problem of the color line.* W.E.B. Du Bois Papers (MS 312), Special Collections and University Archives, University of Massachusetts Amherst Libraries, 1868–1963. http://credo.library.umass.edu/view/full/mums312-b216-i004. Accessed 15 July 2020.
Dumitrescu, Irina. 'Heel Turns: The History of Modern Celebrity'. *Times Literary Supplement*. 20 September 2019, no. 6077, pp. 3–5.
Dyson, Freeman J. *The Sun, the Genome, and the Internet.* Cambridge University Press, 1999.
Edelstein, Dan, and Chloe Edmondson. *Networks of Enlightenment: Digital Approaches to the Republic of Letters.* Oxford University Press, 2019.

Egejuru, Phanuel. 'Shailja Patel: Rebel and Renaissance Woman'. *Pambazuka*, 14 May 2009, http://www.pambazuka.org/en/category/books/56260. Accessed 15 July 2020.

Ehrenreich, Barbara. *Fear of Falling: The Inner Life of the Middle Class*. Harper Perennial, 1990.

Ekine, Sokari. 'Contesting Narratives of Queer Africa'. *Queer African Reader*, edited by Sokari Ekine and Hakima Abbas, Pambazuka Press, 2013, pp. 78–92.

—. 'Scammers Targeting Gay Men in Ghana'. *Black Looks*, 14 September 2009, http://www.blacklooks.org/2009/09/scammers_targeting_gay_men_in_ghana_kenya/. Accessed 15 July 2020.

Ekine, Sokari, and Hakima Abbas, editors. *Queer African Reader*, Pambazuka Press, 2013.

Ekwensi, Cyprian. *Jagua Nana*. Penguin Classics, (1961) 2018.

Emenyonu, Emmanuel. *Cyprian Ekwensi*. Evan Bros, 1974.

Epprecht, Marc. 'Sexuality, Africa, History'. *American Historical Review*, vol. 114, no. 5, December 2009, pp. 1258–1272.

Equiano, Olaudah. 'The Interesting Narrative of the Life of Olaudah Equiano, Or Gustavus Vassa, The African Written By Himself'. The Project Gutenberg, 17 March 2005,
https://www.gutenberg.org/files/15399/15399-h/15399-h.htm
. Accessed 31 July 2020. Originally published on 24 March 1789.

Fihlani, Pumza. 'South Africa's Lesbians Fear 'Corrective Rape''. *BBC News Online*, 30 June 2011, https://www.bbc.co.uk/news/world-africa-13908662. Accessed 15 July 2020.

Fiorini, Reinaldo, Damian Hattingh, Ally Maclaren, Bill Russo, and Ade Sun-Basorun. 'Africa's Growing Giant: Nigeria's New Retail Economy'. McKinsey, December 2013, https://www.mckinsey.com/business-functions/marketing-and-sales/our-insights/africas-growing-giant-nigerias-new-retail-economy. Accessed 15 July 2020.

Forsey, Jane. 'Appraising the Ordinary: Tensions in Everyday Aesthetics'. *Proceedings of the European Society for Aesthetics*, vol. 5, 2013, pp. 237–245.

Frank, Barbara E. 'Field Research and Making Objects Speak'. *African Arts*, vol. 40, Ceramics in Africa, 2007, pp. 13–17.

Foucault, Michel. *The Care of the Self: The History of Sexuality, Volume 3*. Random House, 1988.

—. 'Of Other Spaces'. *Diacritics*, vol. 16, no. 1, 1986, pp. 22–27.

—. *The History of Sexuality, Volume 1*. Penguin, 1981.

—. *Discipline and Punish: The Birth of the Prison*. Translated by Alan Sheridan, Allen Lane, 1977.

Furniss, Graham. 'Hausa Creative Writing in the 1930s'. *Readings in African Popular Fiction*, edited by Stephanie Newell, The International African Institute, 2002, pp. 11–17.

Garland, Muthoni. 'Odour of Fate'. *Storymoja*, 8 September 2008, http://storymojaafrica.co.ke/main/2008/09/odour-of-fate/. Accessed 15 July 2020.

Gbolahan, Rasaq Malik. Untitled Facebook Post. Facebook, 19 February 2019, 9.00am, https://www.facebook.com/rasaq.m.gbolahan. Accessed 15 July 2020.

—. Untitled Facebook Post. Facebook, 8 December 2018, 4.25pm., https://www.facebook.com/rasaq.m.gbolahan. Accessed 15 July 2020.

—. 'FOR OSHOYIMIKA (WOLE SOYINKA) @ 84'. Facebook, 13 July 2018, https://www.facebook.com/rasaq.m.gbolahan/posts/1867558863267318. Accessed 15 July 2020.
—. 'Your Love'. *The New Black Magazine*, 15 July 2014, http://thenewblackmagazine.com/view.aspx?index=3328. Accessed 15 July 2020.
—. 'Kofi'. Facebook, 23 September 2013, https://www.facebook.com/rasaq.m.gbolahan/posts/1561211800568694. Accessed 15 July 2020.
Giddens, Anthony. *The Transformation of Intimacy: Sexuality, Love, and Eroticism in Modern Societies*. Stanford University Press, 1992.
Gikandi, Simon. 'The Work of the Book in the Age of Electronic Reproduction'. *PMLA*, vol. 127, no. 2, March 2012, pp. 201–211.
Gilroy, Paul. *The Black Atlantic: Modernity and Double Consciousness*. Verso, 1993.
Goffman, Ervin. *The Presentation of Self in Everyday Life*. Pelican Books, 1971.
Gomez, Antonio Garcia. 'Competing Narratives, Gender and Threaded Identity in Cyberspace'. *Journal of Gender Studies*, vol. 19, 2009, pp. 27–42.
Gyimah, Miriam C. 'Dangerous Encounters with the West: Gender, Sexuality, and Power in Ama Ata Aidoo's Our Sister Killjoy'. *Gender and Sexuality in African Literature and Film*, edited by Ada Uzoamaka Azodo and Maureen Ngozi Eke, Africa World Press, 2007, pp. 213–228.
Habermas, Jürgen. *The Cultural Transformation of the Public Sphere*. Translated by Thomas Burger with Frederick Lawrence, MIT Press, 1992.
Hall, Stuart. 'The Meaning of New Times'. *Stuart Hall: Critical Dialogues in Cultural Studies*, edited by David Morley and Kuan-Hsing Chen, Routledge, 1996, pp. 223–237.
—. 'The Question of Modern Identity'. *Modernity and Its Futures*, edited by Stuart Hall, David Held and Tony McGrew, Polity Press, 1992, pp. 275–77.
Hanson, Clare. 'Introduction'. *Re-reading the Short Story*, edited by Clare Hanson, Palgrave Macmillan, 1989, pp. 1–9.
Haraway, Donna. 'A Cyborg Manifesto: Science, Technology, and Socialist-Feminism in the Late Twentieth Century'. *Simians, Cyborgs, and Women: The Reinvention of Nature*, Routledge, 1991, pp. 149–181.
Harpold, Terry. 'Dark Continents: A Critique of Internet Metageographies'. *Postmodern Culture*, January 1999, http://pmc.iath.virginia.edu/text-only/issue.199/9.2harpold.txt. Accessed 15 July 2020.
Hetata, Sherif. 'Dollarization, Fragmentation, and God'. *Cultures of Globalization*, edited by Fredric Jameson and Masao Miyoshi, Duke University Press, 1998, pp. 273–285.
Hoad, Neville. *African Intimacies: Race, Homosexuality and Globalization*. U of Minnesota P, 2007.
Hosseini, Bahareh. 'Binyavanga Wainaina and Diriye Osman - The London Session'. YouTube, uploaded by Bahar Films, 4 November 2014, https://www.youtube.com/watch?v=tSfoDfPcbI4. Accessed 15 July 2020.
Internet World Stats. 'Internet Users Statistics for Africa'. *Internetworldstats.com*, 31 March 2019, https://www.internetworldstats.com/stats1.htm. Accessed 15 July 2020.
Islam, Gazi. 'Virtual Speakers, Virtual Audiences: Agency, Audience and Constraint

in an Online Chat Community'. *Dialectical Anthropology*, vol. 30, no. 1–2, 2006, pp. 71–89.

Iwuanyanwu, Obiwu. 'Madding Crowd: For Esiaba Irobi and Kofi Awoonor'. Facebook, 22 September 2013, https://www.facebook.com/obiwu/posts/10151942885136155. Accessed 15 July 2020.

Jackson, Stevi. 'Heterosexual Hierarchies: A Commentary on Class and Sexuality'. *Sexualities*, vol. 14, no. 1, 2011, pp. 12–20.

Jagoda, Patrick. Network Aesthetics. University of Chicago Press, 2016.

—. 'Networks Aesthetics: American Fictions in the Culture of Interconnection'. Duke University, PhD thesis, 2010, https://dukespace.lib.duke.edu/dspace/handle/10161/2293. Accessed 15 July 2020.

Jamison, Anne. *Poetics en Passant: Redefining the Relationship Between Victorian and Modern Poetry*. Palgrave Macmillan, 2009.

Jaouën, Françoise, and Benjamin Semple. 'Editors' Preface: The Body Into Text'. *Yale French Studies*, no. 86, 1994, pp. 1–4. *JSTOR*, www.jstor.org/stable/2930272. Accessed 15 July 2020.

John D. and Catherine T. MacArthur Foundation, The. 'Chimamanda Ngozi Adichie'. *2008 MacArthur Fellows*, 27 January 2008, https://www.macfound.org/fellows/69/. Accessed 15 July 2020.

Johnson, Cary Alan. 'Outlier'. *Outliers: Theorizing (Homo)Eroticism in Africa: A Collection of Essays and Creative Work on Sexuality in Africa*, IRN-Africa, 2008, pp. 40–41. Pdf file.

Joyce, Michael. 'Notes Toward an Unwritten Non-Linear Electronic Text: The Ends of Print Culture'. *Postmodern Culture*, vol. 2, no. 1, September 1991. *Project MUSE*, doi:10.1353/pmc.1991.0030.

Just a Band. 'Forever People (Do It So Delicious)'. YouTube, uploaded by Justabandwidth, 14 March 2010, https://www.youtube.com/watch?v=_mG1vIeETHc. Accessed 15 July 2020.

Kahora, Billy. *The True Story of David Munyakei: Goldenberg Whistleblower*. Kwani Publishers, 2008.

—. 'Munyakei at the Coast'. *Madkenyanwoman* blog, 4 October 2005, http://madkenyanwoman.blogspot.com/2005/10/munyakei-at-coast.html. Accessed 15 July 2020.

Karanja, Ben. 'Makmende Goes After Hitler'. YouTube, uploaded by Ben Karanja, 29 March 2010, https://www.youtube.com/watch?v=kg9n0nnAUlI. Accessed 15 July 2020.

Kelly, Tim, and Rachel Firestone. 'How Tech Hubs Are Helping to Drive Economic Growth in Africa'. *World Bank: World Development Report 2016*, 2016. Pdf file.

Kendrick, Michelle. 'Cyberspace and the Technological Real'. *Virtual Realities and Their Discontents*, edited by Robert Markley, John Hopkins University Press, 1996, pp. 143–160.

Kennedy, Jenny. 'Conceptualizing Social Interactions in Networked Spaces'. *Technology for Personal and Professional Relationships*, 2012, pp. 24–40.

Kiragu, Joe, and Michael Onsando. 'The Labourer'. *Koroga*, 29 July 2013, https://koroga-blog-blog.tumblr.com/image/56773319162. Accessed 15 July 2020.

Kirkpatrick, David. 'Facebook's Founder Goes Public'. *Wired*, August 2010, pp. 48–50.

Kitching, Gavin. *Class and Economic Change in Kenya: The Making of an African Petite-Bourgeoisie.* Yale University Press, 1980.
Knappert, Jan. *Four Centuries of Swahili Verse: A Literary History and Anthology.* Heinemann, 1979.
Knezevic, Borislav. *Figures of Finance Capitalism: Writing, Class, and Capital in the Age of Dickens.* Routledge, 2003.
Koskimaa, Raine. 'The Challenge of Cybertext: Teaching Literature in the Digital World'. *UoC Papers: e-Journal of the Knowledge Society,* March 2007, https://www.uoc.edu/uocpapers/4/dt/eng/koskimaa.pdf. Accessed 15 July 2020.
Krishnaswamy, Revathi. 'Mythologies of Migrancy: Postcolonialism, Postmodernism and the Politics of (Dis)Location'. *Ariel,* vol. 26, no. 1, 1995, pp. 125–146.
Landow, George, and Paul Delaney. *Hypertext, Hypermedia and Literary Studies: The State of the Art.* MIT Press, 1990.
Leddy, Thomas. 'Everyday Aesthetics and Photography'. *Aisthesis,* vol. 7, no. 1, 2014, pp. 45–64.
Lefebvre, Henri. *Critique of Everyday Life.* Verso, 1947.
Leye, Tunde. Comment about book publishing by Nigerian authors. *Krazitivity* listserv, 18 April 2013.
Ligaga, Dina. '"Virtual Expressions": Alternative Online Spaces and the Staging of Kenyan Popular Cultures'. *Research in African Literatures,* vol. 43, no. 4, 2012, pp. 1–16. JSTOR, www.jstor.org/stable/10.2979/reseafrilite.43.4.1. Accessed 15 July 2020.
Lorde, Audre. 'The Erotic as Power'. *Sexualities and Communication,* available at https://uk.sagepub.com/sites/default/files/upm-binaries/11881_Chapter_5.pdf. Accessed 15 April 2019.
Ludot-Vlasak, Ronan. 'Canon Trouble: Intertextuality and Subversion in Queer as Folk'. TV/Series 1 November 2012, http://journals.openedition.org/tvseries/1479; DOI: https://doi.org/10.4000/tvseries.1479.
Lugones, Maria. 'The Coloniality of Gender'. *Worlds and Knowledges Otherwise,* vol. 2, no. 2, Spring 2008, https://globalstudies.trinity.duke.edu/sites/globalstudies.trinity.duke.edu/files/file-attachments/v2d2_Lugones.pdf. Accessed 15 July 2020.
Macharia, Keguro (with Sokari Ekine). *Digital Queer Africa.* Unpublished paper presented at Digital Africas symposium, Amherst College, October 2017.
—. 'Blogging Queer Kenya'. *The African Writer,* August 2012, www.theafricanwriter.files.wordpress.com/2012/08/jcps-macharia-1-final.docx. Accessed 15 July 2020.
—. 'More Notes on Queer Africa: Toward an Intellectual Project'. *Gukira,* 10 January 2010, http://gukira.wordpress.com/2010/01/10/more-notes-on-queer-africa-toward-an-intellectual-project/. Accessed 15 July 2020.
—. '"Slicing the Hunger": Queering Diaspora in Melvin Dixon's Change of Territory'. *Callaloo,* vol. 32, no. 4, Fall 2009, pp. 1262–1273.
—. 'Koroga: Another African Story'. *Koroga,* http://koroga-blog-blog.tumblr.com/links. Accessed 15 July 2020.
Macharia, Keguro, and Wambui Mwangi. 'Koroga: Another African Story'. *Anglistica,* vol. 15, no. 1, 2011, pp. 1–17.
Marx, Karl. *Capital: A Critique of Political Economy.* Progress Press, 1887.
Massaquoi, Notisha. 'The Continent as a Closet: The Making of an African Queer

Theory'. *Outliers: Theorizing (Homo)Eroticism in Africa: A Collection of Essays and Creative Work on Sexuality in Africa*, IRN-Africa, 2008, pp. 50–60. Pdf file.

Mawiyoo, Ngwatillo, and Andrew Njoroge. 'The Writing on the Screen'. *Mad Kenyan Woman* blog, 16 June 2010, http://madkenyanwoman.blogspot.com/2010/06/koroga-writing-on-screen-ngwatilo.html. Accessed 15 July 2020.

McKaiser, Eusebius. 'Shades of the New South Africa'. *African Writing*, October/November 2007, https://www.african-writing.com/mckaiser.htm. Accessed 15 July 2020.

McQuail, Denis. *McQuail's Mass Communication Theory*. Sage, 2005.

Meiji, Dele. 'Mourning Lover'. *Jalada Africa*, 10 June 2014, https://jaladaafrica.org/2014/06/10/mourning-lover-by-dele-meiji/. Accessed 15 July 2020.

Melber, Henning. *The Rise of Africa's Middle Class: Myths, Realities and Critical Engagements*. Zed Books, 2016.

Mitchell, W.J.T. *Picture Theory: Essays on Verbal and Visual Representation*. University of Chicago Press, 1994.

Mochama, Tony. *The Road to Eldoret and Other Stories*, Brown Bear Insignia Publishers, 2009.

—. 'The Road to Eldoret'. *Kwani*, 2008, http://www.kwani.org/editorial/fiction_poetry/11/the_road_to_eldoret.htm. 30 May 2020

Mohammedali, Marziya, and Jim Chuchu. 'Sparks'. *Koroga*, 30 August 2011, https://koroga-blog-blog.tumblr.com/search/sparks. Accessed 15 July 2020.

Mohanty, Satya P. editor. *Colonialism, Modernity, and Literature: A View from India*. Palgrave, 2011.

Mohiddin, Ahmed. 2Ujamaa: A Commentary on President Nyerere's Vision of Tanzanian Society'. *African Affairs*, vol. 67, no. 267, 1968, pp. 130–143.

Moss, Stephen. 'Madonna's not our Saviour'. *The Guardian*, 8 June 2007, https://www.theguardian.com/books/2007/jun/08/orangeprizeforfiction2007.orangeprizeforfiction. Accessed 15 July 2020.

Muthoni, Phyllis, and Jim Chuchu. 'The Sandwich Bar'. *Koroga*, 5 September 2011, https://koroga-blog-blog.tumblr.com/search/the+sandwich+bar. Accessed 15 July 2020.

Mwangi, Evan. *Africa Writes Back to Self*. University of New York Press, 2009.

Namwalie, Sitawa. 'A Daughter's Loss'. Facebook, 22 April 2020, 10.31am, https://www.facebook.com/sitawa.namwalie/posts/10159529582395828. Accessed 15 July 2020.

Newell, Stephanie. *The Power to Name: A History of Anonymity in Colonial West Africa*. Ohio University Press, 2013.

—. 'West African Popular Literatures: Readers, Texts and Gender Perspectives in Local Publications From Ghana and Nigeria'. Unpublished PhD thesis, University of Birmingham, 1998.

—. 'From the Brink of Oblivion: The Anxious Masculinity of Nigerian Market Literatures'. *Research in African Literatures*, vol. 27, no. 3, Autumn 1996, pp. 50–67.

Ngara, Emmanuel. *Art and Ideology in the African Novel: A Study of the Influence of Marxism on African Writing*. Heinemann Educational, 1985.

Nigerian Communications Commission. 'Subscriber Statistics'. 15 August 2015, https://www.ncc.gov.ng/. Accessed 15 July 2020.

Niven-Phillips, Lisa. 'Chimamanda Ngozi Adichie is No. 7's New Face'. *Vogue UK*, 18

October 2016, https://www.vogue.co.uk/article/chimamanda-ngozi-adichie-for-boots-no7. Accessed 15 July 2020.

Nkosi, Lewis. *Tasks and Masks: Themes and Styles of African Literature*. Longman, 1981.

Nkrumah, Kwame. *Class Struggle in Africa*. Panaf, 1970.

Nthiga, Mugambi. 'Makmende Rescues Eve and Gaetano from Taste of Daynjah'. YouTube, uploaded by Mugambi Nthiga, 28 May 2012, https://www.youtube.com/watch?v=tINUcFVlcEo. Accessed 15 July 2020.

Nwoga, Donatus I. 'Onitsha Market Literature'. *Transition*, vol. 4, no. 19, 1965, pp. 26–33.

Nwokolo, Chuma. 'The Inhuman Race'. Facebook, 17 October 2017, https://www.facebook.com/notes/chuma-nwokolo/the-inhuman-race/10155691064148361. Accessed 15 July 2020.

—. 'The Box of Widowhood'. Facebook, 22 November 2015, https://www.facebook.com/notes/chuma-nwokolo/the-box-of-widowhood/10153697790703361. Accessed 15 July 2020.

—. 'Present Tense'. Facebook, 6 November 2015, https://www.facebook.com/notes/chuma-nwokolo/present-tense/10153669237368361. Accessed 15 July 2020.

—. 'True Infidels'. Facebook, 23 September 2013, https://www.facebook.com/chuma/posts/10151924604456458. Accessed 15 July 2020.

—. 'Sudan.Sudan'. YouTube, uploaded by Chuma Nwokolo, 9 July 2009, https://www.youtube.com/watch?v=lGCE8lo3vCg. Accessed 15 July 2020.

Nyabola, Nanjala. *Digital Democracy, Analogue Politics: How the Internet Era is Transforming Politics in Kenya*. Zed Books Ltd, 2018.

Obadare, Ebenezer. 'Playing Politics with the Mobile Phone in Nigeria: Civil Society, Big Business and the State'. *Review of African Political Economy*, vol. 33, no. 107, 2006, pp. 93–111, https://doi.org/10.1080/03056340600671340.

Obiechina, Emmanuel N., editor. *Onitsha Market Literature*. Africana Marketing Publication, 1972.

Odhiambo, Pauline. 'Her Friend's Father'. *Storymoja*, 20 October 2011, https://storymojaafrica.wordpress.com/archives-20102011/stories-2010/her-friend%E2%80%99s-father/. Accessed 15 July 2020.

Oduor, Okwiri. *My Father's Head*. 2013, available at https://mkenyaujerumani.de/wp-content/uploads/2016/12/Okwiri-Oduor-My-Fathers-Head.pdf. Accessed 15 July 2020.

Odutola, Koleade. *Diaspora and Imagined Nationality: USA-Africa Dialogue and Cyberframing Nigerian Nationhood*. Carolina Academic Press, 2012.

Ogola, George. 'The Political Economy of the Media in Kenya: From Kenyatta's Nation-building Press to Kibaki's Local-language FM Radio'. *Africa Today*, vol. 57, no. 3, 2011, pp. 77–95.

Oguibe, Olu. 'Wake for Awoonor'. Facebook, 22 September 2013, https://www.facebook.com/groups/298741450183968/?post_id=590000667724710. Accessed 15 July 2020.

—. 'Connectivity and the Fate of the Unconnected'. *Social Identities: Journal for the Study of Race, Nation and Culture*, vol. 5 no. 3, 1999, pp. 239–248.

—. 'Art, Identity, boundaries: Postmodernism and Contemporary African Art'.

Reading the Contemporary: African Art, from Theory to the Marketplace, edited by Olu Oguibe and Okwui Enwezor, InIVA, 1999, pp. 16–29 .

Ogungbesan, Kolawole. 'The Cape Gooseberry Also Grows in Botswana'. *Journal of African Studies*, vol. 6, 1979, pp. 206–212.

Ogunlesi, Tolu. 'Pétrole'. *Facebook*, 1 August 2010, https://www.facebook.com/toluogunlesi. Accessed 30 May 2019.

—. 'Ich bin ein Berliner, Freiburger, Edinburgher, Londoner …'. *Tolu Ogunlesi* blog, 5 July 2010, https://toluogunlesi.wordpress.com/2010/07/05/this-and-that/. Accessed 15 July 2020.

Okonkwo, Rudolph Ogoo. 'Prisoners of the Sky'. *Outliers: Theorizing (Homo)Eroticism in Africa: A Collection of Essays and Creative Work on Sexuality in Africa*, 2008, pp. 26–34. Pdf file.

Okonkwo, Uche. '#Storyofmyvagina: Old Things'. *Happenings*, 4 October 2016, https://www.happenings.com.ng/lifestyle/2016/10/04/135639-2. Accessed 15 July 2020.

Okpewho, Isidore, and Nkiru Nzekwu, editors. *The New African Diaspora*. Indiana University Press, 2009.

Okunoye, Oyeniyi. 'Ewì, Yorùbá Modernity, and the Public Space'. *Research in African Literatures*, vol. 41, no. 4, 2010, pp. 43–64.

Olofinlua, Temitola. 'Facebook now has 26 Million Active Users in Nigeria'. *Techpoint Africa*, 23 May 2018, https://techpoint.africa/2018/05/23/26-million-nigerians-use-facebook/. Accessed 15 July 2020.

—. '#StoryofmyVagina: Who's Afraid of the Vagina?' *Happenings*, 14 October 2016, https://www.happenings.com.ng/lifestyle/2016/10/14/137425-2. Accessed 15 July 2020.

Onsando, Michael, and Marziya Mohammedali. 'Digital Comfort'. *Koroga*, 1 September 2013, https://koroga-blog-blog.tumblr.com/image/59967965437. Accessed 15 July 2020.

Onsando, Michael, and Jerry Riley. '(Re)member'. *Koroga*, 1 September 2013, https://koroga-blog-blog.tumblr.com/image/59967711946. Accessed 15 July 2020.

Onwutuebe, Ucheoma. '#Storyofmyvagina: Lessons from my Mother'. *Happenings*, 27 September 2016, https://www.happenings.com.ng/lifestyle/2016/09/27/134360-2.

Opara, Chidi Anthony. Email communication. *Nigerian World Forum* listserv, 18 August 2010.

Oriogun, Romeo. 'Gay Boy Blues & Other Poems'. *Enkare Review*, 29 April 2017, https://enkare.org/2017/04/29/gay-boy-blues-poems/?fbclid=IwAR1vsHXfzixqPAwfRTKzPnV9BrN2KHWeCSyBh7Omarv-Uo4cmoLs4nv-Ypg. Accessed 15 July 2020.

—. 'Gay Boy Blues & Other Poems'. Facebook, 29 April 2017. https://www.facebook.com/oriogun/posts/10154690892368719. Accessed 15 July 2020

—. 'Gay Boy Blues'. Facebook, 23 May 2016, https://www.facebook.com/oriogun/posts/10153739761368719. Accessed 15 July 2020.

Osinubi, Tunji A. 'Cinema, African (Anglophone): Representations of same-sex desire in English language films made in Africa or by directors of African descent'. *Global Encyclopedia of Lesbian, Gay, Bisexual, Transgender, and Queer History*, edited by Howard Chiang et al., Charles Scribner & Sons, 2017, pp. 332–342.

Osman, Diriye. 'The Memory Snatcher'. *Black Looks*, 11 October 2013, http://www.

blacklooks.org/2013/10/the-memory-snatcher-a-short-story/. Accessed 15 July 2020.

Osofisan, Femi. 'Wounded Eros and Cantillating Cupids'. *Theorizing (Homo) Eroticism in Africa: A Collection of Essays and Creative Work on Sexuality in Africa*, Outliers IRN-Africa, 2008, pp. 64–78. Pdf file.

Osondu, E.C. 'Waiting'. *Guernica Magazine,* 1 October 2008, https://www.guernicamag.com/waiting/. Accessed 15 July 2020.

Osundare. Niyi. 'Blues for the New Senate King'. *Sahara Reporters,* 29 June 2015, http://saharareporters.com/2015/06/29/blues-new-senate-king-niyi-osundare. Accessed 15 July 2020.

—. *Kiss & Quarrel: Yoruba/English, Strategies of Mediation*, edited by Stewart Brown, University of Birmingham Press, 2000, pp. 15–31.

Otiono, Nduka. Untitled poem. Facebook, 16 March 2019, https://www.facebook.com/groups/1871516933129411/?post_id=2311159952498438. Accessed 15 July 2020.

—. 'Swan Song'. *Camouflage: Best of Contemporary Writing from Nigeria*, edited by Nduka Otiono and D. Okonyedo, Treasure Books, 2006, pp. 290–291.

Owuor, Yvonne Adhiambo. 'Weight of Whispers'. *Kwani*, Kwani Publishers, 2003.

Oyewumi, Oyeronke. 'Making History, Creating Gender: Some Methodological and Interpretive Questions in the Writing of Oyo Oral Traditions'. *History in Africa*, vol. 25, 1998, pp. 263–305.

—. *The Invention of Women: Making an African Sense of Western Gender Discourses.* University of Minnesota Press, 1997.

Partington, Stephen D. Email conversation. *Concerned Kenyan Writers* listserv, 29 November 2009.

Patel, Shailja. *Migritude*. Kaya Press, 2010.

—. 'On New Arts'. *Concerned Kenyan Writers* listserv, August 2010.

—. 'Migritude'. *Black Looks,* 10 March 2010, http://www.blacklooks.org/2011/03/migritude-by-shailja-patel/. Accessed 15 July 2020.

—. 'Last Word: Caught in the Act'. *The Africa Report,* 2 February 2010, https://www.theafricareport.com/9240/last-word-caught-in-the-act/. Accessed 15 July 2020.

—. 'This is How it Feels'. *Theorizing (Homo) Eroticism in Africa: A Collection of Essays and Creative Work on Sexuality in Africa*, Outliers IRN-Africa, 2008, pp. 22–24. Pdf file.

—. 'Two Girls'. *Theorizing (Homo) Eroticism in Africa: A Collection of Essays and Creative Work on Sexuality in Africa*, Outliers IRN-Africa, 2008, pp. 24–27. Pdf file.

Patil, Vrushali. 'Sex, Gender, and Sexuality in Colonial Modernity: Towards a Sociology of Webbed Connectivities'. *Global Historical Sociology*, edited by Julian Go and George Lawson, Cambridge University Press, 2017, pp. 124–41, https://doi.org/10.1017/9781316711248.007.

Phillips, Siobhan. *The Poetics of the Everyday: Creative Repetition in Modern American Verse.* Columbia University Press, 2009.

Porter, Roy. 'Body History'. *London Review of Books*, vol. 11, no. 16, 1989, pp. 11–13.

Pugliese, Cristiana. 'The Organic Vernacular Intellectual in Kenya: Gakaara wa Wanjau'. *Research in African Literatures*, vol. 25, no. 4, 1994, pp. 177–187.

Ray, Prasanta. 'Introduction: Everyday Lifeworlds'. *Pratyaha Everyday Lifeworlds:*

Dilemmas, Contestations and Negotiations, edited by Prasanta Ray and Nandini Ghosh, Primus Books, 2016, pp. 1–25.

Reich, Justin. 'Reworking the Web, Reworking the World: How Web 2.0 is Changing Our Society'. *Beyond Current Horizons*, December 2008, available at https://issuu.com/gfbertini/docs/reworking_the_web__reworking_the_world_-_how_web_2. Accessed 15 July 2020.

Rheingold, Howard. *The Virtual Reality*. Rheingold.com, 1991, https://www.rheingold.com/vc/book/10.html. Accessed 15 July 2020.

Rogaly, Ben, and Becky Taylor. *Moving Histories of Class and Community: Identity, Place and Belonging in Contemporary England*. Palgrave Macmillan, 2009.

Ross, Michael W. 'Typing, Doing, and Being: Sexuality and the Internet'. *Journal of Sex Research*, vol. 42, no. 4, 2005, pp. 342–352.

Russell, Gillian, and Clara Tuite. *Romantic Sociability: Social Networks and Literary Culture in Britain, 1770–1840*. Cambridge University Press, 2002.

Saco, Diana. *Cybering Democracy: Public Space and the Internet*. University of Minnesota Press, 2002.

Sahay, Amrohini. "'Cybermaterialism' and the Invention of the Cybercultural Everyday'. *New Literary History*, vol. 28, no. 3, 1997, pp. 543–567.

Santana, Stephanie Bosch. 'Migrant Forms: Africa Parade's New Literary Geographies'. *Research in African Literatures*, vol. 45, no. 3, Africa and the Black Atlantic (Fall 2014), pp. 167–187.

Schwartzman, Adam. *Ten South African Poets*. Caranet Press Limited, 1999.

Sedgwick, Eve. *Novel Gazing: Queer Readings in Fiction*, Duke University Press, 1997.

Shattuck, Roger. 'The Sphinx and the Unicorn'. *Forbidden Knowledge: From Prometheus to Pornography*, St Martins Press, 1996, pp. 302–312.

Shearer, Elisa. 'Social Media Outpaces Print Newspapers in the U.S., as a News Source'. *Pew Research*, 10 December 2018, https://www.pewresearch.org/fact-tank/2018/12/10/social-media-outpaces-print-newspapers-in-the-u-s-as-a-news-source/. Accessed on 31 July 2020.

Soja, Edward W. 'Thirdspace: Toward a New Consciousness of Space and Spatiality'. *Communicating in the Third Space*, edited by Karin Ikas and Gerhard Wagner, Routledge, 2009, pp. 49–61.

Soneye, Yemi. 'It is Development'. *Saraba 7: The Tech Issues*, 30 November 2010, http://sarabamag.com/saraba-so-far-a-summation-of-all-our-publications/. Accessed 30 December 2018.

Soyinka, Wole. *Death and the King's Horseman*, Methuen Publishing Limited, 1975.

—. *The Interpreters*. Heinemann Educational Books Ltd, 1965.

Spillman, Rob. 'Binyavanga Wainaina by Rob Spillman'. *Bomb Magazine*, 1 July 2011, https://bombmagazine.org/articles/binyavanga-wainaina/. Accessed 15 July 2020.

Spronk, Rachel. 'Sex, Sexuality, and Negotiating Africanness in Nairobi'. *Africa: Journal of the International African Institute*, vol. 79, no. 4, 2009, pp. 500–519.

#Storyofmyvagina. 'Story of my Vagina'. Twitter, https://twitter.com/hashtag/storyofmyvagina. Accessed 15 July 2020.

Tamale, Sylvia. 'Researching and Theorizing Sexualities in Africa'. *African Sexualities: A Reader*, edited by Sylvia Tamale, Pambazuka Press, 2011, pp. 16–62.

Taye, Kiru. 'Thighs Fell Apart'. *Brittle Paper*, 14 February 2014, https://brittlepaper.com/2014/02/thighs-fell-kiru-taye-fall-fan-fiction-erotica/. Accessed 15 July 2020.
Terrell, John Edward, Termeh Shafie, and Mark Golitko. 'How Networks are Revolutionizing Scientific (Maybe Human) Thought'. *Scientific American*, 12 December 2014, https://blogs.scientificamerican.com/guest-blog/how-networks-are-revolutionizing-scientific-and-maybe-human-thought/. Accessed 15 July 2020.
Thomas, Isaac Babalola. Iwe Itan Igbesi Aiye 'Segilola Eleyinju-Ege, Elegberun Oko L'Aiye', Akede Eko Press, 1930.
Tilley-Gyado, Terna. 'Ashewos Anonymous'. Facebook, 15 June 2009, https://www.facebook.com/note.php?note_id=101111261372. Accessed 15 October 2018.
Tilley-Gyado, Terna. 'Spinning With Longing'. *Theorizing (Homo) Eroticism in Africa: A Collection of Essays and Creative Work on Sexuality in Africa*, Outliers IRN-Africa, 2008, pp. 8–10. Pdf file.
The ICC Witness Project. *ICC Witness Project*, http://iccwitnesses.tumblr.com/. Accessed 15 May 2020.
Trask, Michael. *Cruising Modernism: Class and Sexuality in American Literature and Social Thought.* Cornell University Press, 2003.
Trivedi, Harish. 'Translating Culture vs. Cultural Translation'. *91st Meridian*, vol. 4, no. 1, May 2010, https://iwp.uiowa.edu/91st/vol4-num1/translating-culture-vs-cultural-translation. Accessed 15 July 2020.
Udenwe, Obinna. 'Holy Sex'. *Brittle Paper*, 18 May 2015, https://brittlepaper.com/2015/05/holy-sex-pt-1-obinna-udenwe-nigerian-church-literature/. Accessed 15 July 2020.
Umez, Uche Peter. *The Runaway Hero.* Jalaa Writers' Collective, 2011.
—. Email communication. *Ederi* listserv, 3 April 2009.
—. 'A Night So Damp'. *Author-me.com*, http://www.author-me.com/ficto6/nightsodamp.htm. Accessed 15 July 2020.
Unigwe, Chika. *On Black Sisters Street.* Random House, 2009.
—. 'Dreams'. *Eclectica*, January/February, 2004, http://www.eclectica.org/v8n1/unigwe_dreams.html. Accessed 15 July 2020.
United Nations Capital Development Fund. 'Nigeria'. *Countries and Regions*, 2018. https://www.uncdf.org/article/3519/digital-financial-services-in-nigeria. Accessed 15 July 2020.
Wainaina, Binyavanga. 'We Must Free Our Imaginations (1–6)'. YouTube, uploaded by Binyavanga Wainaina, 21 January 2014, https://www.youtube.com/watch?v=8uMwppw5AgU. Accessed 15 July 2020.
—. 'When the Internet Arrived, the Homosexuality Deamon Went Digital'. *Black Looks*, 8 January 2014, http://www.blacklooks.org/2014/04/when-the-internet-arrived-the-homosexuality-deamon-went-digital/. Accessed 15 July 2020.
—. Status update. Facebook, 17 November 2011, https://www.facebook.com/profile.php?id=664287342. Accessed 15 July 2020.
—. 'How to Write About Africa'. *Granta 92,* 2005, https://granta.com/how-to-write-about-africa/. Accessed 15 July 2020.
—. 'Discovering Home.' *Kwani Series,* 2002. Pdf file.
Wallerstein, Immanuel. 'Class and Class-Conflict in Contemporary Africa'. *Canadian*

Journal of African Studies, vol. 7, no. 3, Special Issue: Social Stratification in Africa, 1973, pp. 375–380.

Warah, Rasna. Email communication. *Concerned Kenyan Writers* listserv, 4 November 2009.

wa Thiong'o, Ngũgĩ. *Writers in Politics: A Re-engagement with Issues of Literature and Society*, James Currey, 1997.

—. *A Grain of Wheat*. Heinemann, 1967.

—. *The River Between*. Heinemann, 1965.

—. *Weep Not, Child*, Heinemann, 1964.

wa Thiong'o, Ngũgĩ, and Micere Githae Mugo. *The Trial of Dedan Kimathi*. East African Educational Publishers, 1986.

Waweru, Nducta and Sylvia Gichia. 'Blooming Flower'. *Koroga*, 14 September 2013, https://koroga-blog-blog.tumblr.com/image/61200872683. Accessed 15 July 2020.

Weinrich, James D. 'Strange Bedfellows: Homosexuality, Gay Liberation, and the Internet'. *Journal of Sex Education and Therapy*, vol. 22, no. 1, 1997, pp. 58–66.

Weinbaum, Alys Eve, et al., editors. *The Modern Girl Around the World: Consumption, Modernity, and Globalization*. Duke University Press, 2008.

Whitman, Myne. 'Myne Whitman Writes'. *Myne Whitman Writes*, 11 March 2011, http://www.blogher.com/frame.php?url=http://www.mynewhitmanwrites.com. Accessed 26 June 2017.

—. 'Writing and Publishing in the Age of Social Media'. *Saraba, no. 7: The Tech Issues*, November/December 2010, pp. 5–6, http://voux.sarabamag.com/wp-content/uploads/2012/12/Saraba_7.pdf. Accessed 30 October 2017.

Whitty, Monica T. 'Cyber-flirting: An examination of men's and women's flirting behaviour both offline and on the Internet'. *Behaviour Change*, vol. 21, no. 2, 2004, pp. 115–126.

Whitty, Monica T., and Tom Buchanan. 2010. 'What's in a Screen Name? Attractiveness of different Types of Screen Names Used by Online Daters'. *International Journal of Internet Science*, vol. 5, no. 1, 2010, pp. 5–19.

Winckles, Andrew O., and Angela Rehbein, *Women's Literary Networks and Romanticism: 'A Tribe of Authoresses'*. Liverpool University Press, 2017.

Winiecka, Elżbieta. 'The Literariness of the Net, and the Functioning of Literariness Online: Perspectives for Future Research'. *Forum of Poetics*, vol. 2, no. 1, Spring 2016, pp. 32–47. Pdf file.

Wolff, Richard D. 'The Class Consciousness of Colonialism in Africa'. *Pula: Botswana Journal of African Studies*, vol. 14, no. 2, 2000, pp. 178–185.

Yeku, James. '"Thighs Fell Apart": Online Fan Fiction, and African Writing in a Digital Age'. *Journal of African Cultural Studies*, vol. 29, no. 3, 2017, pp. 261–275.

Zabus, Chantal. *Out in Africa: Same-sex Desire in Sub-Saharan Literatures & Cultures*. James Currey, 2019.

Zedong, Mao. 'Talks at the Yenan Forum on Literature and Art, 2 May 1942'. *Selected Works of Mao Tse-tung*, available at https://www.marxists.org/reference/archive/mao/selected-works/volume-3/mswv3_08.htm. Accessed 15 July 2020.

Index

Abani, Chris 36
Abasi, Crispin Oduobuk-Mfon 106, 169
Abbas, Hakima 76, 81
Abeokuta 159
Abiodun, Rowland 37, 38, 154
Abuja 36, 40, 106, 110
Abuya, Kerubo 57
Achebe, Chinua 3, 15, 31, 33, 34, 35, 70, 136, 137, 144
Adagbonyin, Sonnie Asomwan 51
Adaptation 44
Adebayo, D.O. 122
Adeeko, Adeleke 145
Adejobi, Oyin 76
Adepoju, Lanrewaju 41
Adesanmi, Pius 34, 51, 52, 53, 170
Adesokan, Akin 36
Adichie, Chimamanda 1, 2, 3, 16, 24, 25, 34, 36, 37, 48, 63, 68, 69, 70, 71, 73, 84, 106, 127, 136, 163, 166, 170
Aesthetic agenda 28, 29
Afolabi, Segun 66, 67
   See African Aesthetics
African Aesthetics 38, 146
African art 40, 41
African bodies 18, 84, 86, 109, 110, 111, 113, 167
African Book Writers Limited 32
African condition 85, 148
African cultures 30, 84, 93
African Development Bank 6, 13, 64
African digital age 46
African digital communities 35
African femininity 4
  Female narratives 26
  Female intellectuals 8
  Female nudity 89

African history 5, 85
African homosexual 18, 83, 85, 111
African humanity 144, 170
African identity(ies) 63, 92
African literature 2, 3, 4, 8, 10, 1219, 21, 28, 32, 33, 34, 36, 37, 41, 42, 43, 44, 47, 48, 57, 64, 75, 78, 85–7, 91, 92, 95, 102–4, 111, 115, 137, 143, 147, 163, 165–9, 171
  Canons/canonical 8, 27, 136, 137
  Market 33
  Productions 8
African masculinity 86
African metropolitanity 88
African middle class(es) 6, 9, 69, 167
African modernity 60, 61
African perspective 32, 59
African poetic tradition 50
African poetry 50, 54, 56, 57, 61
African queer voices 81
African queerness 92
African readers 5, 10, 33
  Readership 32, 125
African remediation 44
African Report, The 83
African sexual history 76, 168
  African sexuality and history 17, 18, 76, 84, 114, 115, 168
African societies 7, 19, 40, 50, 79, 87, 165
African Stories 10, 25, 28, 38, 39, 44, 59, 167
African tradition(s) 51, 115, 147
African voices 28, 48
  Online 70
African writer(s) 2, 10, 16, 18, 19, 41, 42, 43, 44, 88, 110, 123, 129, 133, 154, 166

Women writers 33
African writing(s) 33, 34, 36, 83, 143
  Africanwriters.com 12, 36
  African-writing.com 12, 36, 147
Africanness 40, 166
  Africanism ad nauseam 72
Afro hairstyle 45
Afro-diasporic histories and narratives 102
Afro-pessimists 6
Afro-romantics 6, 7
Agenda setters 5, 6
Agony Aunt 2
Aidoo, Ama Ata 33, 82, 83, 86, 87
Aina, Tade 52
Ajayi, Dami 48, 157, 159
Ajayi, J.F.A 48
Akede Eko 17, 29, 30, 120, 122, 124
Akeh, Afam 51, 53
Akinosho, Toyin 36
Akinsoto, Nkem, Nigerian romance writer 11
Ali, Richard, Nigerian writer and publisher 41, 70
Al-Shabab 22
Amazon 11, 41
Amęwa 38
Amutabi, Maurice 31
Amu-Nnadi, Chijioke 51, 152
Anansi the trickster 22
Analogue age 145, 162
Analogue terrain 21
Anglophone Africa 41
Anglophone African literature 8
  Anglophone writing(s) 27, 140
Anthropological perspective 4
Anti-gay bill 95
  Anti-gay coalition 95
  Anti-Sodomy law 80, 95, 99
Anya, Ike 36
Arndt, Susan 49
Art and commercialisation 6
Anti-colonial struggle 32
Artisans, a new network of 31
Artistic endeavours 3, 46, 114, 159, 170

Artistic self-presentation 2
Atta, Seffi 36, 126
Asexual figure 90
Ashewo(s) 113–19, 123–6
Asia 46
Attwood, Feona 140
Audience(s) 1, 10, 12, 13, 53, 56, 57, 68
Audiovisual elements 165
  Audiovisual technology 42
Author(s) 35, 86
  Authorship, notion of 44
Awoonor, Kofi 52
Azikiwe, Nnamdi 17, 29
Azodo, Ada Uzoamaka 115
Azuah, Unoma 81, 90, 91

Baje, Ayo 156
Bakare-Yusuf, Bibi 36
Baldwin, James 83, 85, 100
Balewa, Tafawa Abubakar 31
Bandele, Biyi 24
Bannerji, Himani 88
Barber, Karin 49, 53, 123, 159
Bell, David 9
Beier, Ulli 31
Belgium 66
Bennet, David 116
Benin 113
Berger 125
Berlant, Lauren 168
Berlin 65
Bewaji, Isi Joy 132, 133
Beyoncé 2, 3
Bhabha, Homi 67, 79
Birmingham 66
Bisexuality 99
Black power 86
Black queer(s) 99, 112
  Black queer body 102
  Black queer historicism 84
Blackberry Messenger 41
Black Looks 2, 76, 77, 78, 80, 81, 109, 110
  Blacklooks.org 13
Blaxploitation figure 45
Blog(s) 3, 12, 15, 35, 40, 42, 64–6, 77–9, 92, 109, 117, 119, 122–33, 136, 152, 166

Blogger(s)   23, 75, 86, 134, 150
Blogosphere   2
Blog post   77, 166
Bodily imaginations   114
Body, controlling the   80
  Body politics   16, 18, 81
Boko Haram   4, 22, 148
Bolter, Jay   58
Book age   54, 165
Book publishing   5, 10, 12, 14, 28, 34, 35, 39, 41, 47, 85, 91, 157
Boykin, Keith   107
Brain aneurysm   1
Brittle Paper   136
  Brittlepaper.com   140
Brown, Stewart   155
Brussels   66
Brutus, Dennis   81
Bryson, Mary   88, 108
Buchanan, Tom   109
Burke, Martin   9
Burna Boy   3
Butler, Judith   76

Caine Prize   8, 12, 36, 66
Cameroon   29
Calabar   29, 30
Campbell, Edward, an Oxford-educated Briton   25, 28
Cape Town   103, 106
Capitalism   6, 18, 89, 102, 105, 111, 112, 167
  Capitalist desire   111
  Capitalist exploitation   19
Carey, Mariah   68
Casanova, Pascale   26
Cassava Republics   24
Castells, Manuel   21
Chamberlain Art Foundation   25
Chan, Annie Hau-nung   108
Chemi Chemi literary club   31
Chikezie, Ella   150, 152, 153
Chimurenga.com   12
Christian evangelism   140
Christian lesbian   90
Christianisation   136

Chuchu, Jim   60
Cinematic experimentation   43
Cinematic genre   45
Clark, J. P.   31
Class   6, 9, 15, 16, 18, 22, 24, 32, 49, 54, 60, 61, 63, 65, 68, 69, 71–3, 75, 100–1, 103, 105, 129, 140, 143, 146, 159, 167
  Class-consciousness   6, 15, 16, 60, 61, 63, 65, 68, 72, 171
  Classless Africans   49
  Class system   6
    Aspiration   15
    Boundaries   105
    Class divide   71
    Privilege   60, 160
CNN   70, 106
  African Voices   84
Cole, Jennifer   18
Cole, Teju   3, 10, 24, 34, 48, 71, 72, 106
Colonialism   6, 29, 79, 81, 86, 129, 135, 168
  Colonial anxiety   19
    Hang-ups   86
  Colonial dispensation   99
  Colonial era   32, 51, 89, 115, 130
  Colonial-framed narratives   61
  Colonial rule   7, 15, 19, 31, 48, 130
  Government   34, 99
    Educational policy   31
  Legacy   99
  Modernity   8, 18, 19, 22, 29, 75, 77, 79, 82, 83, 99, 115–16, 130, 134–5, 145, 169
  West and East Africa   32
Collymore, Wambui Wamae Kamiru   39
Compulsory heterosexuality   99, 101
Concerned Kenyan Writers   15, 64
Confino, Alon   39
Conrad, Joseph   47
  Perception of Africa   144
  World view   166
Contemporary Africa   3, 14, 61, 65, 91, 107, 156
  Writer/writing   22, 67
Content on Facebook   42

Coronavirus   1, 57
Corporate entities   23
Corrective rape   106
Cosmic Yoruba   134
Cosmopolitan cities   28
  Authors   66
Cover, Robert   105, 111
Creative artists   2, 6
Creative writing(s)   1, 10, 12, 13, 22, 24, 34, 36, 43, 58, 61, 75, 77, 86, 113, 115, 130, 133, 136, 144, 145, 167, 168, 169
  Workshops   36
  Work   2, 19, 46, 49, 56, 123, 125–6, 165
Crowther, Samuel Ajayi   29
Crime-fighting hero   44
Cultural capital   7, 30, 63, 105
Cultural practices   33, 72, 87, 99
Cultural representation(s)   44, 72
Cultural space   88, 100
Cutler, Richard   53
Cyberspace   3, 5, 6, 12, 13, 14, 16, 19, 21, 24, 43, 47, 48, 49, 50, 51, 54, 57, 60, 61, 63, 64, 66, 72, 82, 83, 87, 88, 89, 92, 93, 93, 94, 100, 105, 106, 107, 109, 110, 111, 120, 134, 136, 138, 165, 166, 167, 168
  Cyber-communities   33, 167
  Cybercultural imaginary   138
  Cyber-framing   5
  Cyber-poet   59
  Cybertexts   49, 57, 59, 141
  Cyberworld, emergence of   58

Dangarembga, Tsitsi   78
Data mining   22
Decolonisation   84, 86
  Agenda   86
Delany, Samuel   102
Dele-Ogunrinde, Folasayo   36
Deleuze, Giles   167
Diabate, Naminata   8
Diasporic folklore   22
Dibia, Jude   81
Didactic Christian texts   32
Diallo, Ayuba   25

Diaspora   5, 30, 38, 65, 77, 82, 84, 101, 102
  Diasporic blackness   84
  Diasporic space   102
  Literary circles   30
  Literature   84
  Productions   99
Digital age   1–6, 9, 10, 13–16, 18, 19, 22, 24, 32, 37, 39, 40, 42, 43, 46, 47, 53, 54, 73, 75, 76, 80, 82, 83, 85, 87, 106, 110, 113, 114, 123, 138, 139, 140, 145–7, 152, 156, 159, 161–3, 169, 171
  Capital   6, 47, 105
  Communities   10, 13, 35, 165
  Conglomerates   8
  Conversations   145, 156
  Culture   3, 8, 9, 33, 161
  Digital generation   49, 82
  Digital publishing   41
  Digital space   6, 7, 9, 10–14, 16, 19, 21, 34–5, 38, 40, 43, 45, 51–4, 56, 61, 72–3, 78, 80, 82, 85–9, 91–2, 94–5, 107–8, 110, 113–14, 119, 121, 123, 131, 137, 138, 141, 143, 146, 148, 155, 162, 165, 167–70
Landscape   2, 50, 53, 90
Literary networks   23, 25, 37, 64, 147
Marketing   3, 162
Media   41, 78, 136
  Broadcasters   41
  Media platforms   44
  Presence   78
Medium(s)   2, 113, 165
Modernity   145, 155, 163
Natives   53, 162
Network   7, 8, 10, 21–4, 25, 33, 35, 42, 44, 46, 52, 63, 65, 75, 119
Participation   7
Pioneer   147
Platforms   7, 34, 81, 134, 140, 149
Presence   2
Public   3, 16, 38, 45, 113, 119, 120, 145, 149, 162, 164, 166
  Public domain   3
Queer   18, 75, 80, 81

Relationships 147
Reproduction 44
Services 35
Technologies 65, 139, 162, 165
Writings 4, 13, 75, 156
Dimock, Wai Chee 72
Disillusionment 33, 34, 144
Dissenting voices 23
Dolby, Nadine 104
Douala 14
Du Bois, W.E.B. 100, 166
Dumitrescu, Irina 3
Durban 28
Dzukogi, Saddiq 48, 51

East Africa 8, 116
  East African Standard 31
East Germany 66
East, Rupert, a colonial officer 30
Eastwood, Clint 44
Ebedi 36
  Residency 36
Ebola fever 166
Economic ladder 15, 51, 70
  Economic power 104
  Emerging economies 127
  Structure 28
Ede, Amatoritsere 36, 48
Edeh, Ifeanyi 52
Edelstein, Dan 22
Ederi 11, 12, 15, 41, 55, 64, 147
  Network 37
Edinburgh 66
Editor(s) 10, 16, 19, 23, 26, 32, 33, 36, 85, 90, 119, 123, 138, 157, 166
Edmondson, Chloe 22
Eindhoven 66
Eji Ogbe 135
Eke, Maureen Ngozi 115
Ekine, Sokari, the British-Nigerian queer activist 75, 76, 77, 79, 109, 110
Eko Akete 29
Ekun-Iyawo 159
Ekwensi, Cyprian 120, 121, 124
El Sadawi, Nawal 78
Eleti-Ofe 17, 29, 30

Email conversation 11, 41, 84
Emecheta, Buchi 78
Emenyonu, Ernest 121, 124
Emergent activist 32
Emerging narratives 102
Emerging voice(s) 10, 14, 16, 18, 19, 54, 82, 87, 123, 168
  Writers 19
Emotional needs 128
English 7, 9, 14, 29, 32, 36, 45, 52, 68, 71, 88, 114, 154, 155
  language 32, 45
Epistemic violence 32
Epprecht, Marc 115
Equiano, Olaudah 15
Erotic choices 82
Erotic literature 134, 138
Erotic writings 130
Europe 7, 10, 16, 17, 19, 35, 47, 65, 82, 126
  Eurocentric
    Anthropological approach 37
    Conception 26
    View of history 6
  Euro-modernity 8, 82, 116, 129
    Euro-modernist Era 15
  European civility 82
  European imagination 70
  European missionaries and colonialists 31, 71
  European modernity 29
  European traditions 41
  Europeanisation 93
Ezeanah, Chiedu 52

FaceTime 1
Facebook 2, 5, 6, 8, 11–13, 24, 40–3, 47–9, 51–4, 57–8, 64, 70, 85–6, 100, 114, 116–18, 123, 131–3, 144–6, 148–50, 152–4, 160–2, 164, 166, 168, 170
  Likes 3
Fagunwa 34
Fanon, Frantz 26
Farafina 24
Female African writers 26
  Equality 79
Female genital mutilation 166

Female sex workers   169
Female sexuality   141
Feminism   86
Feminist   2
    African writing   78
    Icon   3
Fictional narratives   5
    Hero   44
Film   3
    Filmed   1
        dancing   1
    Filmmakers   44
Financial capital   6
Financial impotence   160
Fiorini, Reinaldo   65
Followers   1, 10, 47, 163
    Instagram   1
Formats   2, 48
Forsey, Jane   146
Foucault, Michel   93, 94, 100, 103, 105
Freiburg   65
Futuristic science fiction   45

Gacheru, Margaretta
Garveyism   84
Gay(s)   3, 14, 26, 80–4, 92–4, 99, 100, 102–12, 144, 159, 160, 169
    Africans   3, 94, 103
    communities   92
    Gayness   85
        Gay rights   82, 84, 112, 168
            Gaydar.com   106, 108, 110
    Icons   3
    Lovers   106
    Marriage   101, 103
    Sex   94
Gbolahan, Rasaq Malik   52, 152, 153, 154, 155, 156, 157
Geertz, Clifford   108
Gender binary   88
Gender desire   108
Gender performance   19, 139
    Gender roles   8, 19
Genets, Jean   87
Geocities   12
Ghana   52, 109

Ghanaian   30
    Ghanaian writer   33
Giddens, Anthony   91
Gikandi, Simon   32
Gikuyu people   147
Gilmore, Michael   73
Global audience   3
Global capitalism   9, 18
    Global capital   111
    Global capitalist system   106
Global culture   69
    Global identities   100
    Global interconnectedness   23, 45
    Global literatures   21
        Literary history   31
        Literary networks   23, 25, 34
Global market   11
Global media powerhouses   70
    Global networks   21
Global North   63
Global politics   16
Global South   23, 127
Globalisation   19, 65, 111, 115
    Globalisation, context of   19, 65
Globalised identity   106
    Globalised lifestyle   73
Goffman, Erving   144, 162
Golitko, Mark   24
Gomorrah   93
Google   8, 35
    Google Maps   123
    Search   11
Gordimer, Nadine   163
Grand narratives   125
Granta   25
Guardian, The (UK)   126
Guatarri, Felix   167
Guerrilla war footage   143
Gujarati   32, 88

Habermas, Jurgen   54
Habila, Helon   36
Hakima Abbas   3
Happenings.com.ng   132
Haraway, Donna   138
Harare   27

Harlem   30
   Harlem Renaissance's romantic
      view   143
Harpold, Terry   47
Hausa   7, 15
   Hausa-Fulani People   7
Head, Bessie   70
Heart of digital darkness   47
Hegel   107
Hegemonic power   102
Heinemann's African Writers Series   33
Heteromasculinity   110
Heteronormativity   77, 78, 99, 108, 111, 112
   Argument   95
   Capital   88
   Ideals   75
   Patriarchy   109
   Society   110
Heteropatriarchy   76
   Hetero-patriarchal structures   79
   Narratives   78
Heterosexuality   88, 94, 99, 101
   Heterosexual matrix   76
   Identities   76
   Relationships   76
   Union   90
History, over-simplification of   7
Hoad, Neville   84, 86, 110
Holy Sex   140, 141
Hollows, Joanne   9
Hollywood   44, 45
   Movie   45
Homoerotic experience   94
Homoerotic materials   95
Homogenising tendency   63
Homophobia   18, 26, 77, 79, 80, 81, 82, 83,
   93, 94, 99, 105, 107, 108, 112, 160, 161
   Behaviour   103
   Laws   94
   Rage   109
   State-sponsored   92
Homosexuality   14, 17, 76, 80–6, 92–3,
   99, 101, 107, 111–12, 160
   African   80, 94
      African subjects   84

   Un-Africanness of   80, 86
   Behaviour   95
   Bodies   94, 111
   Criminalisation of   80, 95
   Desire   90, 93
   Homosexualisation   81
   Texts   85
Hosseini, Bahareh   3
Human experience   39
   Human history   2
Human sexuality   94
Hybridity   88
Hyperlinks   51
   Hyper-textuality   51

Ibadan   30, 31, 42, 124, 159
Ibikunle, Olasunkanmi   52
ICC Witness Project   4
   Trial   4
Icon of popular culture   1
Identity   2, 15, 65–6, 72–3, 78, 80, 88, 92,
   100, 105, 110, 118, 123, 144, 165
   politics of   88
Ideologically abject   9
Idowu-Taylor, Babatunde   27
Iduma, Emmanuel   24
Ifa oracle   145
Ifa religious poetry   135
Ifowodo, Ogaga   36
Igbo   70, 72, 135
Igbo women   2
Ikheloa, Ikhide   36
Ilesha   42
Image-text(s)   60, 61
Imaginar(ies)   34, 143
   Western   34
Independent, The (UK)   126
Indian languages   32
Indigenous Kenyan languages   45
Indigenous Nigerian languages   52
Individual authorship   6
Indonesia   66
Information technology   21, 22, 23, 102
   Terminology   22
Instagram   1, 5, 6, 13, 24, 42, 133, 145, 150,
   152, 157, 159, 161, 162

Moments 2
Followership 3
Page 1, 2
Instant messaging 65, 109
Intellectual 2
　Intellectual productions 8
Interconnected entities 21
　Atmosphere of 30
　Groups 22
Intercultural space 105
Internet 3, 10–14, 18, 19, 24, 35, 41, 43, 46, 53, 64, 65, 80, 83, 87–8, 91–5, 103, 105
　Age 34
　Cloud 165
　Dating 106, 107, 110
　Internet-enabled device 23, 64
　Internet sensation 45
　Usage 13, 64
　World Stats 13, 64
Intertextual and intervisual mediation 44
　Link 49
　Intertextuality 83, 84, 159
Irobi, Esiaba 36
Ivory tower 170
Ivy-League professor 166

Jackson, Stevi 105
Jamison, Anne 144
Jesus Christ 90, 91, 161
Jagoda, Patrick 21, 23, 43, 44, 165
Jargon 53
Jevanjee, A.M. 31
Johannesburg 27, 28, 39, 144
John D. and Catherine T. MacArthur Foundation 69
Johns Hopkins University 63, 73
Johnson, Cary Alan 101
Journalism 17, 29, 30, 32, 41, 120, 123, 157

Kabaka Magazine 13
Kaduna 66
Kahora, Billy 36
Kamiru, Wambui 159, 170
　See also Collymore, Wambui Wamae Kamiru

Kampala 27, 28
Kano 42, 133
Karanja, Ben 45
Kardashian, Kim 3
Katsina College 30
Kehinde, Hussein Lanase 156
Kendrick, Michelle 106, 139
Kennedy, Jenny 14
Kenya 4, 7–13, 15, 17, 19, 22–5, 28, 31–6, 38, 41, 45, 47–8, 52, 59, 63–4, 78–9, 85, 88, 91, 102–3, 105, 109, 114–16, 120, 122, 130–1, 133, 144, 146–7, 156, 160, 168, 170
　Cities 36
　Digital networks 37
　Government 34
　Kenyan(s) 1, 4–5, 12–13, 19, 21, 24–5, 28, 32, 44, 47, 53–4, 64, 72, 76, 80, 117, 119, 145, 154, 159, 164, 168
　　Writers 1, 11, 25, 143, 144
　　group 36
　Languages 32
　　Kenyaness 14, 32, 40
　Television Network 41
Kenyatta, Jomo 17, 32, 122
Khartoum 58
Kikuyu 32, 45, 72, 88
　Kikuyu language newspaper 32
　Kikuyu writer 32
　Kikuyuness 32
Kirkpatrick, David 86
Kiragu, Joe 159, 160
Kisumu 42
Kiswahili 88
Knowledge production 170
Koroga 38–41, 43, 59–61, 146–7
　Artists 34
　Koroga network 34
Koskimaa, Raine 5
K'Oyuga, Redscar McOdindo 48
Krazitivity 12, 15, 34, 35, 36, 37, 64, 147
Krishnaswamy, Revathi 9
Kwani 23, 24, 36, 37
Kwani Trust 36

Kwegyir Aggrey, James, Ghanaian educator and intellectual   30

Lagos   9, 14, 17, 27, 29, 30, 39, 42, 47, 65, 66, 83, 104, 106, 113, 115, 121, 123, 124, 126, 133, 144
   Lagos-based publications   29
   Political elites   30
Lamu   36
Lefebvre, Henry   144
Leddy, Thomas   146
Lesbian(s)   16, 26, 81, 82, 83, 92, 94, 99, 106, 107, 108, 110, 112, 169
   African Christian   90
   Lesbianism   91
   Lesbian sex   89
Lasisi, Akeem   51
Leye, Tunde   34
Liberal gay laws   103
Liberal pose   19
Libidinal economy   114, 116, 169
Ligaga, Dina   44, 45
Lilongwe   14
Listservs   11, 12–13, 15, 23, 35–6, 53, 55–6, 58, 64, 84
Literature   3, 5, 10–19, 22, 24–5, 29–36, 39–41, 43, 47–9, 53, 56–7, 60–1, 64–5, 73, 78, 80, 82, 84, 85–7, 91–3, 95, 102–6, 111–13, 115, 120–3, 125, 129, 133, 136–8, 143–8, 163–71
   Culture   9, 37
   History   16
   Literary circle   3, 10, 22, 25, 29, 33–7
   Literary listservs   34, 148
   Literary representations   29, 100, 125
   Literary texts   22, 24, 25, 27, 35, 72, 114
   Literary work(s)   1, 28, 86, 130
   Literature Bureau   30
      Literature for experimentation   6, 36
   Market   3, 10
      Marketplace   25, 26, 29
   Networks   9, 16, 22, 23–39, 41, 64, 67, 125, 147, 165
      Western   27
Lived experience(s)   2, 61, 84, 156, 170

Local film industry   44
Location, dynamics of   22
London   27, 30, 66, 104
Lorde, Audre   19, 131, 132, 134
Los Angeles   104
Lower classes   104, 105
   Characters   71
      Nigerian   70
   Lower middle classes   15
   Lower status   79
Ludot-Vlasak, Ronan   84
Luo   45

MacArthur Foundation, see John D. and Catherine T. MacArthur Foundation
Macharia, Keguro   34, 37, 38, 39, 40, 75, 77, 80, 81, 111, 143, 166, 168
Macmillan's Pacesetter Series   33, 147
Madrid   66
Mainstream gay culture   103
Mainstream ideologies   10
Mainstream media discourse   114
Makerere   42
Magazine   12, 19, 32, 33, 35, 49
Makmende   44, 45
   Makmende films   44
Makokha, Wa Waniohi   156
Manhood, concept of   110
Managing editor   31
Manuscript   11
Marginalisation   7, 29, 49, 112, 165
   Marginalised bodies   18, 85, 91, 111, 167, 168
   Marginalised groups   13
   Of African women   26
Marginality   103
Marketable product   3
Marketers   31
Market economies   25
Marketing   11
Martial-arts animation   45
Marxian understanding   15
Mawiyoo, Ngwatillo   40
Mashada.com   12
Mass media   4
Massaquoi, Notisha   92, 103

Masculinity   79
Mayinka, Sarah Ladipo   36
Mazrui, Alamin   31
Mbari Club   31
Mbuthia, Richard   156
McKaiser, Eusebius   103, 169
McKinsey & Company, *see* Fiorini, Reinaldo
Mecca   153
Media discourses   77
  Landscape   6
  Media space   85, 126
  Technologies   44, 60, 129
Meiji, Dele   138
Melber, Henning   6
Metropolitan centres of the West   39
  Metropolitan perception   9
  Metropolitan space(s)   106
Microsoft   35
Middlebrow literature   33
Middle class(es)   3, 9, 13–18, 26, 28, 32–3, 48–9, 51, 54, 60–1, 63–4, 68, 70–1, 80, 88, 100, 110–11, 127, 160, 167
Middle-class Africans   61, 63, 65, 66, 71, 73, 106, 119, 160
Middle-class audience   63
  Middle-class consciousness   3, 9, 16, 170
  middle-class domination   9
Migritude   49
Militarised masculinities   79
Minna   42
Mitchell, W.E.B.   166
Mochama, Tony   36
Modern Africa   39
  Writers   15, 48
Modern girl   18, 19, 30, 113–15, 118, 120–5
Modern society   93
  Modern state   61
Modern technologies   46, 139
Modernist era   22
Modernist thinkers   144
Modernity   30, 84, 113–14, 126, 129–30, 136, 145, 147, 157
  Notions of   30
Mohammedali, Marziya   60, 147

Mohanty, Satya   135
Molosi, Donald   81
Moral issues   40
  Corruption   85, 115, 119, 122
  Morality, vanguard of   19
Moss, Stephen   16, 63, 70
Mphalele, Es'kia, South African writer and scholar   31
Muholi, Zanele   81
Muigwithania   17, 32
Mugo, Githae Micere   144
Musile, Kato David   81
Musundi, Steve   57
Muthoni, Phyllis   60
Mwangi, Wambui   34, 37, 40, 111, 143, 166, 168

Namwalie, Sitawa   48, 57
Nairobi   9, 14, 17, 27, 31, 36–7, 39, 42, 47, 78, 113, 117, 131, 133
  Brown Bear Insignia publishers   37
  Libidinal economy   39
  Nairobians, middle-class   3
National capitalism   111
Ndibe, Okey   34, 36
Negritude   84
Neirynck, Kristof   69
Neo-Colonialism   26, 168
  Influence   81
  Violence   110
Nerdz Lounge   41
Neruda, Pablo, the Chilean poet   152
New Magazine, The   152
New media   10, 12, 13, 22, 87, 120, 168
  Age   19, 50
  New media space   10, 21, 104, 105
New public   28, 32, 40
New York   27, 30, 35, 105, 106, 144
New Yorker, The, online   69
Newblackmagazine.com   40
Newell, Stephanie   8, 10, 121, 122
Ngũgĩ, wa Mũkoma   10
Ngũgĩ, wa Thiong'o   3, 34, 35, 70, 143, 144, 163
Niger   30

Index

Nigeria   1, 7, 10–13, 15, 17, 19, 22–5, 28–35, 41, 44, 47–8, 63–5, 76, 81, 84, 91, 98–9, 102, 103, 105–7, 114, 116, 120, 122, 130–1, 136, 140, 143–7, 154, 156, 161, 168, 170
   Church Erotica   140
   Communications Commission   13
   Digital news media organisation   43
   Languages   36
      Pidgin English   52
   Literature   12, 35, 136, 138, 146
   Nigerian condition   35
   Nigerian stories   34
   Nigerian writers   5, 11
   Nigeria.com   12, 35
   Northern   30, 31
   Senate House   43
   Women   2
Nigeriavillagesquare.com   12
Nikasimo, Mia   81
Nile River   58, 59
Niven-Phillips, Lisa, *Vogue* magazine's beauty editor   69
Njoroge, Andrew   40
Nnedi, Okorafor   34
Nollywood   44
   Films   143
Non-queer writers   75
Non-straight   99
   Non-straight Africans   105, 168
   Non-straight bodies   167
North America   6, 10, 19, 35, 100, 101, 112
Nthiga, Mugambi   45
Nwapa, Flora   33
Nwoga, Donatus   31
Nwokolo, Chuma   24, 36, 51–2, 58–9, 147–50
Nyabola, Nanjala   64, 115, 131, 163, 165
Nyerere, Julius Kambarage   6

Obadare, Ebenezer   104
Obama, Michelle   2
Obiechina, Emmanuel, the scholarly works of   31
Odhiambo, Pauline   117–20, 124
Odili.net   12

Odu-Ifa   114
Oduor, Okwiri   8
Odutola, Koleade   5, 36, 113, 120
Offline associations   42
Offline community   109
Offline space   88, 91–2, 94, 107, 109–10, 119, 131, 133, 137, 155, 162, 169
   Public engagements   42
Oguibe, Olu   28, 36, 52, 72
Ogunde, Hubert   76
Ogungbesan, Kolawole   107
Ogunlesi, Tolu, the Nigerian author   65, 66, 73
Ogola, George   104
Ogot, Grace   33
Okada Books   24
Okafor, Basil   148, 149
Okediran, Wale, the writer-cum-politician   36
Okewole, Niran   52
Okonkwo, Rudolf   98, 100
Okunoye, Oyeniyi   157
Olofinlua, Temilola   132
Olokun   155
Olorunyomi, Sola   52
Onitcha   31
   Market literature   31, 33
   Pamphlet literature   15
Online communities   47, 109, 119, 134
   Conversations   51
Online dating   108
   Profile   108
Online followers   152
Online forums   45, 53, 73, 126, 131
Online media   10, 47
   Platforms   10
Online public   48, 121
Online readers   53, 119
Online writings   10, 19, 91, 106, 122
   African literature   53, 104
   African space   18
   Literature   61, 84, 136, 139
   Literary publications   8
   Poetry   53, 57
   Publishing   85

Writer   13, 14
    Writing space   86, 102, 167
Onsando, Michael   147, 160
Onwutuebe, Ucheoma   132
Opara, Anthony Chidi   56
Open network   24
Oral networks   22
Oral performances   58
Oral productions   22
Oral sex   135
Oral texts   87
    Traditions   32, 58, 135
Ordinary people   7
Original stories   44
Oriki   154, 156, 157
    Poetry   156
Oriogun, Romeo   10, 81, 160, 161, 162, 163
Osinubi, Tunji Adetunji   76
Osman, Diriye   3, 4, 24, 78, 79, 80, 81, 83
Osofisan, Femi   36, 86, 87, 129, 130, 134, 136, 138
Osofisan, Sola   36
Osondu, E.C.   8
Osu, Ishaya David   48
Osundare, Niyi   43, 48, 159
Otiono, Nduka   53
Owuor, Yvonne Adhiambo   36
Oyewumi, Oyeronke   8, 99
Oyo   46, 113
Oxford   25

Paedophilia   93
Pan-African ideals   14
    Pan-Africanism   18, 30, 84
    Pan-Africanist writers   33
Paressia Book publishers   41
Paris   27, 28
Partington, Stephen Derwent, the Kenyan writer   84
Pastoralist peoples   35
Patel, Shailja   16, 37, 48, 50, 77, 81, 83, 84, 87, 88, 90, 91, 94, 95, 169
Patriarchal authority   93, 131
Patriarchy   2, 78, 79, 80, 89, 131, 132, 141
Phillips, Siobhan   144
Photographic images/imagery   58–9

Pidgin-English   34, 52
Poetic tradition(s)   88, 154, 157, 159
Poetry   5, 10, 13–15, 17, 19, 39, 43, 47–9, 51–4, 56–7, 60, 61, 85–6, 88, 92, 115, 135, 138–9, 144, 152, 154, 155–7, 159, 160–3, 165, 167, 169
    Collection of   56
Political class   85
    Corruption   70
Political landscape   72
Political upheaval   4
Political thoughts   5
Politics   3, 6
    Activism   87
    and Crime   45
    and Culture   36
    and Literature   35
    Debates   51, 54
        Discourses   113
        Engagements   53, 61
Popular culture   1, 5, 47, 115
    Age of   3
    and Literature   3
Popular following   10
Pornography   131
    Pornographic materials   94
Porter, Roy   18
Port-Harcourt   42, 133
Postcolonial world   73
    African politics   92
    Bodies   128
    Contemporary   115
    Era   32, 69, 124
    Experience   10
    Heteronormativity   78
    Migrancy   88
    Order   26
    Postcolonialism   79
    Publishing   157
    Societies   78
    State   18, 33, 81, 85, 88, 93, 128
    Studies   37
    Urban language   45
    Vocabulary   45
Post-independence   86

African writers   75
Power dynamic   34
Power of literature   2
Precarity   2
Precolonial Africa   6, 83
  Precolonial era   76, 79, 113, 149, 165, 169
  Nigeria   15
Pre-internet years   92
Print culture(s)   29, 32, 33, 48, 145
  and Network   29
  Format   84, 138
  Medium   12, 48, 121
  Print age   9, 122
  Printing press   31, 32
  Publication   10, 21, 29, 30, 32, 135
Professional actor   44
Professional middle-class   31
Publishers   10, 11, 12, 23, 26, 29, 31, 35–7, 134
  Houses   3, 6, 11, 39
  Industry   34
  Platforms   127
  Traditional   11
Pugliese, Christiana   32

Quarantine   1
Queer   2, 13, 16, 76–9, 82–4, 86–8, 90, 94–5, 99–100, 108–12, 161, 167, 169
  Africa   81, 103
    African(s)   84, 92–3, 95, 103, 161–2, 167
      African writers   82
  Anxiety   100
  Communities   92
  Desire   79, 87, 91, 104, 163
  Equality   79
  Experience   76, 103, 104
  Identity   90, 91, 102, 103
  Literature   81, 86
  Perversion   100
  Pleasure   89
  Representation(s)   76, 84
  Rights   86
  Text   78, 111
  Voices   81
  Writers   75, 76

Female writers   26
Writing   81, 87
Queerness   88, 112, 161, 167
Queerphobia   81
Quotidian experience   3, 144, 160
  Practices   102
  Quotidian of the Twenty-first-century life   38, 39

R. Kelly, the music of the American R&B singer   106
Racism   22, 98, 99
  in the Diaspora   29
Radical Islamic groups   22
Raji, Remi   36
Ray, Prasanta   159, 160
Reader response   157
Reading public   1, 6, 12, 13
  and Followers   12
Real-life experiences   169
  Real-life characters   61
Rehbein, Angela   22
Religious fundamentalist   4, 89
Repressed identities   168
  Repressed memories   80
Revolutionary peasants   143
Rheingold, Howard   54
Riley, Jerry   147
Robertson, Pat, the neoconservative American televangelist   89
Rogaly, Ben   65
Ross, Michael   91, 94, 124
Royal College for Girls   71
Ruling classes   7, 15, 31, 83, 113
Rural dwellers   72
Russell, Gillian   22
Ruwen, Ruthie   57

Saco, Diana   24
Saharareporters.com   43
Sahay, Amrohimi   138
Same-sex desire   26, 35, 80, 81, 83, 89, 93, 94, 105, 112, 168
  Marriage   81
  Marriage Prohibition Act   81
  Union   103

Same-sex fiction   85
  Erotic writing   87
Santana, Stephanie Bosch   23
Saraba   49
Saraki, Busola   43
Saudi Arabia   153
Schwartzman, Adam   61
Scholar(s)   23, 35, 36, 44, 90, 91, 129, 146, 165
Scriptwriters   44
Sedgwick, Eve   102
Sęgilǫla   30, 120, 121 123, 124, 129, 139
Segun, Mabel   31, 33
Self-fashioning   2, 78, 146, 162
Self-portraits   2
Self-Publishing   11, 34
  Authors   10
Self-realisation   5
Senegalese   26
Sex work   35, 169
  Sex trade   116
  Sex worker(s)   18, 39, 107, 115–16, 125, 161, 169
Sexist stereotype   140
Sexuality   4, 9, 15–18, 30, 48, 76–7, 84–6, 90, 92–4, 99, 101–3, 107, 109, 113–15, 119–20, 122–4, 127, 129, 131, 133, 135, 138, 140–1, 146, 159–60, 163, 167–8, 171
  Convention(s)   92, 99
  Culture(s)   127, 169
  Decorum   114, 122
  Desire(s)   100, 115, 120, 128, 131
  Deviancy   114, 119, 120
  Differences   81
  Discourse of   8
  Experimentation   169
  Explicitness   56, 86, 129, 132
  Fantasy   141
  Freedom   134
  Frivolity   135
  Identities   16, 92
  Illicitness   17
  Intercourse   130, 133
  Liberal   17
  Longing   90, 137, 160
  Market(s)   39, 114, 169
  Norm(s)   18, 39, 91, 114
  Orientation   5, 54
  Other   83, 161
  Politics   18, 75, 80, 84, 87
  Pleasure(s)   88, 122, 131, 133, 136–8
  Rebellion   125
  Relationship(s)   30, 114, 121, 127, 139
  Revolution   17, 133
  Rights   132, 170
  Self   139
  Urges   139
  Violence   109, 110, 168
    Violation   106
Sexually suggestive and provocative   56
Shafie, Termeh   24
Shakespeare, William   81
Shared aesthetics   38
Shearer, Elisa   163
Sheng   7, 44, 45
Shire, Warsan, Kenyan-Somali British writer   2, 6, 10, 24, 163
Shoneyin, Lola   36, 70
Short stories   5, 10–13, 29, 30, 32, 36, 41, 43, 69, 71, 73, 87–8, 92, 105–6, 111, 114, 119, 120, 123–8, 132, 136, 141, 167, 169
  Anthology of   11
Show business   5
Sierra Leone   69
  Civil War   70
Silence, culture of   99
Single story   34, 70, 166, 167
Single African story   170
Sociability   34, 119
Social class(es)   5, 6, 13, 15, 63, 64, 116, 148, 160
  Backgrounds   115
Social commentary   118
Social exclusion   105
Social ideologies   99
Social imaginaries   168
Social interactions   14, 42, 61
Social Media   1, 6, 10, 12, 13, 24, 38, 42, 43, 45, 51, 120, 123, 132, 144–6, 148, 150, 154–7, 159, 161–4, 168, 169, 170

Followers   148, 161
Pages/sites   12, 15, 23, 24, 148, 161, 163
Communities   13
Network   45, 64, 70, 145
Social mobility   9
Social movements   102
Social networks   85, 167
  Channels   11
  Generation   86
  Networking   43, 54, 57, 58, 65, 166
  Spaces   58
Social realism   61
Social relationships   105
Social status   15
  Social strata   7, 156
Social structures   7, 8, 17
Socialism   7
Social-political developments   4
Social-political engagements   4
Societal norms   19, 79
  Values   66
Sodomy   81, 82, 95
Sokari, Ekine, queen activist   2
Soneye, Yemi   49, 50
Sori, Abdulrahman   15
South Africa   7, 25, 103, 105, 148
Soyinka, Wole   3, 15, 31, 75, 81, 82, 83, 84, 98, 99, 107, 154, 155, 156, 157
Spillman, Rob   12
Spiritual sensibilities   79
Status updates   2
Stereotype(s)   63, 122, 143, 166
Stonewall   17
Storymoja   24
Straight   82, 99, 102, 110
Straight Africans   82
Sub-Saharan Africa   32, 161
Subversion   2, 95
  Assertions   32
Sudan   58, 59
Surtees, Rebecca   127
Surveillance laws   23
Swahili   7, 15, 31, 45, 46
Swahili coastal civilisation   46
  Intellectuals   31

Literary traditions   31
Talakawa   7
Tamale, Sylvia   114
Tanzanian   28
Targeted audience   11, 35
Tarikh al-Fattash   7
Tarikh es-Sudan   7
Taveta Chronicle   31
Taye, Kiru   134, 136, 137, 140
Taylor, Becky   65
Tech-savvy African voices   60
Technoculture   138
Technological utopianism   54
TED talks   68
Terrell, John   24
Terrorist networks   22
Text
  Analysis   43
  Genres   41
  Manifestation   58
  mobility of   50
  Multiplicity of   51
Theocracy/ Despotic regime   59
Theological text   114
Thinkers of Nigerian affiliation   36
Third-space consciousness   102
Thomas, I.B.   30, 114, 120, 121, 122, 123, 124, 129, 139
Thomas, Lynn   18
Tilley-Gyado, Tema   98, 99, 100, 114, 118, 120, 124
Traditional media   76
Traditional publishing industry   35
Transatlantic belonging   101
Transatlantic slave trade   22
Transcendental figure   79
Transculturality, the ideas of   100
Transgender   112
Transmedia format   40
  Transmedia space   24
Transnational
  Capitalism   25
  Conversations   73
  Space   60, 100, 102
Trask, Michael   17

Trivedi, Harish   65, 67
Tufiakwa Syndrome   66
Tuite, Clara   22
Tumblr   4, 10, 13, 38, 40
Turnhout   66
Tutuola   34
Twenty-first century   4, 10, 17, 22, 32–3, 36, 38, 41, 43, 58, 63, 66–7, 81, 83, 106–7, 111, 113, 129, 133, 137, 139, 140, 144, 166
    Modernity   145
    Narrative discourse   108
Tweets   43, 133, 145
Twitter   2, 5, 8, 10, 24, 37, 42, 43, 49, 51, 53, 57, 64, 100, 131–4, 145, 150, 170

Udenwe, Obinna   140
Uganda   42
    Ugandan   28
Ujunwa, character in *Jumping Monkey Hill*   25, 26, 28, 170
Umez, Peter Uche   55, 56, 58
Unapologetic generation   41
Underclass   70, 103
Under-representation   169
Unigwe, Chika   36, 48, 70, 125, 126, 169
United Kingdom   2, 52
United States   7, 22. 29, 31, 46
Urbanisation   33, 113
USA-Africa Dialogue   15, 64
Users   45

Verissimo, Jumoke   48
Victims, experience of the   4
Victorian attitude   136
Victorian Era   86
Video(s)   4, 5, 24, 43, 58, 65, 68, 88, 145, 146, 147, 162, 163
Visual performance   61
Visual symbols   34
    Virtual text   59
Visibility   2, 5, 7, 10, 11, 83, 85, 94, 163, 165, 167
Vogue Brazil   1

Waciuma, Charity   33

Wainaina, Binyavanga   2, 3, 4, 5, 8, 12, 36, 80, 111, 143, 144, 163, 166, 170
Wanjaũ, wa Gakaara, Kikuyu writer and journalist   32
Warah, Rasna, the Kenyan writer   11
Warhol, Andy   1
Washington, DC   35
Weate, Jeremy   36
Website(s)   11, 12, 77
    African-owned   12
Weinbaum, Alys Eve   18
Weinrich, James   92
West Africa   8, 22, 29, 31, 145
Whatsapp   1, 24
Whitman, Myne   11, 12
Whitty, Monica   109
Winckles, Andrew   22
Winiecka, Elzbieta   43, 47
Wood, Molara   36
Working classes   15, 17, 19, 61, 103, 143
World wide web   21, 38, 92, 94
Writer(s)   1, 10, 12, 13, 15–18, 29–33, 36–7, 41–3, 53, 73, 75, 80, 82, 85–7, 91, 95, 100, 105, 111, 114–15, 119–20, 122–4, 126, 130–2, 135, 138, 143–4, 147, 150 155–7, 163–70
    Up-and-coming   36
Written text(s)   43, 61, 145
    Written literature   49

Yahoo   12, 35
Yeku, James   44, 137
Yoruba   7, 15, 29, 30, 34, 38, 41, 46, 72, 76, 79, 113, 114, 116, 121, 129, 135, 147, 153–7, 159
    Yoruba art   37
        Artistic discourse   38
        Dictionary   29
    Yoruba Ewì poetry   41
    Yoruba language   145, 159
        Yoruba language novel   30
    Yoruba, old Oyo Kingdom of   46
    Yoruba oral tradition   41
    Yoruba poetic tradition   157, 159
    Yoruba world   38, 153

YouTube 2, 3, 6, 42, 44–6, 48, 80, 88,
    147, 170
  Poems 58

Zabus, Chantal 90, 91

Zimbabwe 5
  Zimbabwean 28
Zuckerberg, Mark, Facebook's
    founder 86

AFRICAN ARTICULATIONS

ISSN 2054–5673

Previously Published

Achebe & Friends at Umuahia: The Making of a Literary Elite
Terri Ochiagha, 2015. Winner of the ASAUK Fage & Oliver Prize 2016

A Death Retold in Truth and Rumour: Kenya, Britain and the Julie Ward Murder   Grace A. Musila, 2015

Scoring Race: Jazz, Fiction, and Francophone Africa   Pim Higginson, 2017

Writing Spatiality in West Africa: Colonial Legacies in the Anglophone/Francophone Novel   Madhu Krishnan, 2018

Written under the Skin: Blood and Intergenerational Memory in South Africa   Carli Coetzee, 2019

Experiments with Truth: Narrative Non-fiction and the Coming of Democracy in South Africa   Hedley Twidle, 2019

At the Crossroads: Nigerian Travel Writing and Literary Culture in Yoruba and English   Rebecca Jones, 2019

Cinemas of the Mozambican Revolution: Anti-Colonialism, Independence and Internationalism in Filmmaking, 1968–1991, Ros Gray, 2020

CPSIA information can be obtained
at www.ICGtesting.com
Printed in the USA
BVHW051950010323
659502BV00008B/109